Sub-National Constitutional Law in Spain

Sub-National Constitutional Law in Spain

Agustín Ruiz Robledo

This book was originally published as a monograph in the International Encyclopaedia of Laws/Constitutional Law.

Founding Editor: Roger Blanpain
General Editor: Frank Hendrickx
Volume Editors: André Alen & David Haljan

Wolters Kluwer

Published by:
Kluwer Law International B.V.
PO Box 316
2400 AH Alphen aan den Rijn
The Netherlands
E-mail: international-sales@wolterskluwer.com
Website: lrus.wolterskluwer.com

Sold and distributed in North, Central and South America by:
Wolters Kluwer Legal & Regulatory U.S.
7201 McKinney Circle
Frederick, MD 21704
United States of America
Email: customer.service@wolterskluwer.com

Sold and distributed in all other countries by:
Air Business Subscriptions
Rockwood House
Haywards Heath
West Sussex
RH16 3DH
United Kingdom
Email: international-customerservice@wolterskluwer.com

Printed on acid-free paper

ISBN 978-90-411-9530-2

e-Book: ISBN 978-90-411-9531-9
web-PDF: ISBN 978-90-411-9533-3

Printed in the United Kingdom.

The Author

Dr Agustín Ruiz Robledo is Professor of Constitutional Law at the University of Granada. He has combined his teaching work with other legal activities; he was a supplementary Magistrate in the Provincial High Court of Granada (1988–1991) and has been Director of the Analysis Advisory Council of the Presidency of the Andalusian Parliament (1996–2004). He has also taken courses in Business Studies and has a Diploma in Business Planning from the Polytechnic University of Madrid. He has widened his studies and research in several centres outside Spain (the Universities of Montreal, London, Florence and Bayreuth, amongst others). He was a visiting academic at University College Dublin in 2011–2012. He has published more than 100 works on his speciality, published in Spain, Italy, Germany, The Netherlands, United Kingdom and Colombia, among the most important of his books being *El Estado autonómico*, *El ordenamiento jurídico andaluz*, *El Síndrome de Fabrizio (Notas Jurídicas de política cotidiana)*, *El derecho fundamental a la legalidad punitiva* and *Constitutional Law in Spain*. He has taken part in a considerable number of national and international conferences, speaking on his special topics, especially in the Constituent Assemblies of Bolivia and Nepal. In addition, he is a regular contributor to the radio and the newspaper El País.

The Author

Table of Contents

List of Abbreviations

Legal Norms

EAA	Ley Orgánica 2/2007, de 19 de marzo, de reforma del Estatuto de Autonomía para Andalucía – Reform of the Statute of Autonomy, Andalusia
EAC	Ley Orgánica 6/2006, de 19 de julio, de reforma del Estatuto de Autonomía de Cataluña – Reform of the Statute of Autonomy, Catalonia.
EAG	Ley Orgánica 1/1981, de 6 de abril, de Estatuto de Autonomía para Galicia – Autonomy Statute, Galicia.
EAPV	Ley Orgánica 3/1979, de 18 de diciembre, de Estatuto de Autonomía para el País Vasco – Autonomy Statute, Basque Country.
LOFCA	Ley Orgánica 8/1980 de 22 de septiembre, de financiación de las Comunidades Autónomas – Organic Act on Financing Autonomous Communities.
LOPJ	Ley Orgánica 6/1985, de 1 de julio, del Poder Judicial - Organic Act on Judicial Power.
LORAFNA	Ley Orgánica 13/1982, de 10 de agosto, de Reintegración y Amejoramiento del Régimen Foral de Navarra, reformada por las leyes orgánicas 1/2001, de 26 de marzo, y 7/2010, de 27 de octubre – Organic Act on Reintegrating and Improving the Provincial Regime of Navarrae, reformed by Organic Acts 1/2001, 26 March, and 7/2010, 27 October.
LOREG	Ley Orgánica 5/1985, de 19 junio, del Régimen Electoral General – Organic Act on General Electoral Regime.
LORMR	Ley Orgánica 2/1980, de 18 de enero, de regulación de las distintas modalidades de referéndum – Organic Act on Regulating Different Forms of Referendum.

List of Abbreviations

LOTC	Ley Orgánica 2/1979, de 3 de octubre, del Tribunal Constitucional – Organic Act on the Constitutional Court.
LRBRL	Ley 7/1985, de 2 de abril, reguladora de las Bases del Régimen Local – Act on Regulation of Bases of Local Regime.
RDL	Real Decreto-ley – Royal Decree-law.
SC	Spanish Constitution of 27 December 1978

General Abbreviations

CiU	Convergencia i Unión
ERC	Esquerra Republicana de Cataluña-Republican Left of Catalonia
FJ	Fundamento Jurídico (Legal Ground)
GCJP	General Council of Judicial Power
PSOE	Partido Socialista Obrero Español
PNV	Partido Nacionalista Vasco
PP	Partido Popular
STC	Sentencia del Tribunal Constitucional-Judgment of Constitutional Court
UCD	Unión de Centro Democrático

Preface

By a chronological coincidence, this book intended to explain Spanish autonomous state to foreign readers is published in the year in which the Spanish autonomous state has become international news due to the great challenge it is facing from the Catalan independence forces that control the Government of that Autonomous Community. Throughout the book and especially in the section dedicated to the Concise description of subnational constitutional history, I have explained, in the most objective way I can, how this challenge is being dealt with legally. However, in this preface I would like to express my personal opinion on the future of the autonomous state and on Spain in general: I share with many citizens and specialists the idea that the autonomous state is very far from having gained the objectives with which it was conceived in the first years of democracy, since it has neither achieved the satisfactory integration of the territories with the greatest desire for self-government nor improved the general functioning of the public powers. However, with all its flaws, it is the form of State that has served us to achieve forty years of democracy and life together. Therefore, looking at our history and paraphrasing Winston Churchill, we can say that the autonomous state is the worst form of territorial distribution of political power that we Spanish have been given, except for all the others. However, the challenge of independence can be an incentive to improve it and make it more inclusive and effective. For this reason, I think that the Spaniards who believe in a united Spain within an increasingly integrated Europe can repeat another well-known phrase, in this case of Antonio Gramsci: 'I am a pessimist because of intelligence, but an optimist because of Will.'

General Introduction

§1. The Subnational Units: Names and Territory

1. The Spanish Constitution of 1978 called the subnational entities into which the Spanish State is organized territorially by the name of Autonomous Communities; the constituent assembly sought especially to avoid the two expressions that had been used in the past in Spain to organize the compound State – 'State' in the 1873 draft federal Constitution and 'region' in the 1931 Constitution. In this way, it wanted to organize a State with greater autonomy for subnational authorities than in the regional State but less than in a federal State. Moreover, the Constitution does not consider the Communities as entities existing prior to it or to the Spanish State (as in the USA), but rather that their autonomy is based on the Constitution of 1978, although some territories have been autonomous, independent even, in the past (paragraph 7). Moreover, unlike the vast majority of constitutions that create a compound State (either federal like Germany or regional like Italy), the Spanish Constitution does not include a list of the regions but in its Article 2 merely declares the right of 'nationalities and regions' to autonomy, creating in Title VIII a set of procedures for provinces who wish to exercise this right through the adoption of a 'Statute', not a constitution. Thus, the unitary State was favoured (which under Franco, rather than unitary, should be called centralist), and it could be transformed into a compound State, which many experts believe is similar to a federal State.

2. Therefore, the Spanish autonomous State falls within the group of compound States denominated as a 'devolutionary federal system', whereby a State organized as unitary is transformed into a compound one. This process began immediately after the first democratic elections on 15 June 1977, as the government restored by Decree-law the Generalitat (Government) of Catalonia, abolished by Franco and created many 'Provisional Autonomous Regimes', so that as soon as the Constitution came into force, on 29 December 1978, the constitutional procedures to form neoautonomic regions began and was carried out in a short period: in 1979 the Statutes of the first two, the Basque Country and Catalonia, were approved while the last of the seventeen statutes were approved in 1982. Attached is a Table of Communities (Table 1), ordered by date of approval of the Statute, which is the system used in the Spanish State for the list of Communities. It also sets out the number of reforms that have taken place (strictly speaking, not including changes to its financial rules) and the number of Statutes that have been approved for each Community up to 31 July 2015.

Table 1 The Autonomous Communities

Community	*Date of First Statute*	*Reforms*	*Number of Statutes*	*Statute Now in Force*
The Basque Country (País Vasco)	18 December 1979	0	1	Organic Act 3/1979, 18 December
Catalonia	18 December 1979	0	2	Organic Act 6/2006, 19 July
Galicia	6 April 1981	0	1	Organic Act 1/1981, 6 April
Andalusia	30 December 1981	0	2	Organic Act 2/2007, 19 March
Asturias	30 December 1981	3	1	Organic Act 7/1981, 30 December
Cantabria	30 December 1981	3	1	Organic Act 8/1981, 30 December
La Rioja	9 June 1982	2	1	Organic Act 3/1982, 9 June
Murcia	9 June 1982	4	1	Organic Act 4/1982, 9 June
Valencia	1 July 1982	2	2	Organic Act 1/2006, 10 April,
Aragón	10 August 1982	2	2	Organic Act 5/2007, 20 April
Castile-La Mancha	10 August 1982	4	1	Organic Act 9/1982, 10 August
Canary Islands	10 August 1982	1	1	Organic Act 10/1982, 10 August

Community	*Date of First Statute*	*Reforms*	*Number of Statutes*	*Statute Now in Force*
Navarra	10 August 1982	2	1	Organic Act 13/1982, 10 August
Extremadura	25 February 1983	3	2	Organic Act 1/2011, 28 January
Balearic Islands	25 February 1983	2	2	Organic Act 1/2007, 28 February
Castile and Leon	25 February 1983	2	2	Organic Act 14/2007, 30 November
Madrid	25 February 1983	3	1	Organic Act 6/1982, 7 July

Note: The number of reforms does not take into account changes in the financial rules of the Statutes because they themselves say that these changes are not considered 'reforms'.

§2. Types of Subnational Units of Constitutional Dimension

I. The Autonomous Communities

3. Spanish Constitutional history has two precedents on how to transform the unitary State, the Federal Republic of 1873, which established a system of decentralization for Spain (which unfortunately was aborted before being put into practice) and the 'integral State' of the Second Republic in 1931, which conceived decentralization only for certain territories, those that demonstrated a strong desire for self-government. The constituent authors of the 1978 Constitution attempted an intermediate model between the two: Article 2 of the Constitution recognizes the right to autonomy in two different forms, nationalities and regions, and then develops this fundamental policy decision so that, without saying so, it could decentralize the State throughout by creating two types of communities: political, characterized by having a Legislative Assembly, and the other administrative, unable to pass legislation.

The maximum range was designed for the 'nationalities', in order to resolve the problem of integration of Basque and Catalan nationalism in Spain which, with great social support had been demanding self-government for their territories for a century. On the other hand, administrative autonomous 'regions' were intended to transform the centralized organization of the State, which in 1978 was considered undemocratic and inefficient, and so had to be replaced by another, thought then to be technically superior and closer to citizens. This very positive perception of autonomy has declined over the years, especially with the economic crisis that began in Spain in 2008, as many citizens believe that the Communities are part of the problem because on one hand they have created many economic rules that hamper the functioning of the single market and on the other, because they think autonomous institutions have high economic costs of operation that do not correspond to their level of effectiveness.

4. Once the Constitution was adopted, the Communities launched the formation processes; this idea of two types of communities (or the logic of duality) remained in effect only in 1979 and 1980, at the time of adoption of the Statutes of the Basque Country and Catalonia, and was later replaced by a logic of homogeneity (sometimes referred to as 'one size fits all') which sought, and achieved, that all Autonomous Communities should have their own legislative power. Both major parties of that time (Unión de Centro Democrático (UCD) was in government and Partido Socialista Obrero Español (PSOE) in opposition) signed 'regional agreements' on 31 July 1981, in which they agreed to approve Statutes of Autonomy nationwide with differences only in the degree of autonomy, but not in their nature: all communities would have an assembly elected directly by the people with the ability to pass laws, but a few scored higher degrees of autonomy in Article 149 of the Constitution, and others only enjoyed the lesser powers granted by Article 148.

In this change of the logic of duality to homogeneity, Andalusia played a special role because in 1980 a referendum was held to achieve full autonomy; it was a political victory (55% of Andalusians voted for it), but not legal (an absolute majority was needed in the eight provinces that make up Andalusia, but was only gained in seven), which resulted in an intricate legislative process that ended in a generous interpretation of the Constitution for the autonomy of Andalusia which obtained its own legislative power through the adoption of two special Organic Acts (paragraph 11). It opened the way for all others to have it too: if Andalusia could obtain a Statute with a Legislative Assembly without having achieved the provincial quorum of the absolute majority laid down in Article 151 of the Constitution, but did so with the generous support of the legislature, then Navarra could not be prevented from using the first additional provision to achieve its Legislative Assembly as its Provincial Council had been prepared since 1979. Pre-autonomous bodies of the Canary Islands and Valencia, which had redirected their autonomous *iter* from Articles 151 to 143 of the Constitution, pressed in a similar sense, producing a cascading effect that resulted in regional pacts of 31 July 1981 and the inclusion of a Legislative Assembly in all Statutes of Autonomy. Thus, the Autonomous State effectively came into force, designed by the binomial of Constitution-Statutes (or perhaps we should say eighteen polynomial terms), leaving aside the qualitative distinction of nature between the different Communities and other administrative policies, to replace it with a quantitative difference between the Communities of full autonomy or first degree and those of the second degree or delayed autonomy.

II. The Autonomous Cities

5. In addition to the seventeen communities there are two autonomous cities, Ceuta and Melilla in North Africa, although their Assemblies have no ability to pass laws, so that they can be considered from a strictly legal point of view as regions (Orders of the Constitutional Court 201 and 202/2000 of 25 July). However, in practical politics, their performance is very close to that of the Communities so that today they are part of many coordination bodies between the State and the Communities and the Conference of Presidents and sectoral conferences.

III. Local Authorities: Municipalities and Provinces

6. Unlike federal Constitutions, which do not often rule on the local government of each Member State, the Spanish Constitution states in Article 137 that the State 'is organized territorially into municipalities, provinces and Autonomous Communities that may be constituted. All these entities shall enjoy self-government for the management of their respective interests.' Nevertheless, the subsequent constitutional articles make a substantial difference between the autonomy of local and that of the autonomous communities, as the latter enjoy legislative and governmental powers that shape them as a political autonomy, greater than the local autonomy, granting them 'political and administrative power over the municipalities and provinces that are included in its territory' (STC 84/1982, December 23, case *Presupuestos Generales del Estado 1982*). In any case, this superiority does not become as high as that which California and other American States exercise over their local bodies, which can regulate without the intervention of the Federation, while in Spain the basic regulation of local government is the responsibility of the State, the Communities starting from that general legislation to develop their own (paragraph 136).

§3. Method of Formation of Subnational Units

7. The Spanish State was established in the late fifteenth century by a process of the aggregation of independent kingdoms: first by the union of the Crowns of Castile and Aragon, through the marriage in 1469 of Isabella I of Castile and Ferdinand II of Aragon, and afterwards by the conquest of the Kingdom of Granada in 1492 and Navarre in 1515. For nearly two centuries, this union maintained the different realms with their own various institutions, but creating some common institutions. The grand unification occurred in the early eighteenth century when King Felipe V, who was the grandson of Louis XIV and therefore raised in French centralism – abolished the institutions of the four kingdoms of Aragon (Aragon, Catalonia, Balearic Islands and Valencia). For good measure, the 'Nueva Planta decrees' were taken because in the War of Succession (1701–1714) those territories did not support Felipe as the new king of Spain and preferred Archduke Charles, and as an example that they kept their own institutions, the three Basque provinces and Navarre even had customs borders with the other Spanish territories.

The liberal State strove to continue this unification, so that the 1812 Constitution established a unitary State and market unity, which most of the later constitutions kept, except for the draft 1873 federal Constitution and Constitution of 1931 which established the *integral* State. For its part, the Franco dictatorship (1936–1975) was based on extreme centralism. As a reaction, democrats identified autonomy with democracy and after the elections of June 1977 they were prepared to transform the unitary State into a compound one. Interestingly and contrary to what happened in the United States, after the return to democracy in Spain the parties of the left have been more disposed to increase the powers of sub-constitutional bodies than those of the right.

8. To transform the unitary State into a compound one, the Constitution of 1978 used what is technically known in Spain as 'the dispositive principle'; after declaring the right to autonomy of the nationalities and regions, it established several procedures that allowed these nationalities and regions (not specifically identified in the Constitution) to become Autonomous Communities through the development of a Statute of Autonomy, defined as its 'basic institutional law', which sets out its institutions and powers. Therefore, the statute serves a function similar to the constitution of a Member State of the Federation, but with one important difference: the statute does not independently develop the Community but only makes it a project submitted to Parliament. I return to this point later (paragraphs 10 and 12). For now, we shall focus on the idea that the Constitution does not enumerate nationalities and regions. It only refers to 'bordering provinces with common historic, cultural and economic characteristics, island territories and provinces with a historic regional status (Article 143.1 SC).

9. The two general procedures – according to what we have called logic of duality – established in the 1978 Constitution the 'right to autonomy', which are first, the standard procedure (Article 143 SC), and second, an extraordinary, more complicated procedure but which grants greater autonomy (Article 151). To complement that extraordinary procedure, the second transitional provision enables the territories which in the past had a statutory plebiscite to move to the second phase of this procedure, thus avoiding the complicated process of a new referendum. It was certainly an objective formula to distinguish between regions and enabled the Basque Country, Catalonia and Galicia, which were the only ones that had endorsed a statute in the 1930s, to become political autonomous communities quickly. It is precisely for this reason that in the Spanish terminology they are often referred to as 'historical nationalities'. In addition to these two main procedures, the Constitution provides special procedures for the African cities of Ceuta and Melilla as well as a closing clause by which, as an exception to the device, the courts themselves could create an autonomous region. Moreover, the first additional provision makes reference to respect the historic rights of the territories with traditional laws (known as fueros), a provision that was exploited by Navarra to access the highest level of autonomy by a special procedure used only for it (paragraph 13).

10. The first, the ordinary, autonomous procedure (Article 143 SC) was easy to achieve and can be grouped into three phases:

(1) The initiative, to be taken by all interested Provincial Councils and two-thirds of the municipalities whose population represents, at least, the majority of the electorate of each province or island.
(2) The draft Statute of autonomy to be drawn up by an assembly of the members of the Provincial Council and parliamentarians (deputies and senators) elected in the territory.
(3) The State Parliament to enact it into law as an Organic Act.

Autonomous Communities whose statutes were approved between 1982 and 1983 were constituted by this procedure. In chronological order they are: Asturias, Cantabria, La Rioja, Murcia, Valencia, Aragon, Castile La Mancha, Canary Islands, Extremadura, Balearic Islands and Castile and Leon.

11. The extraordinary procedure is much more complicated than the previous one, designed so that only areas with a strong will to self-government will be encouraged to choose it. Or it can be considered just as an excuse to prevent the Constitution being accused of favouring the historical nationalities: using this procedure any territory could achieve maximum autonomy. It has two very distinct phases, the first to prove the territory's will to autonomy (Article 151.1 SC) and the second is the drawing up of the Statute (Article 151.2 SC). As already noted, the Basque Country, Catalonia and Galicia could go directly to the second stage because the second transitional provision of the Constitution gave validity to the referendums that had been used to pass their own Statutes in the 1930s, during the Second Republic. The rest of the territories that wanted maximum autonomy had to undergo a very complicated procedure: the initiative lies with the Provincial Councils concerned together with over three-quarters of the municipalities in each province, representing at least a majority of the electorate of each of them. This had to be ratified in a referendum by a majority of voters in each province.

Only Andalusia dared to follow this procedure, where a referendum was held in February 1980 that achieved that quorum globally, in all eight provinces, but in one of them, the province of Almeria, where, although the supporters of autonomy won, the vote only reached 44% of total census. So, after a year of debate, the Government of the UCD, and PSOE, the main opposition party, agreed that the formation of the Community would continue under the extraordinary procedure, even though it did not meet exactly the requirements of Article 151.1 of the Constitution. To achieve this, the Organic Act on referendum arrangements was modified so that the courts, at the initiative of the deputies and senators of Almeria, could meet the will of the voters in that province, as shown in Table 2.

Table 2 Final Results of Ratification of Referendum Initiative of Andalusia Held on 28 February 1980 (Question: Do You Give Your Agreement to the Ratification of the Initiative, under Article 151 of the Constitution, to Be Acted upon by the Procedure Laid Down in that Article?)

Province	*Electors*	*Voters*	*Votes in Favour*	*Votes Against*	*Voting Papers in Blank*	*Null Voting Papers*	*Percentage of Votes in Favour as Proportion of Potential Votes*
ALMERÍA	279,300	142,769	118,186	11,092	12,307	1,184	42.31%
CÁDIZ	664,109	407,493	367,065	13,412	24,147	2,869	55.27%
CÓRDOBA	521,027	362,616	312,419	20,339	27,528	2,355	59.95%
GRANADA	535,926	335,060	283,777	20,491	29,012	1,780	52.95%
HUELVA	307,943	186,748	165,976	6,808	12,897	1,067	53.89%
JAÉN	468,804	296,417	234,746	29,610	29,876	2,304	50.07%
MÁLAGA	661,825	392,379	346,819	20,822	22,020	2,718	52.40%
SEVILLE	991,422	720,338	643,299	29,864	42,423	4,750	64.89%
TOTAL	4,430,356	2,843,820	2,472,287	152,438	200,210	19,027	55.80%

Source: BOE, No: 115, 13 May 1980, p. 10,346.

12. After verifying the will to autonomy, the development of the draft Statute began, which was the responsibility of an Assembly composed exclusively of deputies and senators of the territory. Then the project was submitted to the Parliament, although not by the usual process for an organic act, as if the Statute were to follow the ordinary procedure but rather the draft Statute of the extraordinary procedure was discussed in the Constitutional Commission of the Congress with the Delegation of the proposing Assembly. The vote of a majority of the members of each of the parties was needed for approval. The resulting text was then presented to a referendum of the citizens of the territory concerned, and if they approved it, the Congress and the Senate submitted it to a 'ratification vote'.

Only four autonomous Statutes were developed by this procedure, but they were the first to be approved: the Basque Country and Catalonia, both in 1979 and those of Galicia and Andalusia in 1981. In 2006 and 2007 new statutes were developed for Catalonia and Andalusia (although the Organic Acts bore the name of "reform" of the above statutes), with referendums in both territories. What catches the attention about those twenty-first century referendums is the low number of citizens who voted: 2,570,478 in Catalonia, representing 48.85% of the electorate and 2,217,833 in Andalusia, just 36.28% as shown in Table 3.

Table 3 Autonomy Referendums Held in Spain (Question: Do You Approve the Draft Statute of Autonomy for … ?)

Date	*Territory*	*Electoral Roll*	*Voters*	*Yes*	*No*	*Blank*	*Null*	*Turnout (%)*	*Yes (%)**	*No (%)*	*Blank (%)*	*Null (%)*
25/10/79	País Vasco	1,565,541	921,436	831,839	47,529	31,419	10,649	58.86%	90.28%	5.16%	3.41%	1.15%
25/10/79	Cataluña	4,421,965	2,639,951	2,327,038	204,957	93,784	12,576	59.70%	88.15%	7.76%	3.61%	0.48%
21/12/80	Galicia	2,172,898	614,218	450,556	121,448	28,381	13,833	28.27%	73.35%	19.77%	4.62%	2.26%
28/10/81	Andalucía	4,543,836	2,430,603	2,172,577	170,190	69,873	17,963	53.49%	89.38%	7.00%	2.87%	0.75%
18/06/06	Cataluña	5,310,103	2,594,167	1,899,897	533,742	137,207	23,321	48.85%	73.24%	20.57%	5.29%	0.90%
18/2/17	Andalucía	6,186,072	2,217,833	1,920,944	207,955	67,853	21,081	35.85%	86.61%	9.38%	3.06%	0.95%

* The yeas, nays, blank and null votes are calculated on the total votes cast.
Source: Compiled from official data at http://www.congreso.es/consti/elecciones/referendos/index.htm

13. During the nineteenth and twentieth centuries the old 'Kingdom of Navarra', which even had customs borders with the rest of Spain, became a constitutional province, although it enjoyed administrative and financial autonomy, recognized in the Jurisdictions Amendment Act 1841, which remained in force for nearly 150 years until 1982. The 'Provincial Council' of Navarra continued to exist even during the Franco dictatorship, but obviously it was not then a democratic institution. This Provincial Council, elected by popular vote in 1979, agreed with the central government to constitute itself into 'Navarra' with some institutions and a level of autonomy similar to that of the first degree Communities, as well as maintaining its special financing regime, the 'economic agreement' (paragraph 36). To do this, the Government sent to Parliament an organic bill which, following the historical tradition, was called 'Improvement of the Jurisdiction of Navarre', which was processed in a single reading (i.e., the deputies and senators only had the opportunity to vote for or against it but could not propose amendments). This regime has been amended twice to increase the level of independence, always using the same parliamentary procedure of the single reading: slightly modified by Organic Act 1/2001, 26 March, and more profoundly by the Organic Act 7/2010, 27 October. Despite the official name of 'Foral Community' and basing its autonomy on the first additional provision of the Constitution, Navarra is a region similar in nature to the other sixteen Communities, as the Constitutional Court declared on the first occasion that the government of Navarra argued that the general rules of the autonomous State were not applicable to it (STC 16/1984, 6 February, case *Gobierno de Navarra*).

14. Article 144 of the Constitution provides that Parliament may authorize a province that has no historical regional body to be constituted into Autonomous Community and by this means the Organic Act 6/1982, 7 July authorized the creation of Madrid, as requested by its Provincial Council, which did not want to be incorporated into Castile-La Mancha, the other constitutional possibility based on the geographical and historical situation of the capital of Spain and its province. The Statute was drafted the following year following the procedures of Article 143 so that Madrid is a common regime Autonomous Community, without any special regime, unlike what occurs in some compound States with their 'Federal Districts'.

§4. Concise Description of Subnational Constitutional History

15. When in 1983 Parliament completed the approval of the seventeen Statutes of Autonomy, the neoautonomic communities could be divided into two groups: the communities with greater autonomy (Basque Country, Catalonia, Galicia, Andalusia and Navarra) with legislative and executive powers in matters as fundamental to citizens as education and health, and those with fewer powers (Asturias, Cantabria, La Rioja, Murcia, Aragon, Castile-La Mancha, Extremadura, Balearic Islands, Castile-Leon and Madrid). In between these two groups, the regions of Valencia and the Canaries achieved a degree of autonomy similar to that of the first, although not directly in the Statutes, and these were handled by the normal procedure, so more matters could not be included than those indicated in Article 148 of the Constitution, being almost all management responsibilities traditionally assigned to local government. Therefore, State organic acts were passed for the express purpose of increasing their autonomy, the Organic Act 12/1982, 10 August, on transfer to the Community of Valencia of competences in matters that were the responsibility of the State (known as LOTRAVA) and Organic Act 11/1982, 10 August, on Complementary Transfer to the Canaries Islands (LOTRACA).

It must be pointed out that all Communities had either greater or lesser levels of autonomy and had a legislative assembly, so that the logic of duality, which could be inferred from the constitutional distinction between nationalities and regions and guarantee of legislative powers only for some communities, was replaced by a logic of homogeneity, with differences in the degree of autonomy but not in their nature.

16. As the Constitution itself allows ordinary autonomous communities to expand their competences after five years (Article 148.2), all communities that had not transmitted their Statutes by the procedure of Article 151 of the Constitution, in the following years began the processes of statutory reform to fit them for maximum autonomy. This process was especially favoured because in 1992 some neoautonomic pacts were concluded between the government (at that time controlled by the PSOE) and the Partido Popular (PP), the main opposition party, which two years later would win the general election. Thus, in 1994–1999 the statutes of autonomy of the second level were reformed, so leading their communities to a similar level of autonomy to that of Catalonia and the other Communities of the first degree, especially in the two major issues that in Spain were important in the provision of government services, namely, education and health.

17. In the Basque Country and Catalonia the movements to reform their laws also occurred in the early years of the twenty-first century, no doubt motivated by their own desire for self-government, but also by the desire to enjoy greater autonomy than that obtained by the ordinary Communities, thereby demonstrating the dispositive principle that feeds a centrifugal spiral in the autonomous State that has proved difficult to deactivate: the territories with greater awareness claim a higher level of autonomy, but those with less (or their political elites) do not want to be left behind and so demand any advance that the former obtain.

Thus, the Basque Parliament in December 2004 approved a draft Statute whose very title indicated their maximum will to self-government: 'Political Statute of the Community of Euskadi' (the Basque Country). The Congress of Deputies totally rejected this project in February 2005 as unconstitutional. The two great national parties, PSOE and PP, which had voted against it in the Basque Parliament, voted against it in Congress, while Basque and Catalan nationalists supported the proposal: 313 votes against, 29 in favour and 2 abstentions. After this rejection, and even at the time of writing, no reform bill has been reintroduced, in part because the nationalists would not lower their aspirations and in part because the two Basque autonomous governments that have been formed since then (socialist, 2009–2012 and another, nationalist, from December 2012) have focused on the fight against the economic crisis.

18. In November 2005, the draft reform of the Statute of Autonomy of Catalonia, approved by the Catalan parliament in September of that year, was presented to Congress. While the Basque text had had only nationalist support, this Catalan project received the affirmative vote of the Catalan Socialists (then governing in coalition with ERC and IC) and PP voted against. This different view was also reflected in Congress: PSOE argued that the Catalan project should be dealt with as a bill, opening up an opportunity to present amendments, PP considered that it should be rejected from the outset, as had been done with the Basque bill. Logically, PSOE won because although their majority in Congress did not reach an absolute majority, it had the support of all the nationalist parties (197 votes in favour, 146 votes against and one abstention).The bill received multiple amendments in Congress, most of them designed to curtail the powers of the Catalan *Generalitat* (Government) and bring the text within the limits set by the Constitution.

The final text was approved in March 2006 by Congress and two months later, in May, by the Senate. The many changes in the draft Statute did not convince the PP, nor yet ERC, the independence party that had supported the project. It considered that the changes approved by Parliament denatured the proposal of the Catalan Parliament, so that it opposed the new text both inside and outside Parliament when seeking endorsement by Catalan citizens. It campaigned for the 'no' vote in the referendum of 18 June 2006, so agreeing with the PP, but for diametrically different reasons; this did not prevent 73.9% of Catalan voters who went to the polls that day from voting yes, but only 49.4% of the electorate voted. This low percentage of voters did not invalidate the result because, as a general rule, an autonomous minimum quorum of votes to ratify a referendum is not necessary – unlike what happens in other European countries but as we have seen, it is demanded by the Spanish Constitution in Article 151.1. Be that as it may, the truth is that after the Statute was passed and came into force, the PP took its opposition to the Constitutional Court, with its broad appeal on grounds of unconstitutionality lodged in July 2006, which for its importance deserves a separate section.

19. If until then the few appeals that had been lodged against the Statutes of Autonomy were limited to challenging the constitutionality of any particular item, PP's appeal against the Catalan statute departed from precedent in two major aspects: first because never before in our modern constitutional history had there been an appeal against a Statute endorsed by the citizens of a territory, and second, never had so many items been the subject of appeal. Of course it was also the first time that a Statute had been approved without consensus. This point seems to me extremely important because if until 2006 something had characterized the deployment of the autonomous State it was consensus – not without previous disagreements – of the great Spanish parties, first achieved in 1979 in the processing of the Statute of the Basque Country and Catalonia, and then the solution given to the Andalusian autonomous initiative in 1980, as well as the autonomous agreements in 1981 and 1992. If from the political point of view this consensus was important, it was no less so from the legal and constitutional point of view because the Statutes have always moved in a territory defined by a reading of the Constitution generously in favour of autonomy.

20. And again the Catalan Statute took another step in the direction of autonomy, but without the backing of more than three-fifths of the Congress and Senate, the majorities needed to amend the Constitution, but with only enough votes to overcome the absolute majority of Congress fixed at 176 deputies (it obtained 189 votes for the PSOE, CiU, PNV, IU-ICV, CC-NC and BNG), 154 against (PP, ERC and EA) and two abstentions (CHA and Navarre-Bai). In the absence of consensus and with PP appealing the new Catalan Statute before the Constitutional Court, the Court was in the very difficult position of having for the first time to judge a Statute, a quasi-constitutional text approved by the Catalan and Spanish Parliaments, which also enjoyed the added legitimacy of having been endorsed by the Catalan people. In its Judgment 31/2010, 28 June the Court responded to this challenge in a way that, from a technical point of view, seemed reasonably useful for the maintenance of the autonomous State, annulling a few items and reinterpreting others to give them a meaning fully consonant with the Constitution. However, in Catalonia it was felt as a serious attack on its self-government. So much so that in July 2010 a demonstration against the ruling was organized in Barcelona, which was attended by the President of the Generalitat and other authorities and former authorities, which, according to the city police, brought more than one million people on to the streets.

21. The subsequent Catalan autonomous elections in November 2010 resulted in the return to power of the nationalist party Convergence and Union Coalition (CiU), but without an absolute majority. Precisely to gain this and following the success of the independence demonstration of 11 September 2012, the president of the Generalitat called autonomous elections for 25 November 2012. However, its radical new programme did not bring CiU the desired majority but rather it suffered a major setback, although it remained the largest party (going from sixty-two to fifty seats). The party that did obtain significant electoral growth was the independence party, Esquerra Republicana de Cataluña (ERC), which for the first time won second place (twenty-one seats, twenty for the Socialist Party and nineteen PP). To form a government CiU and ERC signed an 'Agreement for the national Transition and to ensure Parliamentary stability for the Government of Catalonia'; in this Agreement the parties committed themselves, (which is what interests us here) to hold a referendum on self-determination in Catalonia in 2014. Therefore, on 23 January 2013 the Catalan Parliament approved a Declaration 'of sovereignty and the right of the People of Catalonia to decide', which was approved by eighty-five votes in favour, forty-one against, two abstentions, and five who did not vote.

A year later, the Parliament of Catalonia approved Law 10/2014, of 26 September, 'non-referendum popular consultations and other forms of citizen participation' that allowed the President of the Generalitat to call a 'non referendum consultation on the political future of Catalonia' in November 2014. The reaction of the Government of the nation was to appeal the Declaration, the Law and the Decree before the Constitutional Court, which in all three cases has granted the appeal (SSTC 42/2014, of 25 March, 31/2015 of 25 February and 32/2015 of 25 February). Legally prohibited from holding the referendum, the President of the Generalitat called elections for October 2015 which were won by a coalition for independence

(Junts per si) and in November of that year it adopted a declaration to start a process of independence (seventy-two votes for and sixty-three against), which the Government immediately appealed before the Constitutional Court, which considered it unconstitutional (STC 259/2015 of 2 December). Beyond the legal dispute, the political problem is of great magnitude, if the slight independence majority persists in building an independent State and the Spanish State stands firm in fulfilling the constitutional order, confrontation is inevitable and the State will have to activate the coercive mechanisms that the Constitution confers on it such as Article 155 which allows the Government, with the prior authorization of the Senate, to take all measures necessary in order to compel the Community to fulfil its constitutional obligations.

22. The Catalan Statute of 2006 opened a new round of reforms with new Statutes much longer than before. For example, the Catalan Statute of 1979 had 57 items while the new one has 223, which are also longer: the 1979 Statute occupied eight pages of the Boletín Oficial del Estado (BOE), the 2006 requires no less than 42. In a way this is reminiscent of the structure of the Constitutions of the Member States of the United States, which are longer than the federal Constitution. Fortunately, after misunderstandings between the PSOE and the PP in processing the Catalan Statute, the two major parties understood that although a statute could legally be adopted by an absolute majority in Congress, it was much better that it should receive broader support, so afterwards they agreed on processing seven autonomous Statutes and the extremely important reform of the financing system. Thus, the Andalusian Statute of 2007 followed in the footsteps of the Catalan, although the vast majority of its controversial Articles were obviously retouched in a more clearly constitutional sense, and the same happened with the Statutes of Valencia (processed in Congress before the Catalan, but inspired by it), Balearic Islands, Aragon, Castile-Leon, Navarre and Extremadura. Unfortunately, confrontation was again produced in 2014 by approving the PP reform of the Statute of Autonomy of Castile-La Mancha (Organic Act 2/2014 21 May) to reduce the number of its members which was totally opposed by PSOE.

23. The length and content of the Statutes have changed, but as the Constitutional Court decision on the Catalan Statute STC 31/2010 highlights, that has not changed the nature of the territorial distribution of political power, nor will it end the dialectic differentiation – equality between territories. Therefore, we can say that the wave of new – and very long – Statutes has brought us the *Neoautonomic State*. Another thing is that due to the economic crisis the centrifugal movement that has been prevalent in the evolution of our State is broken and the central Government has now embarked on a movement to recover its competences, which finds some support in the discomfort which some social sectors feel with the Autonomous State. In a certain way that centripetal reflux had already begun with the reform of Article 135 of the Constitution, which established a clause of a balanced budget for all levels of government, and attributed to the central government the ability to implement measures to achieve it (paragraph 84).

§5. PROFILE OF THE POLITICAL STRUCTURE OF SUBNATIONAL GOVERNMENTS

24. If Title VII of the Spanish Constitution is read carefully, it will be noted that Article 147 remits the regulation of the autonomous institutions to the respective Statute. However, Article 152 itself specified that Communities with greater autonomy had to have a Legislative Assembly. As already mentioned above, what the constituent assembly meant by this dual regime was to attribute a political organization only to the nationalities, leaving the regions without legislative capacity. But the silence of Article 147 was used when preparing the Statutes to copy what was said in Article 152. So that all communities adopted the parliamentary system as a modern version of 'rationalized parliamentarism': citizens directly elect the Parliament and this in turn chooses the head of government, enjoying some institutional mechanisms that reinforce its position such as the constructive censure motion (paragraph 111).

25. Unlike federal States, in Spain the Autonomous Communities do not have their own judicial power, although they do have jurisdiction over the management of the 'the Administration of the Administration of Justice' (paragraph 114). In addition, the new statutes provide some autonomous Councils of Justice as a way to participate in the government of the Judicial Power, but the specific way in which they will do so corresponds to how Parliament decides to amend the LOPJ (Organic Act of Judicial Power), which was not in the plans of the Popular Party government elected in autumn 2011. In 2013 it adopted a reform of that Organic Act that profoundly modified the governing body of judges, the General Council of the Judiciary, but without regard to any such autonomous councils, which currently sleep the peaceful sleep of the just in the Statutes that have incorporated them, or as the Anglo-Saxons say, have been left 'on the book' or 'on the back burner'.

26. Thus, all Autonomous Communities have a unicameral Parliament representing the people of the Community and a President and a Government that exercises legislative power and holds executive power. Most of the Statutes prefer to use the term 'Parliament' instead of 'Legislative Assembly', which the Constitution uses, although some use the traditional name for Spanish Parliaments – 'Cortes' (Castile-León, Aragón and Valencia, for example). Equally, the Statutes use less the term 'Governing Council' – the constitutional term – and prefer to speak of 'Government', as a way to highlight its importance symbolically. The relationship between the autonomous legislative and executive bodies is regulated very similarly in all the autonomous systems (paragraphs 110–111). For a long time the most important difference was the ability of the Autonomous Presidents of the Basque Country, Catalonia, Galicia and Andalusia to dissolve their parliaments before the end of their mandate and call elections, while other parliaments could not be dissolved during the four-year term. This has enabled the first four Communities to hold elections when their president has seen fit, usually not coinciding with other elections, while the other fourteen have held their elections every four years when municipal elections were held, namely on the fourth Sunday in May. At least in theory, this difference is disappearing in the twenty-first century since the new Statutes already approved assign to the President of the Community the ability to dissolve Parliament on the same terms as Andalucía (paragraph 108).

§6. The Purposes and Functions of Autonomous Statutes, Especially in Contrast to the National Constitution

27. The Constitution defines the Autonomous Statute as the 'basic institutional Act' of the Community, so that from the point of view of the autonomous system its function is similar to that of a sub-constitution in a federal State. However, the Statute has a general function, affecting both the respective Community and the central State that is unknown in federal States: the Statute serves to delineate competences between the central State and the Community. This feature of the Statutes, affecting the State's competences, is unknown in the federal government because in it the powers of the central government of a federation are determined by the Constitution itself and tend to be the same throughout the country, while in the Autonomous State these competences depend indirectly (via residual clauses) on what the Statute confers on each Community, and as a result the State powers tend not to be identical throughout the national territory. This in some circumstances is considered a positive characteristic of the system in that it allows a few communities to have more power than others ('asymmetrical federalism').

28. Precisely in the Spanish doctrine and the jurisprudence of the Constitutional Court itself, the concept of the 'constitutionality block' is used to designate the set of laws made by the Constitution, the Statutes of Autonomy and other laws delimiting competences (such as LOPJ and LOFCA) used by the Constitutional Court to determine whether a contested jurisdiction is the competence of the State or the Community. Moreover, within this 'block' some laws that assign competences such as the laws of transfer and delegation of Article 150.2 of the Constitution, which have been used both to increase the competences of some communities such as the already mentioned LOTRAVA and LOTRACA or Organic Act 6/1997, 15 December on the transfer of executive powers in terms of traffic and vehicle circulation in the Catalan Community. This is also included within the 'block' in order to give some consistency to the system, delegating State powers to the Communities to avoid the intervention of the two administrations, as in the case of the Organic Act 5/1987, 30 July, on the State Delegation of Authority in the Autonomous Communities in relation to road transport, as amended by Organic Act 5/2013, 4 July. In any case, strictly speaking there are seventeen constitutionality blocks because the statutes are not identical, although there is a certain tendency to harmonization.

29. The constitutionality block has undertaken the task of dividing social reality into subjects very thoroughly, so that in the first twenty years of life of the Constitution, the 22 rules of Article 148.1 and 32 of Article 149.1 of the Constitution resulted in about 300 competences in the Statutes of Autonomy. This number has increased exponentially in recent years as the Statute of Autonomy of Catalonia of

2006 specifically set out the content of autonomous competences in each social area, a technique followed by the Statute of Andalusia and, with slight variations, by others processed later. The reason for this casuistry in the enumeration of the competences that compose each autonomous statute has been that of bringing together all the constitutional jurisprudence, always focusing it in a manner conducive to the Autonomous Community so that in the future it could not make an interpretation different and favourable to the State. Hence this attention to detail has been dubbed the 'shield' of autonomous competences.

§7. The Form of Autonomous Statutes

30. Following the European and Spanish constitutional tradition, the Statute of Autonomy is a written text contained in a single Act, which under Article 81 of the Constitution will be an Organic Act. However, it is a law drawn up under a special procedure, whose core consists in reconciling two wills (especially in the procedure of Article 151.2 SC): the general will of the Spanish nation, embodied in Parliament, and that of the specific nationality, expressed through their Parliamentary representatives and by referendum. Because of that nature of agreed law, which cannot be changed at the sole discretion of the Spanish Parliament (as with other laws), the Statutes of Autonomy should be considered as a special organic act. Some authors, among whom I include myself, believe that their rank is higher than other organic acts, both because of the special procedure for processing them as well as for their content as the founding norm of a legal sub-order (paragraph 42). Moreover, by admitting that the Statute is superior to the organic act we can reason in logical terms on the position of the autonomous law in the Spanish legal system: the autonomous law is inferior to the Statute while it has the same status as State law. If, on the other hand, it is argued that the Statute is not superior to State law then we would affirm the paradox that the autonomous law is inferior to the Statute but equal to State law, which would also be equal to the Statute. A contradiction that those who deny the superior hierarchy of the Statute can only circumvent by stating that law does not apply the same rules as in mathematics, so the transitive property cannot apply.

31. Article 147 of the Constitution stipulates that the Statute of Autonomy must contain:

(a) The name of the Community which best corresponds to its historical identity.
(b) Its territorial boundaries.
(c) The name, organization and seat of its own autonomous Institutions.
(d) The powers assumed within the framework laid down by the Constitution and the basic rules for the transfer of the corresponding services.
(e) The procedures to reform its content.

The first two statutes approved in 1979, the Basque and Catalan, complied with this mandate, so that two relatively short texts were in line with those adopted by the Second Republic. Thus they contained the name and territory of the Community, a basic regulation of institutions (with frequent remissions to the autonomous legislation), statutory reform procedures and the competences of their respective communities. If anything, they included some items that went beyond matters strictly listed in Article 147 of the Constitution such as a reference to the rights of the Basques and Catalans (which they solved by saying they were recognized in the Constitution) and Articles dedicated to autonomous financing.

The Galician Statute and all subsequent ones followed the same structure, although the fourth Statute, the Andalusian, made some significant changes that most statutes then followed. Thus, in the general provisions certain objectives of the Community were introduced, such as full employment, access to culture, etc. This type of *programmatic law* found theoretical justification in the role of 'basic institutional law' that the Constitution assigns to the Statutes.

32. The new statutes approved since 2006 are much longer than the others, exceeding in length the Spanish Constitution, as happens in the USA where the constitutions of the Member States are longer than the federal Constitution. The greater length of the new Statutes is because they now contain declarations of rights, a detailed regulation of autonomous competences and other matters not previously included, such as the external action of the Communities and legal instruments that reinforce the role of governments, the decree-laws, which until then only the central government could make. Scholars have argued over the constitutionality of this new structure, especially the inclusion of a catalogue of rights. However, the Constitutional Court, relying on an institutional norm of the Statute, has endorsed these decisions (SSTC 247/2007, 12 December, case *Reforma del Estatuto de Autonomía de la Comunidad Valenciana and* 31/2010, 28 June, case *Reforma del Estatuto de Autonomía para Cataluña*).

33. Thus, the new structure of the Statute of Catalonia, which was then more or less followed by the other Statutes, is as follows:

Preamble Preliminary section (Articles 1–14)
Title I. Rights, obligations and governing principles (Articles 15–54)
Title II. Institutions (Articles 55–94)
Title III. Judicial power in Catalonia (Articles 95–109)
Title IV. Powers (Articles 110–173)
Title V. Institutional relations of the Generalitat (Articles 174–200)
Title VI. Funding of the Generalitat (Articles 201–221)
Title VII. The reform of the Statute (Articles 222–223)
Additional Provisions
Transitional provisions
Repealing provision
Final provisions

§8. Financial Position and Relationship Between State and Subnational Components

34. The Spanish Constitution states that the Autonomous Communities have financial autonomy, which is based on the principles of coordination with the State Treasury and solidarity among Spaniards. And it orders that autonomous powers in financial matters will be regulated in an organic law, as well as 'the rules for settling the conflicts which may arise, and the possible forms of financial cooperation between Autonomous Communities and the State' (Article 157). Thus, the Statutes are in second place, unlike what happens in the USA and other federal States, where the binomial federal Constitution – the State Constitutions – remains to establish the basic principles of the system of financing. In Spain, these principles have been established by the Organic Act 8/1980 of 22 September, Financiación de las Comunidades Autónomas (LOFCA), (Financing of the Autonomous Communities) which has been amended six times (1989, 1996, 1998, 2001, 2009 and 2012) to adapt it to the progressive deployment of the Autonomous State in the sense of increasing both the financing of the Communities and their responsibility for their management, while preserving the unity of the economic policy which is reserved for the State powers necessary to ensure stability and economic development. Moreover, the constitutional reform of 2011 changed Article 135 to order all Public Administrations to be governed by the principle of budgetary stability, so that there could not be a structural deficit greater the margins fixed by the EU. And to ensure this mandate the Constitutional Court remitted an organic act which fixed the structural maximum limit permitted to the State and each Autonomous Community according to its PIB. This was done by Organic Act 2/2012, 27 April on Budgetary Stability and Financial Sustainability.

35. The current system, which was agreed between the State and the Autonomous Communities in July 2009, is regulated basically by two important laws: Organic Act 3 /2009, 18 December, amending Organic Act 8 /1980 22 September and Law 22 /2009, 18 December, approving the financing system of the common regime of the Autonomous Communities and Cities with a Statute of Autonomy. The system established two major ways to finance the Communities: taxes and funds to meet three main aims: to improve the provision of autonomous services, including everything relating to the welfare State, cutting the financing differences between Autonomous Communities and increasing the financial autonomy of the Communities. To achieve this, it adopted, among others, two major decisions:

(1) To guarantee to all citizens, regardless of the Autonomous Community in which they reside, equality in funding basic public services (education, health and social services), which devotes 80% of resources through various collaboration techniques among which are the creation of Autonomous Convergence Funds (State-funded) and the Guarantee Fund of Fundamental Public Services, which is funded 75% from tax revenues of the Autonomous Communities and additional resources from the State.
(2) To increase the financial autonomy of the Communities both through their greater participation in State taxes (and up to 50% in income tax and VAT) as

attributing greater legislative capacity in the total ceded taxes (inheritance tax, for example) or those ceded in part (PIT).

36. The Basque Country and Navarre are an exception to this common financing regime since, based on the traditional laws, both their Statutes and LOFCA determine that their financing will be the regime of economic agreement, which later became a special law of the State.[1] In it the competent institutions of both communities (the three Provincial Councils of the Basque Country and the Navarre Parliament) will autonomously determine their taxes and other regulatory elements of taxes; such regulation must maintain an overall pressure (but not tax on tax) equal to the rest of the State. Furthermore, while in the early days of the regular funding scheme the bulk of tax revenues was collected by the State and then distributed to the Communities as legally established, in the economic agreement regime it is always the Provincial Councils (three Basque and Navarre) which collect most of the taxes and they are the ones who give the State a 'quota' or 'contribution' for the common services or 'general charges' of the State.

37. Meanwhile, within the common system, the Canary Islands have a special tax regime for historical and geographical reasons, which the Constitution recognizes (Additional Provision 3) and which incorporates the relevant European principles of recognition of the Canaries as the outermost region of the European Union (Article 349 TFEU). In essence this scheme is based on the commercial freedom of import and export and customs and tax exemptions on consumption, such as the absence of value added tax (VAT), which is a lower tax burden in its territory. For their part, the autonomous cities of Ceuta and Melilla also have certain specialties in their tax system, such as the absence of VAT.

1. These acts are: Law 12/2002, 23 May, *por la que se aprueba el Concierto Económico con la Comunidad Autónoma del País Vasco*, amended by the Law 7/2014, 21 April and the Law 28/1990, 26 December, *por la que se aprueba el Convenio Económico entre el Estado y la Comunidad Foral de Navarra*, amended by different laws, the last of which is Ley 14/2015, 24 June.

Part I. The Sources of Autonomous Legal Systems

Chapter 1. Statute of Autonomy

§1. The Legal Nature of the Statute of Autonomy

38. The Spanish legal system uses the word Constitution only for the supreme norm, the Constitution of 1978. This, in turn, applies the term 'Statute of Autonomy' to the 'basic institutional norm of each community', the State 'recognizes and protects them as an integral part of its legal system' (Article 147.1 EC). This same Article 147 includes the subjects to be included in each statute, such as the name, the organization of autonomous institutions and competences, although in the neoautonomic state, the new Statutes go far beyond these foreseen provisions and acquire a very similar structure to that of the Constitution, even setting out a declaration of rights (paragraph 20).

39. It is not easy to determine what type of legal norm the Statute of Autonomy is. Experts hold different theories, often in close connection with their particular (and legitimate) position on the delicate balance between the competences of the State and the Autonomous Communities taken by the Constitution. So let us begin by first noting their differences with other similar norms of compound States and then study the traits that are accepted by the vast majority of academic authorities, to end with the most controversial feature: whether or not the statute is a norm agreed between the territory concerned and the State.

40. The Statute of Autonomy is a norm characteristic of the autonomous State, which has important differences with both the constitution of a federal State, starting with the title, of course, as it does with Italian 'Statuti':

(a) The Statute is not legally comparable to the Constitution of a Member State of a Federation, because the nationalities and – much less the Autonomous Communities – lack the constituent power that belongs only to the Spanish people as a whole (Article 2 SC) an idea on which the Constitutional Court has insisted (STC 42/2014, March 25, case *Declaración de Soberania de Cataluña*). Starting from the idea that autonomy is not sovereignty – as the Constitutional Court usually asserts, the Statute is not approved exclusively by the Autonomous

Community, but also by the State Parliament, which is involved in its preparation. This deprivation of the capacity unilaterally to decide its content makes the Statute a legal text lower than an Autonomous Community constitution. Paradoxically, however, from another point of view, that of its role within the overall system, it is a superior norm or at least with an overall effect that a sub-Constitution does not have. While this cannot affect the competences of the central State, which are fixed in the Constitution, the Statute can do this, as the competences of the State are not only those reserved to it in the Constitution (basically in Article 149.1 SC) but all those which the Statutes have not attributed to their respective communities (residual clause of Article 149.3 SC).

(b) Nor is the statute an Autonomous Community law – in the style of Italian Statutes, which are approved by the regions and then formally ratified by the Italian Parliament – because the approval of a Statute in the Spanish Parliament is not simply a formal requirement of integration and efficiency, but it is a constitutive act, which decides on the specific content of the statutory text; in the Spanish tradition bills that are remitted to Congress are usually amended profusely. Therefore, there is no alleged difference between the Statute and the organic act that that approves it. Thus, the Constitutional Court has categorically stated: 'The approval of the Statute of Autonomy by an Organic Act is not a simple formal dressing of a proper autonomous norm, but rather the incorporation, final and decisive, of the will of the [Spanish] State legislature to the configuration of what, by its content, constitutes the basic institutional norm of each Autonomous Community' (STC 99/1986, 11 July, case E*statuto de Autonomía de Castilla-León*, FJ 1).

(c) The statute is not, unlike the Statutes of special Italian regions, a constitutional law, that is, a law which, once approved, becomes independent of the Constitution. Rather, it remains subject to it and its provisions must always be interpreted in accordance therewith. Our Constitutional Court has often reminded us, 'while there is a relationship of primacy between the Federal Constitution and that of the federated members, without implying hierarchical subordination of the latter, in our law the Statute of Autonomy has to be conceptualized as a constitutional norm hierarchically subordinate to the unique Spanish Constitution, as the latter has been interpreted by the Constitutional Court' (STC 31/2010, 28 June, case *Reforma del Estatuto de Autonomía de Cataluña*, FJ 12).

41. If we now turn to the positive side, to what a Statute of Autonomy is, we can list four characteristics on which there is no great doctrinal or academic controversy:

(a) The Statute, as defined in Article 147.1 of the Constitution, is the 'basic institutional norm of each community'. Therefore, from a functional point of view, its role is similar to that of the constitution of a Member State: to govern, as the fundamental norm, the performance of an autonomous entity.

(b) Article 81.1 of the Constitution gives the Statute the form of an organic act, being integrated, and Article 147.1 reminds us of this to avoid misunderstandings –in the State legal system. So the first Statute, that of the Basque Country, was approved as the 'Organic Act 3/1979 of 18 December on the Statute of

Autonomy of the Basque Country' and Article 27.2 of the LOTC refers to 'The Statutes of Autonomy and other organic acts'.

(c) From the two features above a third is extracted: the dual character of the Statute, since it belongs to the general system of the State and at the same time, it is the superior norm of a new partial legal order, the autonomous legal system.

(d) The Statutes are processed differently from ordinary laws, especially the four statutes (Basque Country, Catalonia, Galicia and Andalusia) transmitted by the special procedure under Article 151 of the Constitution. Similarly, they can only be amended in accordance with the procedures that they themselves have established (Articles 147.3 and 152.2 SC). Therefore, a statute cannot, despite being an organic act, serve as a law of transfer or delegation of competences, as these laws (Article 150.2 of the SC) are a unilateral product of the State, and therefore the general Parliament could modify them freely. In the words of the Constitutional Court: 'The Statutes of Autonomy, despite their form of organic law, are neither useful nor constitutionally correct instruments, by their nature and mode of adoption, for transfers or delegations of authority in a matter of State ownership permitted under Article 150.2 of the Constitution' (STC 56/1990, 29 March, case *Ley Orgánica del Poder Judicial*, FJ 5).

42. Experts do not agree whether all the features mentioned so far alter the nature of organic law of the Statute processed by the special procedure under Article 151 of the Constitution. For some, they do not, as the Statute is an organic law, but for others it is a complex act, so that, even taking the form of an organic law, it is agreed between the State and the territory, thereby becoming a different kind of norm. The first authors focus their argument that, under Article 151.2.4 of the Constitution, the adoption of the Statute is always a free act of the Spanish Parliament; politically, it is very unlikely that it would reject a draft law approved in a referendum, but it can legally do so. In my opinion, it is an agreed norm because both the autonomous initiative and the development of the draft Statute apply only to representatives of the nationality or region, with whom the State Parliament has to agree the final text, and only if that was not possible would the draft be dealt with as a bill. But even in that case (whose uniqueness is proved by the fact that all four special Statutes and the two reforms have been agreed upon), the Constitution requires that the Statute be accepted by the nationality, whose electoral body must ratify it by referendum. Therefore, the statute is not only an organic act with a special approval process and reform. It is a complex act that eludes the free will of Parliament.

§2. The Position of the Statutes in the Legal System

43. As the Spanish specialists disagree on the legal nature of the Statute they also disagree about its place in the system of sources. Thus, if it is argued that the Statute's nature is that of an organic act, logically it will be argued its position is that of an organic act, the same as other organic acts; however, those of us who believe that it is an agreement think that its position in the legal system is superior to the organic act; an opinion that also has the advantage of explaining it very simple form, as Ockham's razor requires – why the Statute is superior to the autonomous law and this is equal to State law: simply because the Statute is superior to both (paragraph 30). However, while this controversy has important theoretical implications it has few practical consequences, given the doctrinal unanimity on how the Statute relates to the rest of the system: it is subordinate to the Constitution and is superior to the autonomous norms, but may be amended by State laws. Nor is its role in the system put in doubt: it is the most important norm in the constitutionality block, which is the set of rules that delimitates the competences between the State and the Autonomous Communities; therefore, it can be used as a parameter to determine the constitutionality of other laws. But we shall look more closely at these relationships of the Statute with the Constitution, the autonomous laws and State laws.

44. The Constitution as the *lex superior* of the Spanish legal system assumes, first, that the Statute is subordinate to it and therefore cannot contradict it since otherwise it will be declared a nullity as decreed by the Constitutional Court, under Article 163.1.ª) of the Constitution and more accurately replicated in 27.2 LOTC: a) 'the Statutes of Autonomy and other organic laws' are subject to judicial review. That said, we cannot ignore that, in practice, when the Constitutional Court has had to judge the constitutionality of a statutory provision when its wording has seemed contrary to the Constitution, it has preferred to use the technique of interpreting it according to the Constitution, sometimes even 'reading' a meaning into the statutory norm contrary to its own literal meaning, as was seen in no few items in the Catalan Statute that were 'saved' in STC 31/2010. These interpretations, certainly somewhat forced, enabled the Court to declare only a limited number of items unconstitutional. And it should be noted that the fact of judging the constitutionality of the statute after it has been voted for by the citizens of a Community can lead to a political conflict of great importance if the political forces of that territory oppose the legitimacy of popular endorsement against the legitimacy of the Constitutional Court. This happened, unfortunately, in 2010 when the main Catalan political parties held a demonstration against the Judgment 31/2010, held in Barcelona on 10 July 2010 with an impressive number of attendees, including the president of the Community. Very different was the situation created a year later when the Constitutional Court annulled in its Judgment 30/2011 Article 51 of the Statute of Andalusia attributing control of the Guadalquivir River to the Autonomous Community – and the Andalusian political competences did not even discuss that judgment. In any case, this situation of judging a statute after it has been voted for by the citizens could be avoided if a statute were allowed to be voted on after being approved by Parliament and before being voted on by the citizens. That is why the main Spanish parties, the PP and the PSOE, agreed to approve Organic Act 12/2015 to retrieve the earlier preliminary appeal for bill of Statutes of Autonomy. And much better than any legal technique is the political awareness that a basic institutional norm of this importance should only be amended with the agreement of the major political parties, an agreement that has not always been achieved (paragraph 22).

45. The Statute as the 'basic institutional norm' of the Autonomous Community (Article 147.1 SC) is the 'foundational norm' of a legal sub-system and, therefore, all the norms that come from the institutions that the Statute creates are subordinate. The relationship of these with the Statute is a hierarchical one; therefore, no law passed by an autonomous parliament can be contrary to the Statute. If that happens, the principle of conservation of legal acts would force an interpretation in accordance with the Statute and only if that is not possible should the law be expelled from the legal system. However, the judicial body responsible for monitoring the subjection of a rule to the Statute varies in response to its rank: in the case of regulations, control rests with the Contentious-Administrative Court, as provided in Article 153.c) of the Constitution; while that of normative provisions having the force of law is attributed solely to the Constitutional Court (Articles 153.c) SC, 45.1 EAA, 27.2 LOTC), which has this jurisdiction by virtue of holding the monopoly control of the constitutionality of laws. Therefore, we could consider the possibility of independent control of the autonomous laws when, without violating the Constitution, they are contrary to the Statute. An example would be an autonomous law to establish a five-year term for the legislature, instead of four as established in all the Statutes. However, the Constitutional Court has denied that possibility because it would be a violation of the 'monopoly of rejection of acts with the force of law reserved to the Court by Article 161 SC' (STC 31/2010, 28 June, FJ 32).

§3. The Content of the Statute Reserved by the Constitution

46. As already referred to in the introduction (paragraphs 31–33), not only does the Constitution state that the Statute is the basic institutional norm of each autonomous community and sets the procedure for drafting it, but expressly establishes its content (Article 147.2), so differentiating it from what happens in federal states such as the USA, where the references made by the Constitutions of the Federation on the content of the Constitutions of the States are almost non-existent. However, the mandate of Article 147.2 has been interpreted as a minimum content that the Constitution reserves to the Statutes, without thereby prohibiting the incorporation of other mandates consistent with the character of basic institutional norm. Moreover, the matters reserved to the Statute are to ensure the participation of the nationalities and regions in their adoption. That is, the function of these statutory reservations is to act as a limit against the State legislature, which is absolutely excluded, but not against the autonomies. This implies that the Statute itself may well take a concrete decision that the Constitution attributes to it (say, appointing the capital of the Community) or defer it to a later time for the adoption of an autonomous institution. In the words of the Constitutional Court: the Constitution is not violated when 'even without fixing the seat by name, it establishes which body will determine it, when and where it will have to be done and by what majority, which is perfectly consistent with an interpretation, there are no reasons to reject it as we understand Article 147.2.d) as only a relative statutory reservation' (STC 89/1984, 29 September, case *Estatuto de Autonomía de Castilla-León-1,* FJ 7). We see now the four express reservations of Article 147.2 are hereby reduced to three as the name and delimitation of the territory are included in a single paragraph.

I. The Name and the Territory of the Community

47. The Statutes of Autonomy have given their Community the name considered most suitable for 'historical identity' (Article 147.2a SC), which in most cases is done by simply using the proper name of territory: Basque Country, Catalonia, Galicia, etc. However, some statutes have introduced a qualifier to that name: Principality of Asturias, Community of Madrid and Region of Murcia. It should also be noted that the official name of two communities is only the name in their own language: Illes Balears (Balearic Islands) and Comunitat Valenciana (Valencia).

48. When indicating the territory of the Autonomous Communities the first Statutes referred to the territory of the provinces that were integrated into them, because the provinces already had precisely delimited boundaries. However, rather than doing so directly, most of them used a circumlocution: they preferred to refer to 'municipalities' integrated within the provinces. The 1979 Catalan Statute referred to the 'comarcas' (regions) that make up the four Catalan provinces and the 2006 statute fails to mention, even indirectly, these local authorities much discussed by the nationalist forces and notes that the territory of Catalonia is that corresponding to the geographical and administrative boundaries of the Generalitat. In any case, the territory is defined by reference to municipalities, regions, provinces or to the limits of the Community. The legal problem is to define exactly what is included within the concept of 'territory' of the Communities; certainly an important issue to determine the scope of its action, because the legal system is limited by the principle of territoriality, expressly stated in the Statutes of Autonomy. In the words of the Constitutional Court: the territory is considered as the 'spatial scope of applicability of the laws and actions of the Autonomous Community (STC 99/1986, 11 July, case *Estatuto de Autonomía de Castilla-León-2,* FJ 4). This implies that the Constitutional Court has consistently held that the competences of the Autonomous Communities are 'confined to its territory, although this does not prevent the exercise of the competences of one Autonomous Community from having repercussions beyond it'. (STC 38/2002, 14 February, case *Parque Natural Cabo de Gata,* FJ 6).

49. Clearly, the territory consists of the mainland, as a horizontal space in which human activity takes place; but there have been doubts about the inclusion of the maritime zone and the territorial sea. In our legal history, the Supreme Court had ruled that the maritime zone itself is part of the territory of the coastal municipalities, while the territorial sea was not. This distinction has been accepted by the Constitutional Court, which in one of its first judgments, recalled the jurisprudence of the Supreme Court stating that ports and the maritime zone are part of the coastal municipalities, adding that 'it seems clear that the same doctrine should apply to the division of the national territory in the Autonomous Communities (Article 137 of the Constitution), especially when the division of the country into Autonomous Communities is now complete' (STC 77/1984, July 3, case *Ordenación Urbana de Bilbao*, FJ 3). The consequences of including the maritime zone in the autonomous territory were immediately reflected in the competences of the Communities. So the autonomous competence on land use, permitted under Article 148.1.3 of the Constitution and then set out in all the Statutes, included coastal administration because 'there is no doubt that the coast belongs to the territory' (STC 149/1991, 4 July, case *Ley de Costas*, FJ 1).

50. Conversely, the Constitutional Court has denied that the territorial sea forms part of the autonomous territory because the territory of the municipalities that make up the communities has never been extended to the sea. The consequence of the exclusion of the territory for the competences is that only exceptionally can autonomous competences be exercised over the territorial sea, which will require that 'there is an explicit statutory recognition only when it is essential for the exercise of the jurisdiction of those who hold it' (STC 3/2014, 16 January, case *Autorización de instalaciones de generación eléctrica en el mar territorial,* FJ 3). The practical example of what this doctrine means is given in the same judgment: Communities cannot intervene in the energy production facilities in the territorial sea because they are not located in their territory. Thus, while they have the power to authorize windmills on land, they cannot do so at sea. And the exclusion of the territorial sea applies even in the Canary Islands where the Statute provides that 'the territory of the Autonomous Community of the Canary Islands comprises the Canaries Archipelago'. Therefore it is the State and not the Community that can issue authorizations for exploration and research permits under the seabed (STC 8/2013, 17 January, case *Ley del sector de hidrocarburos*).

II. The Autonomous Communities' Own Institutions

51. Article 147 of the Constitution provides that the Statute must contain the name, organization and seat of its own autonomous institutions. For the first degree Communities Article 152.1 specifies the institutions that the Statutes must include:

(a) A legislative assembly elected by universal suffrage under a system of proportional representation, with a just representation of the various territories.
(b) The President of the community is elected by the Assembly from among its members and appointed by the King. The same Article 152 defines the functions of the President: directing the Governing Council, representing the Community and the State's ordinary representation in the latter, understanding by this the set of public authorities (State-Community) and not the ordinary representative of the central government, which is the Government Delegate, that is, a delegate appointed by the central Government to direct State Administration in the territory (Article 154 SC).
(c) A Governing Council with executive and administrative functions.

Without being an institution of the Autonomous Community, as the judiciary is unified throughout the State (Articles 117.5, 123 and in 152.1 SC itself), these Statutes shall also create a High Court of Justice which shall head the judiciary within the territory of the Autonomous Community.

52. As these institutions only have to be included in Statutes prepared by the procedure of Article 151.2 and the Constitution remains silent on other institutions, a systematic interpretation (*inclusius unius, exclusius alterior*) of the Basic Act should have implied that only the Basque Country, Catalonia, Galicia and Andalusia had their own legislatures, a conclusion consistent not only in the light of Articles 147 and 151, but also the distinction between nationalities and regions referred to in Article 2. But we know that this logic of duality in the development the autonomous State was soon abandoned (paragraph 4); thus all Statutes included a Legislative Assembly, a President and a Governing Council. Moreover, some authors have even pointed out that the Constitution creates the paradox of imposing greater limitations, from the organizational point of view, on those Autonomous Communities which generically have greater autonomy, leaving second degree Communities free to create institutions that they consider most appropriate within constitutional principles. Thus they could establish a bicameral parliament, a majority electoral system, etc. This position makes it clear that only a literal interpretation of the Constitution is sustainable, but that a systematic or a historical interpretation is not maintained. Considering these, Article 152 is not a limit but, rather, a guarantee for first degree Communities: whatever may be the will of the drafters of the Statute (and it cannot be forgotten that in the ordinary procedure, the weight of Parliament is well above its weight in the special procedure) the Constitution guarantees a political organization. And as proof of this we see that the ordinary statutes have adopted the institutional organization of Article 152 instead of the theoretical freedom of Article 147 to develop an organizational structure of a different political power.

III. Competences

53. Article 147 also includes among the mandatory contents of the Statute the competences assumed within the framework established by the Constitution and the basis for the transfer of their services. The competences will be extensively discussed in the third part of this book, so now we shall just point out, that as we know, this is the point of the essential difference between the Communities of first and second degree. The Constitution states that these second degree Communities have competences limited during the first five years to the lists of matters set out in Article 148; however, the reforms of the 1990s have led to a blurring of that distinction. Moreover, we must emphasize that to know exactly the meaning of many of the autonomous competences contained in the Statute, it is necessary to consider the constitutional mandates as many of the competences defined in the Statutes as 'exclusive' in truth are not so, both because it is one thing to confer competences on a community, the Statute affects State competences (which loses the competences that the Community gains) and quite another to break 'the framework of Article 149.1 SC so denaturing the content that is specific to each subject and gives it its recognizability as an institution. What is important in this regard is the Statute of Autonomy, being a norm with limited territorial effect; if on occasions it may have to clarify the scope of the matters of State competence, it does so to encourage greater specificity of autonomous competences that correlate with it and in doing so it does not prevent the full deployment of its own State competences regulated in

Article. 149.1 of the Spanish Constitution' (STC 247/2007, 12 December, case *Reforma del Estatuto de la Comunidad Valenciana*, FJ 10).

54. The consequences of this way of understanding the autonomous competences contained in a Statute is, first, that we must always interpret their mandates in accordance with the provisions of the Constitution to respect State competences and, second, that when that interpretation is not possible, the Constitutional Court will have no choice-if it is asked, of course – but to declare that the statutory mandates that encroach upon the State competences are unconstitutional. For example, the Constitutional Court declared contrary to the *Lex Legum* Article 75.1 of the Statute of Autonomy of Castilla-León that attributed to that Community the competences of the legislative development and implementation over the waters of the Duero Basin supra-community because despite limiting it to waters which originated in Castilla-León and Portugal derived without crossing another Autonomous Community, it meant infringing 'the competences reserved to the State by Article 149.1.22 SC and exercised by it through state legislation on water deploying integrative function and reduction of the unit which is their own' (STC 32/2011, 17 March, case *Reforma del Estatuto de Autonomía de Castilla-León,* FJ 7).

§4. Other Contents of the Statute Derived from the Basic Institutional Norm of the Community

55. As the basic institutional law of a community, the content of the Statute is not limited to the matters reserved by Article 147.2 of the Constitution; it can contain all the provisions, when permitted by the Constitution, that serve that function. In fact, the Constitution itself provides that the Statute may declare the official use of their particular languages (Article 3.2), recognize own flags (Article 4.2), regulate the appointment of the autonomous senators (Article 69.5), etc. But in the deployment of the Autonomous State the Statutes have increasingly included more subjects; two texts particularly mark what might be called the enlargement of the basic institutional rules of the Communities: the Andalusian Statute of 1981 that established 'objectives of the Community', which were followed by other Statutes, and the Catalan Statute of 2006 which dramatically increased the extent of the first Statute of 1979, becoming much longer than the Spanish Constitution itself, a trend which one way or another the Statutes subsequently approved have then followed: long preamble, introduction of a declaration of rights, detailed development of competences, including external action, in particular in relation to the European Union, etc. (paragraph 32). There is nothing unconstitutional about it because 'the constitutionally lawful content of the Statutes of Autonomy includes both what the Constitution expressly provides, as well as the content, even if not expressly stated in the Constitution, it is a completely appropriate connection to the aforementioned constitutional provisions, an appropriateness to be interpreted as referring strictly to the function the Constitution entrusts to the Constitution Statute, as basic institutional rule to carry out the functional, institutional and regulatory competence of each Autonomous Community' (STC 247/2007, 12 December, case *Reforma del Estatuto de la Comunidad Valenciana*, FJ 12).

56. The normative value of these statutory provisions, which are not required by Article 147 of the Constitution, is heterogeneous. While some cannot be doubted, even their transgression is sanctioned by the Penal Code (as for example insults to the flag) others are provisions that can be understood as recommendations or even obligations to the Community but which can never be interpreted as mandates binding on the central State, such as the multiple references that the new Catalan Statute makes to the participation of the Community in State functions (health and hydrological planning, drafting legislation for children, etc.) and according to the Constitutional Court they do not divest the State legislature of the power to determine 'freely the expressed participation, their specific content and specific manner of articulation, and ownership of state powers and freedom in their exercise must be safeguarded and belongs to the agencies and institutions of the State' (STC 31/2010, 28 June, *case Reforma del Estatuto de Autonomía de Cataluña*, FJ 104). In short, there are other provisions that although denominated as 'rights' (such as Valencia's right to water) are actually – according to the case-law of the Constitutional Court – mandates to the legislature and not genuine subjective rights. Moreover, there are other mandates, I would add on my own account and risk, whose ability to bind has not been evidenced in all the years of the existence of the autonomous State; they are programmatic norms lacking practical efficiency. One example is demonstrated when the Andalusian Statute of 1981 declared that the aim of the Community was 'industrial development as the foundation of the harmonious growth of Andalusia', and in reality not only has the Autonomous Community economy not been based on industry (rather on construction and tourism), but industry in Andalusia has grown less than in the rest of Spain.

§5. Models of Statute: Original Statutes and Derived Statutes

57. The Basque and Catalan Statutes were developed in parallel to each other and the Constitution – so that their respective drafts were presented in the record of Parliament on the same day that the Constitution entered into force: 29 December 1979. Both Statutes coincided in their willingness to fully develop the autonomy of their nationalities, so they have very similar Articles on the 'jurisdictional order', as well as in the basic configuration of the design of institutions (Parliament, President-Government). However, underneath this similarity there are differences that stem from the characteristics of the Basque Country: the new community integrated in its political organization the provinces of Álava, Guipúzcoa and Vizcaya, which already enjoyed a 'foral' (local, special) scheme of self-government, including a special financing system (paragraph 36). Therefore, the Statute of Autonomy not only created an Autonomous Community but was also 'the most decisive element updating the systems of the three historic provinces integrated in the Autonomous Community of the Basque Country' (STC 76/1988, 26 April, case *Ley vasca de Territorios Históricos,* FJ 5). That gave it a special political organization with much weight in the provinces. For example, the three chose the same number of deputies; the provincial councils have many competences, especially in the assessment and collection of taxes, etc.

58. Logically, these characteristics of the Basque Country prevented the Basque Statute from being a model for other statutes, although some specific provisions have been followed, such as deferring the choice of capital to a decision of the Parliament, an idea that other territories where there had been a controversy over the capital, like Galicia, Andalusia, etc. then took. For that reason, and because Catalonia has always been seen by the rest of Spain as the most advanced territory, the Catalan Statute was the great model inspiring the other statutes in the 1980s, both those of the other two special Statutes, Galicia and Andalusia, as well as the ordinary Statutes that were approved later and that in the 1990s were reformed to increase the level of their competences. Thus, Catalonia has been regarded as the driving force of the autonomous State and its status as an original Statute that the vast majority of territories have been imitating.

59. In the twenty-first century Catalonia has continued that role of leader of the autonomous State and its Statute of 2006 has been a source of inspiration for all new Statutes approved thereafter. Therefore, the new Statutes of Valencia, Andalusia, Balearic Islands, Aragon, Extremadura and Castilla-León have adopted a very similar structure to the Catalan Statute: long preamble, new titles dedicated to rights and foreign policy, detailed lists of competences, etc. However, these Statutes have been careful to avoid some trouble spots of the Catalan statute such as describing itself as 'nation' or attributing to itself State competences and which forced the Constitutional Court in its famous judgment of 31/2010 either to interpret twenty-seven items of the Catalan Statute as in accordance with the Constitution, or to declare another fourteen unconstitutional in some point. Even so, there have already been two judgments in which Articles have been annulled-Articles on water in the Andalusian (STC 30/2011) and Castile-Leon Statutes (STC 32/2011).

§6. Processes for Amendment (Alteration) and Revision (Replacement)

60. Article 147.3 of the Constitution remits the amendment procedure to the Statutes themselves stating that in all of them the approval of the State Parliament is necessary through an. In general, the Statutes have used that Constitutional authorization to strengthen the complex nature of the act of the Statutes, unchangeable by a single will. Thus Statutes enjoy a high rigidity, unknown to other organic laws, demonstrating their special, quasi-constitutional nature. Table 1 sets out both the dates of adoption of the Statutes and the dates of amendments.

Interestingly, although the Spanish legal language distinguishes (as does the Constitution itself) between revision and reform to indicate whether it is a complete replacement of the legal norm or only some of its Articles, the Statutes always use only the word 'reforma'. Thus 'reforma' is used in the Organic Act 7/2013 of 28 November on the reform of Organic Act 4/1982 of 9 June on the Autonomous Statute of the Region of Murcia, which changes only one Article and occupies just two pages of the BOE, and the Organic Act 6/2006, of 19 July, amending the Statute of Autonomy of Catalonia, which changes one text for another and occupies 42 pages of the BOE.

61. The Statutes drafted under the ordinary procedure in general give the initiative for their reform to the Autonomous Government and Parliament and to the State Parliament. However, so far the State Parliament has never initiated a reform which has always come from the autonomous legislatures. For the reform bill to become law it must be approved by the autonomous Parliament, usually with a quorum of two-thirds, although some statutes reduce this to an absolute majority when the purpose of the amendment is to extend the powers of the Community, as permitted by Article 148.2 of the Constitution (e.g., Asturias and Murcia). It must also be approved by an organic law by the State Parliament, as required by Article 149.3 of the Constitution itself and repeated in every Statute.

In the new Statutes approved since 2006 such as those of Valencia, Aragon and Extremadura, the position of the Community in the *iter legis* is reinforced by various techniques, such as allowing the autonomous parliaments to withdraw the draft reform from the State Parliament 'at any time during its processing prior to the final vote in its totality' and authorizing the convening of a referendum after its approval by the State Parliament if so decided by the Autonomous Parliament.

62. The reform of a statute prepared under the procedure of Article 151.2 requires, besides the participation of the Autonomous parliament and the State Parliament, the approval by referendum of the registered voters as mandated by Article 152.2 of the Constitution. Of the four statutes prepared under this procedure, it is interesting to mention now that the role of the Autonomous Community has been enhanced, so that, when drafting the Statute the central Parliament had the 'last word' (with the vote of ratification), but with this reform it is now the Community that makes the final decision as the referendum takes place after the State Parliament has approved the organic law reform. If the reform is intended to deal with organizational aspects (simple alteration of the organization of powers of the Autonomous Community), the four Statutes further reduce the role of the Spanish Parliament to establish a procedure we may call special and the new Statute of Andalusia describes as 'simplified':

(1) Preparation of draft amendment/reform by the autonomous Parliament.
(2) Consultation with the *Cortes* (central Parliament).
(3) If within thirty days the central Parliament declares itself not affected by the reform of the text, it will be submitted to a referendum.
(4) Finally, central Parliament approval by an organic law is required. The Statutes have considered this approval as an act necessary only to comply with Article 147.3 of the Constitution that requires an organic law to amend the statute.

Chapter 2. Types of Community Law

§1. Autonomous Laws

63. A distinctive feature of a compound State is the plurality of state legislatures; the seventeen Spanish Autonomous Communities can approve general norms with the force of law, which have a similar legal nature to State law. Thus, using traditional definitions, we can say that the Autonomous law is a binding general and abstract legal mandate for citizens, public authorities and courts. When equated with State law, their relationship is governed by the principle of competences, not hierarchy. Therefore, Autonomous law serves to enforce the reserves of law established by the Constitution in many matters (e.g., to regulate private property) and the only way to eject it from the system, unlike its repeal by another law of equal or higher rank, is by a decision of the Constitutional Court.

64. The main difference between State and Autonomous law lies in the strong limitation imposed by the principle of territoriality on autonomous systems, which both prevents the autonomous laws from regulating matters outside its territory and its provisions from taking effect beyond its territorial limits. The Constitutional Court has from its first decisions avoided declaring contrary to the Constitution autonomous laws regulating matters located within its territory even though they may have consequences outside it because that 'would inevitably, purely and simply, deprive it of all its capacity to act' (STC 37/1981, 16 November, case *Centros de Contratación de Cargas*, FJ 1). The LOTC has introduced another important difference between the two laws: relying on the text of Article 161.2 of the Constitution that allows the Government to ask the Constitutional Court to suspend the autonomous law under appeal and this automatically suspends it for five months. This has become a common practice of all Spanish Governments regardless of their political orientation. However, when the Communities appeal a State law, it is not suspended, applying the principle of presumption of constitutionality.

65. Another constraint faced by many autonomous laws comes from the technical division of powers, hence the existence of horizontal governmental competences (especially in economic planning which is projected in many areas) and by the distribution of matters where the basic law is the competence of the State and its development that of the Communities (paragraph 133). Both techniques entail State laws being able to determine the content of the autonomous laws, so that although they have the same range as State laws, in practice many of them are limited by the provisions of State law. Perhaps for this decline in their regulatory margin, Communities sometimes pass laws with content typical of the provisions of the executive, such as the expropriation of some specific goods or the approval of a town development plan. The Constitutional Court, without denying that such individual laws have a place in the Spanish legal system, has demanded a series of requirements that to date several autonomous laws, subject to appeal to the Constitutional Court, have not met. An example is the Law passed by the parliament of the Canary Islands 2/1992 of 26 June expropriating certain buildings adjoining the

Canary Parliament without justifying why it chose these and not others also contiguous (STC 48/2005, 3 March). Equally, Act 6/2007 of Castile and Leon, approving the autonomous project 'Environment City' was declared unconstitutional as it undermined the right to effective judicial protection of citizens who could not challenge its content (typically administrative) before the ordinary jurisdiction.

§2. Special Law: Laws of Absolute Majority and Budgetary Laws

66. What one might call the liberal Spanish State legislation pyramid was very simple: Constitution, law and regulation. Over time, that scheme introduced new rules, such as legislative decrees and decree-laws, both approved by the Government, but comparable with those laws enacted by Parliament. The 1978 Constitution further complicates matters both because it created the Autonomous State, with new legislative powers, and it established special laws drafted by the general legislative power itself, such as the organic act and the budgetary law. However, when creating their own autonomous legal system, the Statutes of Autonomy of 1979 only expressly contemplated autonomous law and regulations. However, and without giving it any special name, the Statute of Catalonia and afterwards almost all the others, demanded an absolute majority to pass several controversial laws, such as the electoral laws. This requirement has been expanded with the statutory reforms, while the new Catalan Statute stipulates that an absolute majority is required to legislate over ten matters, a trend that has been followed by other statutes, so that a quorum is required to pass language laws, the electoral system, the territorial structure of the Community, the transfer of community powers to municipalities, the regime of the President of the Community, the popular legislative initiative, etc.

67. Article 66.2 of the Constitution distinguishes between the legislative power of the State Parliament and the approval of the budget. This approval is made by law but, according to a vigorous decision of the Constitutional Court, it is a special law that differs from the others by its content and by certain characteristics in the procedure to pass it. The Statutes of Autonomy have similarly configured their budgetary laws. Thus, the Councils of the Autonomous Communities monopolize the development of the budget, its processing is given priority over other laws and the amendments that involve increased spending or reduced revenues can only be processed if the respective Government Council gives its assent. As for the content of the Finance Act, it must contain all the expenditure and income of the public sector of the Autonomous Community while not being able to create taxes. It is precisely because these characteristics make them different from other laws that the Constitutional Court has refused to allow the budgetary law to contain terms that are not directly related to expenditure and income. Thus, the practice of using regular budgetary laws, which had been very common in both the State and the Communities to modify substantive laws ended in the 1990s (STC 178/1994, 16 June, case *Presupuestos Generales del Estado para 1990*).

§3. Legislative Decrees

68. All autonomous parliaments can delegate the possibility of issuing rules with the force of law to their respective Governments. While the first statutes did not establish any specific mandate in this regard and the delegation was without statutory basis, the subsequent trend has been to regulate the decrees thoroughly in the Statute, to the point that some of them (such as the Catalan and Andalusian) even say, in my opinion superfluously, that they cannot delegate laws reforming the Statutes. Similarly, they are also prohibited from delegating budgetary laws and those that require qualified majorities in Parliaments. As the Constitution does for the State, the Statutes establish two types of delegation: one that is made to innovate the legal system, which will be a basic law and the other to recast the texts of several laws into what will become an ordinary law. Just as has happened in the State, the basic law is rarely used in the Communities and is on track to disappear through disuse (only Catalonia and Valencia have ever used it and they have not done so since 1994), while ordinary delegation is much more common to pass legislative decrees. It is certainly illogical that the legislature refuses to discuss in depth the laws regulating a matter and to delegate this responsibility to the executive. It is much more logical to remit the task of clarifying the applicable legislation on a subject, a technical function which the executive may well undertake in favour of legal certainty and always under the control of both Parliament and the courts.

§4. Decree-Laws

69. Until 2006 no Autonomy Statute provided for the possibility of passing decree-laws, but Organic Act 1/2006 of 10 April on reform of the Organic Act 5/1982, of 1 July, the Statute of Autonomy of Valencia chose that source of law, copying it from the provisions of the State Constitution. This was followed by the new Catalan Statute of Autonomy and then all the others, such as those of Andalusia and Extremadura. In general the regulation made by the Statutes is similar to that of the Constitution: Legislative Decrees may be issued in cases of extraordinary and urgent need, but may not affect the rights established in the Statute, the electoral system or the institutions and must be validated within thirty days, being able to be passed into law by the urgent procedure. In my opinion, the usefulness of Decree-laws at the autonomous level is highly debatable because it is a rarely justified invasion of the legislative power, especially if we bear in mind that the autonomous legislatures are unicameral and also their regulations provide mechanisms to process bills quickly. However, in recent years the autonomous governments have seen otherwise, to the point that in some legislatures (such as Andalusia 2012–2015) they have approved more Decree-laws than laws (thirty-five versus nineteen). The Constitutional Court, following its general doctrine, admitted that the economic crisis could justify the urgency of the autonomous Decree-laws (STC 93/2015, 14 May, case *Decreto-ley andaluz 6/2013, de medidas para asegurar el cumplimiento de la Función Social de la Vivienda*).

§5. REGULATIONS

70. Historically in Spanish law the government has always had the capacity to adopt regulations to develop the law. Therefore, most State laws often direct the central government to issue regulations necessary for developing the law in question, and the Autonomous Communities can enact autonomous laws for their respective Governing Councils, making regulations known as 'executive'. Moreover, the legislatures of both the State and Autonomous Communities can issue regulations without an express legal mandate since both the Constitution and the Statutes of Autonomy expressly recognize their regulatory power; however, in that case they may only do so in matters not reserved to law; therefore, the normal scope of these 'independent regulations' is the organization of the Administration itself, while they are seldom addressed directly to the citizens. In any case, whether executive or independent, regulations are norms below the law. Therefore, Spanish judges, to whom the Constitution does not grant the power to refuse to apply a law it deems unconstitutional (it must consult with the Constitutional Court), do have that power in the case where an unconstitutional or illegal regulation has to be applied, they may even annul it, so that the regulations of the Governments of the Autonomous Communities can challenge the High Courts of the Communities against those of the Autonomous Governments. Moreover, judges of lower courts can raise to these higher courts a 'question of illegality' to declare contrary to law certain Articles which the judge has previously refused to apply when delivering judgment, a similar system to the question of unconstitutionality that the Constitution created for laws that judges deem have violated it.

Chapter 3. Jurisprudence

§1. The Jurisdictional Control of Autonomous Norms

71. The Spanish autonomous communities do not have their own judiciary or 'statutory' courts, like the Constitutional Court, to take charge of ensuring that the autonomous laws are in accord with the Statute. Moreover, the Statute of Catalonia of 2006 established that the opinions of an advisory body such as the Council of Statutory Guarantees are binding when they report on the projects of law and bills of Parliament 'that develop or affect the rights recognized by the Statute' (Article 76.4 EAC). The Constitutional Court found that that provision was an invasion of its exclusive jurisdiction to control the laws, so it declared it unconstitutional and void (STC 31/2010, 28 June, *Reforma del Estatuto de Autonomia para Cataluña*). Therefore, control of the autonomous laws that might violate its Statute of Autonomy is done exclusively but indirectly by the Constitutional Court: if an appeal or question of unconstitutionality against an autonomous law is lodged accusing it of violating the Statute and the Court considers that it is indeed contrary to the Statute, then the Court would declare that it has also violated the Constitution because if it were maintained in force it would be a reform of the Statute for reasons other than those envisaged by the Constitution. Thus that autonomous law would be 'unconstitutional and against the statute'. This latter description actually falls within the former based on the provisions of Article 161.1 a) of the Constitution and Articles 27, 28.1 and 39 of the Organic Act of the Constitutional Court (STC 36/1981, 11 November, case *Inmunidad de los diputados vascos*).

§2. Other Important Sources for Interpretation of Statues of Autonomy

72. The Spanish Constitution provides that the Council of State is the highest advisory body to the government, an institution of great prestige with its roots going back to 1526, when Emperor Charles V founded it, and its liberalism was endorsed by the Constitution of Cadiz 1812. However, all Autonomous Communities have ended up creating similar bodies, often under the name of Consultative Council, made up of prestigious jurists or people who have held important positions in the Community (former presidents) to whom is attributed the function of ensuring (as set out in the Statute of Castile-la Mancha) 'the observance of the Constitution, the Statute of Autonomy of Castile-La Mancha and the entire legal system'. In general, the opinions of these advisory councils are important for autonomous institutions because, although they are not legally binding, the fact that they are written by experts gives them an authority that politicians cannot easily ignore. And their intervention is required in almost all communities for virtually all policy initiatives of governments: draft reforms of the Statute, laws and executive regulations, also implementing rulings when the autonomous government wants to bring an appeal of unconstitutionality or a conflict of competences, etc.

Chapter 4. Political Actions to Reform the Statues of Autonomy

§1. Reform Policy of the Statutes Within the General Political Actions of the State

73. In Spain the reforms of the Statutes does not rest exclusively with the Autonomous Communities, as in most federal States, but rather the State also intervenes because the Statutes are always approved by Spanish Parliament. Therefore, the statutory reforms are very close to national politics. In general, we can say that these changes in the basic texts of the Communities have not responded as much as they have in the United States to reflect the struggle of interests of social groups within each Autonomous Community and the desire of local political elites to gain more power against the central government. This is because, as we have already had occasion to explain, the Spanish Constitution does not, unlike the American, make a complete division of responsibilities between the State and the Autonomous Communities, but the State reserves a minimum to itself (Article 149.1) and allows the rest to be assumed by the Autonomous Communities as established by its Statute (paragraph 8). This *dispositive principle* was intended at the time to establish two types of communities, those of the nationalities and those of the regions; in practice it led to a logic by which the Communities in the early years had fewer competences (as in Aragon and Extremadura) They wanted to reform their statutes to match those with greater autonomy, which they eventually achieved in the 1990s. And given the prestige that the autonomies enjoyed for many years in Spain, all local organizations of national parties were in favour of greater autonomous power. Even the national parties themselves made two pacts to develop the autonomous state in the direction of greater equality between communities than that which could be deduced from a literal reading of the Constitution: first in July 1981 they agreed that all autonomous governments would have a Legislative Assembly, so the differences between them would not be of quality (some with their own legislatures and others without it), but of quantity: the first degree (such as Catalonia, the Basque Country and Andalusia) had more powers than those of the second. And later, in February 1992 they agreed on a comprehensive reform of the Statutes of second degree to increase their competences, especially in education and health.

74. The origin of the Autonomous State is above all an attempt to meet the demands for self-government of Catalonia and the Basque Country, which historically have been channelled through their own parties, especially CiU in Catalonia and the Basque Nationalist Party (Partido Nacionalista Vasco (PNV)). These parties have worked in Parliament as lobby groups in the sense that when the largest party in general elections has not won an absolute majority Convergencia and the PNV have lent it their support in exchange for higher degrees of self-government. For example, this happened in the legislatures 1993–1996 and 2004–2008 with socialist governments and in 1996–2000 with a PP conservative government. In these three legislatures the nationalist parties supported the central government, which in return, agreed to legal changes to increase the power of the Autonomous Communities in general and, particularly, for Catalonia and the Basque Country.

75. In addition to these enhanced powers by the *ordinary* way of state laws, some of the communities with greater autonomy in the early twenty-first century proposed reforms of their statutes to increase their self-government, first the Basque Country, with a failed bill and afterwards Catalonia. In these cases there was a great division within each community between supporters of reforms and those who opposed them. The first relied mostly on their right to self-government while the latter argued that the reform did not respect the Spanish Constitution. As we know, the reform of the Basque Statute was rejected by the Spanish Parliament in 2005 (paragraph 17) while the Catalan was approved, but in 2010 the Constitutional Court ruled that some Articles violated the Constitution (paragraph 18). Interestingly, this reform of the Catalan institutions spread to the Andalusian, who immediately began to prepare a new statute, obviously inspired by the Catalan, which had already been approved in 2007, with the majority of its most controversial aspects watered down. In turn, another group of Communities has followed this path motivated it seems in not being less than the Catalan Community, rather than by each community's own needs.

§2. The Autonomous Policy of Reform of the Statutes Compared with Ordinary Politics of the Communities

76. Since the statutory reform policy is closely linked to the general policy of the State and that of Catalonia, which has a clear lead in this matter, then it cannot surprise us that the policy of reform and the ordinary statutory policy of each Community are very mixed, responding to different logics. In general, the confrontation in the autonomous politics of each Community is marked, first and obviously by ideological differences between parties, but sometimes also by their national strategies, which have resulted in situations that do not contribute to the prestige of politics as the art of the common good. Thus in the past there have been cases of Communities fighting with the central government whom they accused of not respecting the order of competences when that Government completely changed its attitude, not just in politics but also in the legal sphere with the withdrawal of appeals and conflicts of unconstitutionality against State rules which to the new Government did not seem unconstitutional. Thus two very obvious cases were changes in the attitude of the Andalusian Autonomous Community (controlled by PSOE) when the socialist party won the 2004 elections and took control of the national government and the Galician conservative party in 2011 when the PP conservative party won the general elections.

Part II. Forms of Subnational Government

Chapter 1. General

§1. Introduction

77. Unlike the Constitutions of the classical federated States, we have seen that the Spanish Constitution does not itself create any subnational entity with political capacity, but it establishes a series of procedures which State institutions cannot arbitrarily curb – in order to create them under the name of Autonomous Communities. Once created, the Constitution guarantees both the existence and the competences of the Communities, which technically is achieved by converting the Statute of Autonomy into an agreed Act, which cannot be freely modified by the State (paragraph 42).

78. In addition to that way of creating the Statutes, the Constitution safeguards the position of the Autonomous Communities by various legal techniques, beginning with its Article 2: 'It recognizes and guarantees the right to autonomy of the nationalities and regions of which it is composed and the solidarity amongst them all.' Then, in Title VIII the competences of the State are established and it sets out those which the Communities can assume remitting this decision to the Statutes. Therefore, the Constitution and Statutes make up the 'constitutionality block' of each Autonomous Community which fixes the competences of both spheres in each autonomous territory. As a guarantee of this autonomy, that block can only be modified by reforming the Constitution or Statutes, which in both cases require rigid procedures (paragraph 60). In addition, disputes that may arise (and over the years there have been many) in their interpretation are resolved by the Constitutional Court which, as in all composite States, performs an essential function of delimiting the actions of the public authorities.

79. The territorial integrity of the Autonomous Communities is guaranteed because its territory is set out in each Statute of Autonomy. Some of these statutes have established special provisions on the possibility of altering their territory, thinking especially in 'enclaves' or territories of a Community completely surrounded by another Community due to historical reasons. The most important example is the County of Treviño which is located in the Basque Country, but belongs to Castile-Leon. To date, there have been no territorial alterations, nor does it seem easy to do so in the future both due to political constraints (no Autonomous Community leader wants to see the territory reduced), and legal difficulties as the

Statutes like that of Castile-León have created some very complicated procedures that have to be satisfied if these changes are to be made.

80. A special case of provisions on territorial enclaves is Gibraltar, a territory ceded by Spain to the United Kingdom by the Treaty of Utrecht of 1713 and considered by the United Nations since 1963 as a territory subject to decolonization. However, the Andalusian Statute, using an elaborate circumlocution in order not to name it, states 'the expansion of the Autonomous Community provinces to historical territories not integrated into another Autonomous Community will be resolved by Parliament, with the prior agreement of the parties concerned and without entailing reform of this Statute, once these territories have returned to Spanish sovereignty'. Put more directly: the Statute of Autonomy of Andalusia states that the hypothetical integration of Gibraltar in Andalusia will be a decision of Parliament, which could also choose a special regime of autonomy for the Rock outside Andalusia. This latter specification is somewhat legally superfluous (it is the Constitution that attributes this power to Parliament), but certainly desirable from the political point of view.

81. Neither the Constitution nor the Spanish laws guarantee as a general feature a policy of *intrafederalism*, as does the European law which provides for representation of its Member States in its most relevant institutions. However, in Spanish political practice the territorial origin of the members of the central State organs is taken into account, especially in that most visible to citizens, the Government, where the various presidents who have governed during the democracy have sought to form their teams with people from different Spanish territories, but without applying any rigid quota. The parties also seek to integrate representatives from all the territories in their governing bodies.

82. In any event, the Senate is expressly defined by the Constitution as 'the chamber of territorial representation'. But after that definition, the composition of the Senate is based on both the Communities and the provinces, and what is more, the weight of these is greater than that of the Communities:

(a) In each province, four senators are elected, except in the three island provinces, where the constituencies are the islands: three senators in each of the large islands (Gran Canaries, Tenerife and Mallorca) and one for the small: Ibiza-Formentera, Menorca, Fuerteventura, Gomera, Hierro, Lanzarote and La Palma; in addition, the cities of Ceuta and Melilla elect two senators each. In total, citizens directly elect 208 senators by this route.
(b) Each Legislative Assembly of the Autonomous Communities chooses one senator plus one other for every million inhabitants, which in 2016 made up a total of fifty-eight senators.

And they have been distributed in recent legislatures as follows:

Autonomous Community	VII Legislature (2000–2004)	VIII (2004–2008)	IX (2008–2011)	X (2011–2015)	XI (2016) and XII (2016-)
Andalusia	8	8	9	9	9
Aragon	2	2	2	2	2
Asturias	2	2	2	2	2
Balearic Islands	1	1	2	2	2
Canary Islands	2	2	3	3	3
Cantabria	1	1	1	1	1
Castile-La Mancha	2	2	2	3	3
Castile and León	3	3	3	3	3
Catalonia	7	7	8	8	8
Extremadura	2	2	2	2	2
Galicia	3	3	3	3	3
La Rioja	1	1	1	1	1
Madrid	6	6	7	7	7
Murcia	2	2	2	2	2
Navarra	1	1	1	1	1
Valencia	5	5	5	6	6
Basque Country	3	3	3	3	3
Total	51	51	56	58	58

83. In general, this mixed composition of the Senate (266 senators of whom only 58 are elected by the Communities) does not have too much political or academic support and therefore most politicians and experts believe that it should be changed to give more relevance to the Communities, but despite this unanimity in the diagnosis, the Constitution has not been reformed at this point in time, among other reasons because there is disagreement on what model should replace the current one: while some think they have to go to the American model, in which the citizens of each community directly elect senators in Autonomous Community constituencies, other prefer the German model in which Autonomous Community governments make up the Senate. Admittedly, there have been some other reforms that high light the territorial character, such as allowing the use of Autonomous Community languages in their parliamentary activities.

84. With regard to its functions, the Senate is one of two chambers of the Spanish Parliament, but in general it is subordinate to Congress even in the processing of the Statutes of Autonomy (paragraphs 9–14) and other functions directly related to territorial autonomy, such as the authorization of agreements between Communities (Article 145.2 SC) and the drafting of the Act on the Inter-Territorial Compensation Fund (Article 158.2 SC). However, the Constitution has reserved a couple of important functions of the Senate in relation to the Autonomous Communities.
First, Article 150.3 puts it on a par with Congress when assessing the need to enact laws to harmonize the regulatory provisions of the Communities, as the Constitution requires an absolute majority in each of the two chambers. Moreover, Article 155 of the Constitution makes it the guarantor of autonomy in a rather delicate process technically known as 'State coercion': if the central Government considers that a Community is not fulfilling its constitutional obligations, it will need authorization from the absolute majority of the Senate Plenary session to 'adopt the necessary measures' to oblige it to do so. This Article has not been developed generally by the Spanish legislation, so that both the cases in which it could be applied and the measures that could be taken, have given rise to very lively discussion in recent years due to the challenge of the independent parties like the Catalan nationalists, who govern that Community. The only law that makes specific reference to its application is the Organic Act 2/2012 of 27 April on Budgetary Stability and Financial Sustainability (LOEPSF) in three highly technical cases, in which they could be applied, recopying them, almost verbatim, from Article 155 of the Constitution: if the Autonomous Community fails to adopt 'enforceable measures' that the Government requires to avoid excessive deficits, then the Government, after authorization by an absolute majority of the Senate, 'may take the necessary measures to oblige the Autonomous Community to implement enforcement measures. For the execution of the measures the Government may issue instructions to all the authorities of the Autonomous Community' (Article 26 LOEPSF).

85. Finally, Article 159.1 of the Constitution gives the Senate power to appoint four members of the Constitutional Court, the supreme interpreter of the Constitution and arbiter of conflicts of competences between the State and the Communities. Since 2007 the LOTC determines that these appointments have to be made based on the proposals of candidates made by the seventeen autonomous parliaments, a decision that the Constitutional Court considered compatible with the Constitution and that highlights 'an unequivocal constitutional willingness to integrate the territorial structure of the State into the composition of the Constitutional Court' (STC 49/2008, 9 April, case *Articulo 16 LOTC*).

§2. Political Parties

86. Since the early years of the restoration of democracy, the Spanish political system has been characterized by the dominance of two major parties, one centre-right (UCD from 1977 to 1982 and since then the PP) and the other centre-left, the PSOE, who have taken turns in the central government. However, in the Autonomous Communities the party system has been more plural due to the existence of territorial parties, some of which have even more electoral support than the two major national parties. Thus, CiU and the PNV have ruled most of the time in their communities, Catalonia and the Basque Country in 1980. Other parties are Esquerra Republicana de Catalunya, Compromis (Valencia), Coalition Canaria, and Partido Aragonesista and Bloque Nacionalista Galego. All of them have ruled at some time in their communities in coalition with one of the two major parties.

87. In 2014 the two major parties lost many votes in favour of two other political forces, Podemos (left) and Ciudadanos (centre) who obtained good results in the European elections of that year and subsequently in local and autonomous elections of 2015 (in round terms, 15% and 7% respectively). This has meant that from that year only one Autonomous Community maintains an absolute majority (Galicia, which held elections in 2013) while in the other sixteen absolute majorities have been replaced either by coalition governments (as in Asturias, Cantabria and the Canary Islands) or by pacts in the legislatures in which the party that won most votes governs and has the support of another party not incorporated into the government (e.g., in Andalusia, Catalonia and Madrid).

88. From the legal point of view, the parties are mentioned in the Spanish Constitution of 1978, defined as a "fundamental instrument for political participation" (Article 6) and their regulation is attributed to an organic act (currently the Organic Act 6/2002). Therefore, the Autonomous Communities cannot pass laws to regulate them and references in the Statutes are very specific, such as when they may intervene in the election of the President of the Autonomous Community (paragraph 106).

§3. Miscellaneous (Referendum, Popular Initiative, Delegation of Power, etc.)

89. When the Constitution was drafted in 1977 and 1978 and after forty years of dictatorship, the constituents were very concerned about consolidating the then weak political parties. Therefore, as just noted, the parties are enshrined in Article 6 of the Constitution as the fundamental instrument for political participation and therefore also the techniques of direct citizen participation, such as the referendum and the popular legislative initiative appear shyly *cum grano salis*. Today both some parties and experts believe that more prominence should be given to these techniques of direct participation as the real alternative when organizing a democracy is not direct democracy versus representative democracy, but between plain representative democracy or Westminster model (named for the Palace of the British Parliament, not given to referendums) and a representative democracy with institutions of direct participation of citizens or the Swiss model – the Swiss are often called upon to decide in a referendum that is also followed in many states of the United States. As an additional precaution, the Constitution reserves to the State the authorization of the call for referendums, whether State, Autonomous Community or local (Article 149.1.32ª), so that the Communities cannot call a referendum or any other type of 'consultation that, despite the name, is technically a referendum, that is, 'a consultation whose aim strictly refers apparently to the electoral body and externalized through an electoral process' (STC 103/2008, 11 September, case *Ley del Parlamento Vasco 9/2008, de convocatoria y regulación de una consulta popular*).

90. This general prohibition by the Constitution against the techniques of direct democracy was also copied in the first Statutes of Autonomy, so that hardly any of them regulate direct participation techniques. Thus, they are limited to ordering that an autonomous law may regulate the popular legislative initiative. But they did not establish anything about the referendum or on the revocation of authorities, a technique known to be more characteristic of America than Europe. In the following years the Communities approved these laws of legislative initiative in terms similar to the Organic Act 3/1984 de iniciativa legislativa popular (on popular legislative initiative) in the State, so that a large number of citizens are required (e.g., 75,000 in Andalusia), to prevent it from being exercised in sensitive areas such as taxation and the Autonomous Parliament is free to accept or reject the initiative to start a vote known as to 'take into consideration'. It is far, therefore, from the Swiss system in which the legislative initiative is envisaged for all kinds of laws (including the Constitution) and in which laws must be voted for in a referendum when so demanded by 50,000 citizens and 100,000 for constitutional reforms.

91. The Statute of Autonomy of Catalonia of 2006 does not change the regime of legislative initiative, but does introduce the popular consultations as 'a right' of citizens (Article 29) that the Autonomous Community or 'Generalitat' must regulate 'except as provided for in Article 149.1.32 of the Constitution' (Article 122). This provision was interpreted by the Constitutional Court in the sense that the power to regulate (and not just summon) any referendum is the responsibility of the State, while the Generalitat may itself regulate surveys, public hearings, participation forums and any other instruments of popular consultation except referendums (STC 31/2010, 28 June, case *Reforma del Estatuto de Autonomía para Cataluña*). Regardless of the legal interpretation of this Article, it has been much debated politically because it was understood that it could serve as a legal basis for the call for a referendum on the link between Catalonia and Spain, defended by some nationalist forces, in the style of the referendums on Quebec sovereignty held there late in the last century. The other Statutes of what we have called the Neoautonomic State (paragraph 23), also included the possibility of referendums, but clearly reserved to the State the power to regulate referendums, which avoided any risk of invasion of State powers (Article. 50 of the Valencian Statute, 78 of the Andalusian, 71.27 of the Aragonese, etc.).

Chapter 2. Head of the Subnational Governmental Unit

§1. The Organ of the Subnational Unit (Designation)

92. As is well known, the Spanish Constitution provides that the Head of State is the King with symbolic and representational functions unrelated to daily politics, whose most important figure is the Prime Minister, (called the President) who is elected by the Congress of Deputies. This dual design Head of State, Head of Government, is typical of parliamentary systems, and does not apply in the Autonomous Communities where the Constitution itself establishes a single model: the President of the Community 'shall be responsible for directing the Governing Council, which constitutes the supreme representation of the respective Community as well as the State's ordinary representation therein' (Article 152 SC). However, the same Article of the Constitution states that the President of the Community shall be 'elected by the Assembly' (paragraph 106), so designing a parliamentary system in which the President of the Community is, above all, the chief executive and not a neutral figure with only symbolic functions.

§2. Legal Status (Privileges and Immunities, Inviolability, Personal Power, etc.)

93. The fact that the Constitution requires that the Presidents of the Communities are members of the Autonomous parliaments (Article 152.1.) means that they have the same prerogatives as Deputies: semi-immunity and inviolability and also almost all statutes attribute to their Presidents the special jurisdiction of the Supreme Court for criminal liability for any crime he is accused of, although the Statutes of the Basque Country and Catalonia prefer to attribute this competence to the High Court of Catalonia, unless their Presidents were accused of an offence committed outside the territory of the Community. In that case they order that the competent court is the Supreme Court. For civil liability for acts committed in the exercise of office (not therefore by any fact, as it does with criminal responsibility), almost all statutes confer jurisdiction on the High Court of the respective Community, although some (such as Andalusia) prefer the special jurisdiction of the Supreme Court also in these civil cases.

94. The Autonomous Community presidents are prohibited from undertaking other public functions other than, in addition to their own office, that of a parliamentarian; they are also required to give absolute dedication so they cannot perform any other work, professional or business activity. This exclusive dedication to their office is reinforced by the Acts of Governing on the creation of Cabinets or Councils of the Presidency – separate from Councils of Government with the aim of providing policy and technical assistance to President. The Autonomous Communities have copied the model implemented in the central State, which in turn is a copy of the American system, with the obvious difference that the respective constitutions designed two models of different government: the American presidential and European parliamentarian.

§3. COMPETENCES

95. When we study later the Executive Power we will see the functions of the President as a member of this power. Now we shall just set out their functions related to their symbolic role:

(1) The 'ordinary' State representative function assigned by the Constitution implies that the President represents the unity of the state as a system (most Presidents promulgate Autonomous laws 'on behalf of the King'), but he does not represent the central institutions of State, this function is performed by the Government Delegate (Article 154 SC).
(2) The President of the Community is the 'supreme representative' of the Autonomous Community. However, this representation is not political – for all the Statutes reserve this to the respective parliament-but symbolic and legal: he represents the unity of the Autonomous Community legal system and is the legal representative of the Autonomous Community as a legal entity. Therefore, he represents the Community in relations with other State institutions, signing conventions and cooperation agreements with other autonomous communities, convening the Autonomous Community elections, etc.

Chapter 3. The Legislature

§1. The Organ of State (Designation)

96. In Spain all Autonomous Community parliaments are unicameral and their members are elected directly by the citizens for a term of four years, although it can be dissolved in the cases established by the instances set out by the Statutes. The number of parliamentarians depends on the population of each community. Thus, in the least populated region, La Rioja, only 35 are chosen, while in Catalonia there are 135 deputies, 129 are chosen in Madrid, Andalusia 109, etc.

§2. Legal Status (Privileges and Immunities, Inviolability, Personal Power, etc.)

97. The collective prerogatives of the Autonomous Community parliaments are typical of a rule of law: regulatory autonomy, governance and budgetary power, which are joined by the inviolability of their headquarters, a prerogative little known in comparative law and that all statutes have taken slavishly from Article 66.3 of the Constitution for Parliament. The most important consequence of this prerogative is the special legal protection received by Autonomous Community parliaments, matched to Parliament in both the Criminal Code (crimes of rebellion, invasion of parliamentary seats, etc.), and the Public Safety Act (serious administrative offence by disturbance of public security against their headquarters).

98. Individual prerogatives for Autonomous Community parliamentarians are as follows:

(1) Inviolability, which is the typical irresponsibility for the views expressed in parliamentary acts and votes cast in the exercise of their duties, even after their mandate has ceased, and that in common law is called the 'speech and debate clause'.
(2) Semi-immunity means that during their tenure deputies cannot be arrested for criminal acts committed in the territory of the Community, except in cases of in flagrante delicto, as mandated by the Constitution for deputies and senators. However, the Statutes have not taken the other characteristic of immunity: the need to seek permission from the House to prosecute an Autonomous Community parliamentarian.
(3) Special courts for Members who will be judged by the Superior Court of the Community when they are accused of a crime committed in its territory, and the Supreme Court for crimes committed outside it. This prerogative is currently very unpopular and several parties have pledged to repeal it.

99. In addition to these prerogatives, parliamentarians have the classic rights of any parliamentarian to perform their duties: to attend and vote at meetings, be a member of at least one Commission, receive the documentation necessary for the development of their work, salary, etc.

§3. COMPETENCES

100. The Statutes of Autonomy include a long series of powers or functions of parliaments which can be summarized into five major groups:

(1) The representative function of the people of the respective Community.
(2) The role of participating in the legislative drafting of the reform of the Statute of Autonomy, which as we have seen in some detail is a norm agreed between the State and the Autonomous Community (paragraph 61).
(3) The legislative function. The *iter legis* in the Autonomous Community parliaments is very similar to the Congress, with its three phases of initiative, deliberation and publication. In the phase of initiative almost monopolized in practice by the Government – it should be noted that some statutes (such as Andalusia, Navarra, etc.) attribute legislative initiative to the Town Councils. The Statute of Catalonia 2006 does not do so, preferring to attribute it to 'the representative bodies of the supra-municipal entities' (Article 62).
(4) The functions of creation, maintenance and control of the Governing Council will be discussed in the next chapter.
(5) The functions related to other public institutions:
   (a) The appointment of members of the autonomous institutions of parliamentary origin, such as the Ombudsman, the Chamber of Accounts, etc.
   (b) The appointment of the Autonomous senators, whom the Constitution requires to be made taking into account criteria of proportional representation of the various political forces in the Chamber (Article 69.5).
   (c) The remission of bills to the Congress of Deputies.
   (d) The presentation of appeals of unconstitutionality 'against regulations having the force of law that may affect the proper scope of autonomy of the Community" (Article 32.2 of the LOTC). Most parliamentary regulations specified that the quorum required for an Autonomous Community parliament to lodge an appeal shall be the absolute majority of its members, thus distinguishing them from Parliament, where it can be lodged with a fraction of the body (fifty deputies or fifty senators).
   (e) The proposal of two jurists to the Senate so that it can choose the four judges of the Constitutional Court.
   (f) Approval of the conventions and cooperation agreements with other autonomous communities whose projects are developed by the Governing Council.

§4. FUNCTIONING (MODE OF OPERATION)

101. The seventeen Autonomous Community parliaments follow the organization and functioning of Congress, so that all have a Plenum (responsible for passing laws and major decisions) and Commissions, which prepare the work of the Plenum. Their governing bodies are the President, the Table and the Board of Spokespersons. Autonomy Statutes have also established the Permanent Council to ensure Parliament's powers are effective when its term has expired or is not in session.

§5. LIMITATIONS

102. As is typical of parliamentary systems, the Autonomous Community parliaments have no limit imposed by other political powers, such as might be the veto of its laws, traditional in presidential systems. Therefore, the only control over Autonomous Community laws is typical of States with constitutional jurisdiction. Its laws can be appealed by the Prime Minister, fifty deputies, fifty senators and the Ombudsman before the Constitutional Court (Article 162 EC), also judges and courts may submit to the Constitutional Court a *question of unconstitutionality* when they have to apply a law they consider contrary to the Constitution and 'whose validity depends on the judgment' (Article 163 SC). In addition, judges and courts may fail to apply an Autonomous Community law that they consider contrary to the Treaties of the European Union or other European norms. Three issues are worth noting for the regulation of the appeal against unconstitutionality made by the LOTC against Autonomous Community laws:

- The Autonomous Community governments cannot appeal the laws approved by their parliaments, which usually is not a problem because the government normally has broad parliamentary support. However, sometimes a minority government (as happened, for example, in recent years in Navarra and Andalusia) has seen how Parliament has passed laws that it considered contrary to the Constitution. The political practice that has been followed in these cases has been to appeal to the central government or fifty senators of the same party as the Autonomous Community government to appeal the law to the Constitutional Court.
- The Autonomous Community governments and legislatures may appeal State laws, but not those of other Communities, thus 'wars' between Communities, are avoided, especially on fiscal issues because sometimes an Autonomous Community grants tax rebates that a neighbouring Community considers 'unfair competition'.
- When the President of the Central Government appeals an autonomous law he/she may ask the Constitutional Court to suspend it for five months, which ascribes a kind of temporary veto on Autonomous Community legislation (paragraph 64).

§6. ELECTION AND QUALIFICATIONS

103. In most Communities the province is used as a constituency, although in island communities (Balearic and Canary Islands) the island is the constituency, and in some uniprovincial Communities (like Asturias and Murcia) the province is divided into smaller districts. The seats are divided among the constituencies in proportion to the population, except in the Basque Country where twenty-five deputies are attributed to each 'historical territory' (the provinces of Alava, Guipúzcoa and Vizcaya). The electoral system is, in the seventeen Communities, proportional using the D'Hondt formula; in addition, most communities have established a constituency electoral barrier, which in almost all cases is so low that it has no practical effect (3% Catalonia and Andalusia, 5% in Valencia, etc.). Unlike these, Canarias has a high electoral barrier: to participate in the distribution of seats a party needs to obtain 6% in the whole Community or 20% on each island, a statutory mandate that according to the Constitutional Court, is not against the proportionality of the electoral system (STC 22/1988, 25 November, case *Reforma de 1996 del Estatuto de Canarias*).

104. The electoral process is not the exclusive competence of the Communities, but also involves the State under Article 81 of the Constitution which stipulates that the general electoral system shall be regulated by organic law and Article 149.1.1ª which establishes the State's exclusive competence on conditions of equality in the exercise of rights. Therefore, the Organic Act, LOREG, regulates that general scheme which also applies to the Autonomous Community elections: active and passive suffrage from the age of eighteen, organization and control of the electoral process, management of election campaigns and funding and repression of electoral irregularities.

Chapter 4. The Executive

§1. The Organ of State (Designation)

105. The Spanish Constitution stipulates that the Presidents of the Communities are elected by autonomous parliaments from among the parliamentarians themselves. Subsequently, the President chooses the other members of the Governing Council (called councillors), without requiring the ratification of the Assembly. The number of councillors is established by the Acts of Government, with the name of each department (Education, Health, Public Works, etc.) but generally allows the President to vary them and also to redistribute functions among the various ministries as considered convenient. Their number is smaller than the number of ministries in the central Government and is usually between nine and fourteen, depending both on the competence level and of the government arrangements in each case.

106. The quorum for the election of the President is established in all Communities as the absolute majority of deputies on the first ballot and a simple majority on the second. If the candidate does not win, then, in all communities the Parliament is dissolved two months after the first ballot, with the sole exception of Castile-La Mancha, where after that deadline the automatic choice of candidate is made from the party which had won most seats. Interestingly, this was the most common model in the last century, which began in the Statute of Autonomy of Andalusia of 1982, but subsequently has been modified in various statutory reforms. The grounds for termination of the President of the Community also results in the cessation of the rest of the executive: the grounds are renewal of parliament, resignation, death or incapacity of the President, approval of a motion of censure and rejection of a question of confidence.

§2. Legal Status (Privileges and Immunities, Inviolability, Personal Power, etc.)

107. Most of the Statutes make no special requirements to be a councillor so the general requirements suffice, namely to be Spanish and legally of age, although some statutes do require residence in the territory of the Community (such as Extremadura). Following the European parliamentary tradition, councillors are neither required nor prohibited from being autonomous deputies, although in practice most are. Those who are will logically enjoy the prerogatives of deputies. And they all have special jurisdiction entitling them to be judged by the Superior Court of their Community when they are tried for a crime committed within its territory and by the Supreme Court for crimes committed outside it. Civil liability for acts committed in the performance of their duties is always tried in the Superior Court of the Community. In general, the laws governing each community demand that councillors devote themselves exclusively to the Community, and establish a strict regime of incompatibilities, forbidding them to exercise any business work or professional activity.

§3. COMPETENCES

I. Functions of the President

108. The functions of the Presidents of the Autonomous Community like Presidents of the Governing Council, and unlike those we have called symbolic functions (paragraph 94), are specified in the laws of each Community government, which generally reinforce their character as the executive leader conferred upon him or her by Statute. Thus, they set the general guidelines for government action; to freely appoint and dismiss councillors; organize the internal workings of the Council (convene its meetings, set the agenda, in case of a tie use their casting vote, etc.); sign the Decrees agreed upon by the Governing Council; ensure compliance of their agreements; raise questions of confidence, etc. In particular, almost all autonomous presidents can dissolve their parliaments without waiting for the completion of the four-year term except in these three cases:

(1) When a censure motion is pending.
(2) During the first session of the legislature.
(3) Before a year has elapsed since the previous dissolution of the Chamber made in advance by the President, a restriction that does not exist in the case of Catalonia, which has resulted in the Community having held three autonomous elections in five years (2010, 2012 and 2015).

II. Functions of All Governing Councils

109. Autonomous governments have allocated a large number of functions, which can be summarized or grouped into three broad categories:

(1) Functions related to Parliament: to approve bills; develop the draft General Budget and conventions and cooperation agreements with other communities, etc. Moreover, almost all the statutes allow legislative decrees to be issued and since 2006, Decree-laws. The Council may also discuss the presentation of the question of confidence, but in this case the final decision is the sole responsibility of the President.
(2) Functions relating to other State institutions: to agree the lodging of appeals of unconstitutionality and conflicts of jurisdiction; to appoint representatives of the Community for sectoral conferences and other State bodies, etc.
(3) Functions related to the management of the Autonomous Administration: it is responsible for approving the regulations for the development and implementation of laws, resolving the allocation of resources that are conferred, approving the structure of the Commissions, appointing and dismissing senior management positions, authorizing expenses, etc.

§4. Parliamentary Control over the Executive

110. All Autonomous Statutes have established regular controls over autonomous governments such as questions, inquiries, requests for appearances of councillors, commissions of inquiry and motions and non-legislative proposals, etc.

111. In the seventeen Autonomous Communities there are two extraordinary controls of the governments, which if approved, involve the dismissal of the Government: the motion of censure and the question of confidence. Generally these are either in the Statutes or in their respective laws of government, all communities have a 'constructive' motion of censure, according to the German model, which requires that such a motion contains an alternative candidate and is approved by an absolute majority of the chamber. The different Autonomous Community systems have taken Article 112 of the Constitution regulating the vote of confidence: the President of the Community may present it, after deliberation by the Council, on its programme or on a declaration of general policy, with the exception of the Valencian Parliament where it can be linked to a bill, modelled on the classic parliamentarianism still used in some countries such as Italy and France. The favourable vote of the majority of deputies is sufficient for its approval.

§5. The Administration and Bureaucracy

112. All Autonomous Communities have established their own administrations, with an organization similar to the State with central services and peripheral administrations. However, unlike federal States, in the Spanish Autonomous State legal regulation of the Administration and officials does not fully belong to the Communities because the Constitution reserves to the central government the 'bases of legal regime of public administrations and the statutory regime of its officials as well as other matters of administrative law such as the common administrative procedure, the basic legislation on administrative contracts, etc. (Article 149.18ª SC). Moreover, the Constitutional Court, – with very good judgment – has stated that the general principles of Title IV of the Constitution established for the State Administration also apply to the Autonomous Administrations. Therefore, they have to act in accordance with the principles of efficiency and hierarchy, their bodies should be created in accordance with the law, access to public service must be based on the principles of merit and ability (which has resulted in the courts annulling competitive examinations that did not fulfil these principles), etc.

Chapter 5. The Judiciary

§1. Judicial Organization

113. Unlike federal States, the Autonomous State designed by the Spanish Constitution does not allow sub-state entities to have their own judiciary. Thus, Article 122 of the Constitution grants the regulation of Judicial Power to the State under an Organic Act (the LOPJ) and Article 149.1.5 includes the administration of justice within the exclusive competence of the State. However, as a reflection of the Autonomous State, Article 152 of the Constitution determines the existence of High Courts of Justice in first degree Communities. The LOPJ has not only extended these courts to all the autonomous territories but, while the courts remain State organs, this Act allows a system of collaboration between the Legislatures of the respective Autonomous Communities and the General Council of the Judiciary to appoint one senior judge out of each three judges to be nominated by the Parliaments of the Autonomous Community that make up the Bench in the Higher civil and criminal courts.

114. The statutes of the first degree Communities (namely the Basque Country, Catalonia, Galicia and Andalusia) attribute to them the powers that the LOPJ (Organic Act of the Judiciary) reserved to the State Government, a competence that by the late nineties all other Communities had taken in the reforms of their Statutes. The expression 'Administration of the Administration of Justice', has been coined to designate these autonomous powers which are related to executive aspects of the Administration of Justice such as economic management, the provision of premises and non-jurisdictional staff, which has a double dependency: solved with the Spanish judicial offices: the General Council of the Judiciary has jurisdiction over judges and magistrates; the central Government over prosecutors and lawyers of the Administration of Justice and the Autonomous Communities over other administrative staff as well as being responsible for supplying the material means for its operation. Some everyday practical problems such as computer connections between different courts of the territory have highlighted how difficult it is to make the system work properly and added economic costs to achieve coordination between the various institutions involved, for which there a Sectoral Conference on Administration of Justice.

115. In order to organize the single Judicial Branch of the Spanish State, the LOPJ ordered the design of the courts using three criteria: specialization, territoriality and hierarchy. The criterion of material specialization of subjects divides the jurisdiction into four jurisdictional orders: civil, criminal, contentious-administrative and social. In addition, there is military jurisdiction, which in recent years has seen its scope narrowed considerably. Article 30 of the LOPJ divides the State for judicial purposes into municipalities, judicial parties, provinces and Autonomous Communities. Of the four territorial divisions into which the State is organized, three coincide with the administrative divisions, so that their limits need not be specified especially for judicial organization. However a specific demarcation for the judicial parties is needed, these being those composed by one or several bordering municipalities pertaining to the same province (Article 32 LOPJ). The scope of judicial parties is established by State law, although the Autonomous Communities have the competence to make proposals to the Government before it draws up the corresponding bill (Article 35 LOPJ).

§2. Mode of Selection of the Judiciary

116. The Spanish system of selection of judges is meritocratic as is traditional in Europe, which in Spain is organized through a competitive examination (called an opposition) to which law graduates can present themselves. Once they have passed that examination they take a six-month course at the Judicial School (which is in Barcelona) and if they pass it they are already judges. Within three years they are automatically promoted to the next judicial category, that of magistrate. In general, all judicial places are covered by a very objective system, although the judges of the Supreme Court and the Presidents of the High Courts and Provincial Courts are elected by the General Council of the Judiciary, which has a leeway for action that sometimes gives rise to criticism as to whether or not the most qualified magistrate has been chosen.

§3. Judicial Review

117. Spain has a concentrated system of control of constitutionality whereby the monopoly of judging whether an autonomous law is in conformity with the Constitution falls to the Constitutional Court, which also has that monopoly if any autonomous law is challenged for violation of its Statute, without the High Courts of Justice being able to perform this function, as the Constitutional Court has pointed out (paragraph 45). According to the Constitutional Court, if an autonomous law is contrary to its Statute of Autonomy without apparently contradicting the Constitution, it would also violate the Constitution which orders that the Statutes can only be reformed by the procedures that they establish. Thus the hypothetical law would breach the Constitution in that maintaining its text contrary to the Statute would function as a covert reform of it (paragraph 71).

Chapter 6. Independent, Non-political Agencies in the Executive or Legislative branch

118. In addition to the Parliament, the President and the Governing Council, the Autonomous Communities have been provided with various institutions of self-government, among which we can highlight the Ombudsman, the Consultative Council, the Chamber of Accounts and the Economic and Social Council, which are largely designed following the appropriate State model. Thus, the Autonomous defenders of the people, or ombudsman, (currently there are nine, after several Communities have deleted them) are commissioned by their respective Parliaments to defend the rights and freedoms of Title I of the Constitution. The Advisory Councils have the role of giving legal advice to their respective governments, while the Chamber of Accounts controls the economic activity of the institutions and autonomous companies. From the standpoint of the State, the main problem of these institutions lies precisely in the division of powers with similar State institutions; to overcome them Parliament has approved various laws such as Act 36/1985, 6 November, which regulates the relations between the Institution of Ombudsman and similar figures in the different Autonomous Communities and Act 7/1988, 5 April on the functioning of the Chamber of Accounts, where various mechanisms of coordination between institutions are established. In addition, various judgments of the Constitutional Court (especially STC 31/2010, 28 June, case *Reforma del Estatuto de Autonomia para Catalonia*) have clarified some aspects of these relations, highlighting the preeminent general character of State institutions, which cannot be excluded from the supervision of the autonomous organizations.

Part III. Rights and Competences in the Statutes of Autonomy

Chapter 1. Rules Concerning Subnational Citizenship and Its Relevance

119. The Spanish Constitution of 1978 attributes to the State the competence to regulate nationality (Article 149.1.2), but not before guaranteeing that no person of Spanish origin may be deprived of it (Article 13). The Civil Code is the state law in charge of regulating the acquisition and loss of nationality, whose main form of acquisition applies the rule of *ius sangini*: Persons of Spanish origin are those born of a Spanish father or mother irrespective of the place where they are born. The Autonomous Communities play no part in acquiring nationality either by birth or in the special ones (by residence in the country, by concession of the Government, etc.).

120. Historically in Spanish public law 'citizen' was the word used to refer to the person as an active member of a State, the holder of political rights and subject to its laws. In the Autonomous State, 'citizen' has continued to be used only in this sense, when thinking about the person and the State, while for the relationship of the individual with the Autonomous Communities 'political condition' or only 'condition' of Andalusian, Catalan, Basque, etc. is used. This condition is simply acquired by residence in a municipality of the Autonomous Community, as the Statute of Autonomy of the Basque Country of 1979, the first to be approved and today still in force, clearly states: 'they will have the political condition of Basques who live in the administrative neighbourhood, in accordance with the General Acts of the State, in any of the municipalities integrated in the territory of the Autonomous Community' (Article 7.1). In addition, the Statutes establish that Spaniards residing abroad and their descendants who have had their last residence in a municipality of the respective autonomous community can also maintain their autonomous status. In both cases, it is always state law (exactly Act 7/1985, of 2 April, on Regulation of the Bases of Local Regime) that determines the residence and therefore the linkage of each Spaniard with a specific Autonomous Community.

Chapter 2. Fundamental Rights and Liberties

121. The autonomous political condition implies the right to vote in the respective autonomous elections, but very few other rights that had not previously been held by a Spanish citizen were granted because the basic statute of the rights of the Spaniard is fixed, first, in the Constitution and, later, in the organic laws of development, which had to be approved by the State Parliament (Article 81 SC). This conclusion is reinforced by studying the system of distribution of competences that expressly reserves to the State the 'regulation of the basic conditions that guarantee the equality of all Spaniards in the exercise of the rights and in the fulfilment of the constitutional duties' (Article 149.1.1 SC). Therefore, the first Statutes were limited to indicate that the rights and duties of their autonomous citizens would be those established in the Constitution.

122. However, after 2006, the new Statutes have included declarations of rights, which the Constitutional Court has considered to be in conformity with the Constitution provided that the rights contained therein do not affect the basic positions of citizens and have a relationship with Autonomous competences. In addition, the Constitutional Court states that they are not 'subjective rights in the strict sense' since they will only imply rights for the citizens when they are regulated by autonomous laws (SSTC 247/2007, 12 December, case *Reforma del Estatuto de Autonomía de la Comunidad Valenciana* and 31/2010, 28 June, case *Reforma del Estatuto de Autonomía para Cataluña*). A concrete example of these statutory rights is the right 'to receive an adequate treatment for pain and comprehensive palliative care and to full dignity in the process of his death' (Article 20 EAC, Article 20 EAA, etc.), which is Constitutional because it is not contrary to Article 15 of the Constitution (as would be the case if the Statutes recognized euthanasia) and is justified by autonomous powers in health matters. These statutory provisions have led to the approval of several autonomous laws regulating this right, as the Andalusian Act 2/2010, of 8 April, on Rights and Guarantees of the Dignity of the Person in the Process of Death and the Canary Act 1/2015, of 9 February, on rights and guarantees of the dignity of the Person before the final process of his life.

Chapter 3. Autonomous Protections of Minorities (Protection of Minorities and Group Rights)

123. There is no tradition of protecting any social group especially in Spanish constitutional history because the liberal state was formed on the basis of equality of citizens and with the aim of ending the privileges of the Ancient Regime. Moving forward on that liberal tradition, the 1978 Constitution considered that it was not enough to enshrine the formal equality of citizens and to prohibit any form of discrimination, but the public authorities must (in the words of Article 9) 'to promote conditions which ensure that freedom and equality of individuals and of the groups to which they belong are real and effective, to remove the obstacles which prevent or hinder their full enjoyment'. Subsequently, the Constitution sets out specific policies for certain social groups such as children (Article 39), Spanish workers abroad (Article 41), handicapped persons (Article 49), the elderly (Article 50) etc. However, it has no special mandate for ethnic, religious or linguistic minorities.

124. Following this constitutional model, the first Statutes of Autonomy also did not include references to minorities, a decision congruent with the silence they adopted on fundamental rights, as we have seen above. However, taking advantage of their competence in social services, several Autonomous Communities began to implement specific policies for the most important ethnic minority in Spain: the Roma, about 300,000 in number, about half of whom reside in Andalusia. Thus, the Andalusian Government in 1985 created the Secretariat for Studies and Applications for the Roma Community, and later launched an 'Integral Plan for the Andalusian Roma Community', establishing the 'Andalusian Roma Award'. These public policies have been reflected in the statutory reforms of the twenty-first century, so that the Andalusian Statute of 2007 declares among the objectives of autonomy the promotion of 'the necessary conditions for the full integration of minorities and, in particular, the Roma community for its full social incorporation' (Article 9.21). For its part, the Catalan Statute of 2006 orders that the public authorities 'should promote intercultural relations' and guarantee 'the recognition of the culture of the Roma people as a safeguard of the historical reality of this people' (Article 42).

Chapter 4. The Distribution of Competences Between the State and the Autonomous Communities

125. As we have noted on several occasions throughout this monograph, the Spanish Constitution does not itself undertake a distribution of powers between the State and the Communities, but reserves a minimum competence for that and refers the determination of the autonomous competences to the Statutes of Autonomy. Therefore, at first the State had all the public powers, but as the Statutes were approved, the State lost the powers that the Statutes attributed to its autonomous powers in each Community. For this reason, the Constitution and the Statutes are the 'constitutionality block' where the powers of the Autonomous Communities as well as those of the State are fixed. As there are seventeen Statutes, we could say that there are seventeen 'constitutionality blocks', although the Constitutional Court tends to make homogeneous interpretations of all of them. In addition to the Statutes, the constitutionality block also integrates other rules such as the organic laws of transfer and delegation of Article 150.2 of the Constitution, which allow State competences to be transferred to the Autonomous Communities. Thus, in the 1980s and 1990s, several laws were adopted to homogenize competences such as Organic Act 5/1987, of 30 July, on the Delegation of State Powers in the Autonomous Communities in relation to road and cable transport (as amended by Organic Act 5/2013, of 4 July) and another to increase the specific powers of a Community, such as Organic Act 6/1997 on the transfer of executive powers in matters of traffic to Catalonia.

126. Article 149.1 of the Constitution reserves to the State the 'exclusive competence' over 32 matters. But if we read the description of those 'matters' we find not only matters (nationality, immigration, Defence and the Armed Forces, etc.), but also powers on a specific subject (Commercial, criminal and penitentiary legislation, labour legislation). For this reason, Article 149 uses both the American technique of reserving a complete matter to the State, and the German technique of sharing a subject, distinguishing between law and implementation. In addition, Article 149.1 of the Spanish Constitution employs another technique that was only sporadically used by the German Constitution: in several cases, it only reserves to the State the 'basic legislation', 'bases' and 'basic laws'. That not only shares a subject but also its legislation, in such a way that the division of powers between the State and the Communities is established within the legislative power attributing the basic legislation to the State and the complementary legislation to the Autonomous Community.

127. When the Constitution attributes to the exclusive competence of the State a 'set of activities, functions and legal institutions relevant to a sector of social life' (i.e., to a matter as defined by the Constitutional Court, STC 123/1984, 18 December, case *Centros de coordinación operativa*), it is employing the technique of a federalist distribution of dual competences: it is carrying out a strict separation between the State and autonomous spheres, awarding all the functions to the first – both legislative and executive – and none to the latter. Article 149.1 of the Constitution subjects the following matters to this system:

- Regulation of basic conditions guaranteeing the equality of all Spaniards in the exercise of their rights and in the fulfilment of their constitutional duties.
- Nationality, immigration, emigration, status of aliens, and right of asylum.
- International relations.
- Defence and the Armed Forces.
- Administration of Justice.
- Customs and tariff regulations; foreign trade.
- Monetary system: foreign currency, exchange and convertibility.
- Determination of the official time.
- General financial affairs and State Debt.
- External health measures.
- Sea fishing.
- Merchant navy and registering of ships; lighting of coasts and signals at sea; general-interest ports, general-interest airports; control of the air space, air traffic and transport; meteorological services and aircraft registration.
- Railways and land transport crossing through the territory of more than one self-governing Community; general system of communications; motor vehicle traffic; Post Office services and telecommunications; air and underwater cables and radio communications.
- Public works of general benefit or whose execution affects more than one self-governing Community.
- Manufacturing, sale, possession and use of arms and explosives.
- Protection of Spain's cultural and artistic heritage and national monuments against exportation and despoliation; museums, libraries, and archives belonging to the State, without prejudice to their management by the self-governing Communities.
- Public safety, without prejudice to the possibility of creation of police forces by the Self-governing Communities, in the manner to be provided for in their respective Statutes of Autonomy and within the framework to be laid down by an organic act.
- Statistics for State purposes.
- Authorization of popular consultations through the holding of referendums.

128. When a Statute fully assigns a matter to its Autonomous Community, it has a monopoly of legislative and executive power in that area, without the State being able to carry out any activity on it in the territory of that Community. The matters thus regulated are very few (basically their institutions of self-government), because almost always the State has some degree that allows at least a minimum of activity in that area since many of its competences are 'horizontal' and allow it to intervene in multiple spheres. For example, its competence on the general electoral system allows it to regulate aspects of the autonomic elections; equality in the property laws allows a certain legislative capacity in town planning, attributed exclusively to the Autonomous Communities, etc.

129. Some sections of Article 149.1 of the Constitution reserve to the State legislation on certain matters and the Statutes have attributed the competence of execution to their Communities; that is, to say the former has the normative capacity

– which according to the Constitutional is ample: both the State parliamentary laws and the regulations of the Government – while the Communities will have the executive function.

Thus, the following matters are the responsibility of the State:

- Commercial, criminal and penitentiary legislation; procedural legislation, without prejudice to the necessary specialties in these fields arising from the peculiar features of the substantive law of the Autonomous Communities.
- Labour legislation, without prejudice to its execution by bodies of the Autonomous Communities.
- Civil legislation, without prejudice to the preservation, modification and development by the Autonomous Communities of their civil law, *foral* or special, whenever these exist.
- Legislation on copyright and industrial property.
- Legislation on weights and measures.
- Legislation pharmaceutical products.
- Legislation on compulsory expropriation.
- Legislation on hydraulic resources.

130. In these matters in which the State is responsible for the legislation, the Communities can only issue administrative acts in compliance with State regulations. However, they can approve laws to organize the autonomic administration that has to perform this function by virtue of its competence of organization of the autonomous institutions. For that reason, all the autonomous governments have a Councillor of Labour (or Employment) to execute the labour legislation and the majority has created a Council of Labour Relations whose objective is to facilitate both consultation and cooperation between the Autonomous Administration and the organizations and trade unions, such as collective bargaining among social partners.

131. With a frequency unprecedented in comparative law, Article 149.1 of the Constitution uses the complex technique of distributing the same legislative competence over a given matter between the State and the Autonomous Communities. In addition, it does so without ever using the same concept:

(1) Sometimes the 'bases' of certain matters are reserved to the 'exclusive competence' of the State:
   - The regulations concerning credit, banking and insurance.
   - General economic planning.
   - Health matters.
   - the legal system of Public Administrations and the status of their officials
   - The regulation of mining and energy.

(2) In other sections, the State reserves the 'basic rules' of other matters:
   - Basic rules relating to the organization of the press, radio and television and in general, all mass communications media without prejudice to powers vested in the Autonomous Communities for their development and implementation

– Basic rules for the implementation of section 27 of the Constitution, in order to guarantee the fulfilment of the duties of public authorities in this matter.

(3) Finally, in others, the 'basic legislation' of a third group is reserved to the State:
- Basic legislation and financial system of Social Security, without prejudice to the implementation of its services by the Autonomous Communities.
- Basic legislation on contracts and administrative concessions
- Basic legislation on environmental protection, without prejudice to powers of the Autonomous Communities to take additional protective measures.
- Basic legislation on woodlands, forestry and cattle trails.

132. The legislative powers of the Autonomous Communities in these matters – which since the reform of the Statute of Catalonia are called 'shared competences' – are characterized by depending on the State legislative competence to the point that their constitutionality depends directly on their adequacy to the State bases, which the State may modify as it deems appropriate; So that if at any given moment an autonomous law is constitutional it may become unconstitutional if the state bases subsequently change. This occurred to the Act of Extremadura 9/1995 on the public function of Extremadura, which correctly developed State Act 30/1984 on measures for the Reform of Public Function, but which became unconstitutional when Act 13/1996 was amended in a sense incompatible with the Extremadura law (STC 1/2003, 16 January, case *Ley 5/1995 de la Asamblea de Extremadura*).

133. The legal regime of basic legislation and basic norms is identical. The bases differ slightly from these two in their executive aspect: in the basic legislation and in the basic norms, their execution is entirely the responsibility of the Autonomous Communities as attributed to it in its Statutes, whereas in the case of the bases the Administration can, exceptionally, carry out executive acts (SSTC 1/1982, 28 January, case of *Cajas de Ahorros* and 57/1983, 28 June, case of *Operaciones de Crédito de las Corporaciones locales*). In order to exercise its competence to regulate the bases of a matter, the State has to approve a formal law that 'expressly designates its character of basic', a requirement that must also be fulfilled 'in the exceptional case that the basic norm is introduced by the Government of the nation in the exercise of its regulatory power (STC 69/1988, 19 April, case of *Etiquetaje de productos catalanes*). However, the State legislature cannot classify freely as 'basic' all the rules it deems appropriate, but only 'the general criteria of regulation of a sector of the legal order or of a legal matter that must be common to the whole State' (STC 25/1983, April 7, case *Cuerpos nacionales de Administración local*).

134. Summarizing the Spanish competence regime, it can be said that when a matter has been delivered entirely to one of the two territorial powers of the jurisdictional order, either the State or the Autonomous Community, to which it belongs, it will have the monopoly both of its normative regulation and of executive action, the other being completely excluded from these functions. If the said matter is autonomous, it is possible for the State to have jurisdiction over it by any of its horizontal titles that qualify the 'exclusive competence' qualifications that the Statutes perform. When the competence regime is based on the sharing of the matter according to the distribution of legislation / enforcement, the State is responsible both for the drafting of laws and that of the executive regulations of those laws; the Communities have the competence to execute the administrative acts and they have reflexive regulatory power to organize them as the Administration deems appropriate that must execute the State legislation, they can even develop their own policy on the matter. Finally, when the legislation of a subject is shared according to the dichotomy bases / complementary legislation, the State has the capacity to establish by law the general principles of that matter (exceptionally they can be established also by means of regulation) and the Autonomous Community has the competence to legislate the other aspects of the normative regulation of that matter and the responsibility for its ordinary execution (also exceptionally the State can perform some executive acts when the constitutionality block reserves the bases to it).

Part IV. Local Government

Chapter 1. Constitutional Status of Local Government under the National Constitution

135. In Spanish constitutional history municipalities were conceived as autonomous entities of political participation and election by the citizens, although the distinct political forces maintained differences in the way these principles were developed. Therefore, in the Constitutional Parliament of 1977–1978, it was not difficult to consider them as autonomous entities elected directly by the citizens, although it was not specified whether the mayor would be directly or indirectly elected (Article 140 SC). In the Constitution of 1812 the province was created as a territorial organization immediately superior to the municipality, a liberal creation that has remained unchanged ever since and that the Constitution of 1978 recognizes defining it as 'a local entity, with its own legal personality, arising from the grouping of Municipalities'.

136. Unlike what happens in the United States and other federal states, in Spain the local bodies cannot be regulated by the Autonomous Communities but rather it is the State that also has competences over them, so that the Constitutional Court frequently refers to the 'bifrontal character' of the local regime. What is more, the State competence is more important than the autonomous since the Constitution reserves to the former the 'Basic rules of the legal system of Public Administrations' (Article 149.1.18), which means that the State determines the basic principles or criteria in matters of organization and competences of the local bodies throughout Spain. Currently these principles that bind all Autonomous Communities were established by the State in Act 7/1985, 2 April, on Regulation of Bases of Local Regime (LBRL). In addition, the regulation of local elections is made by the State in Organic Act 5/1985, 19 June, on General Electoral Regime.

137. Although the Constitution remits the regulation of local authorities to the law without further details, the Constitutional Court has stated that this remission does not allow the legislature to regulate them freely, but rather the Constitution establishes an *institutional guarantee* of local autonomy that both the State and the autonomous legislators must respect. Thus, they cannot maintain non-jurisdictional controls that subordinate the will of the local authorities to those of the State (STC 4/1981, 2 February, case *Ley de Bases de Régimen Local 1953*) or suppress the powers of the *Diputaciones* (deputations) reducing them to mere protocol bodies (STC

32/1981, 28 July, case *Diputaciones Catalanas*). In addition, laws on local authorities must take into account the general limits established by the Constitution, the obvious ones such as fundamental rights, but also less obvious ones such as the reservation of tax law. Therefore, a State or autonomous law that is limited to creating a tax and allows municipalities to effectively regulate it violates that reservation of law established by Article 133 of the Constitution (STC 233/1999, 16 December, case *Ley de Haciendas Locales*).

Chapter 2. Status of Local Government under the Statutes of Autonomies

138. The first Statutes of Autonomy approved after the entry into force of the Constitution – Basque, Catalan and Galician – had only a generic reference to local authorities, as part of the territorial organization of the Community and in the section on competences conferred exclusive autonomy on 'local regime, without prejudice to Article 149 (1) 18 of the Constitution' (Article 9.4 EAC-1979). The Andalusian Statute of Autonomy of 1981 also followed this technique for its municipalities, but changed it completely for the provinces: it regulated its governing body, called Deputation, in more detail so that, on the one hand, the Community could delegate competences to it and, on the other, for the Deputations to become the territorial administration of the Communities. The other Statutes of Autonomous Community multi-provincial followed this model because it was one of the points of the Autonomous Agreements of 1981 (paragraph 4). However, when the various autonomous elections were held in 1982 and 1983, the neoautonomic governments neither gave their own powers to the Deputations nor used them as their territorial administrations, but organized their own peripheral services just like the State had done and without the opposition of the new Socialist Central Government that had won the October 1982 elections.

139. The Statute of Catalonia of 2006, as in so many other subjects, replaced the scant reference to the local authorities of the 1979 Statute by means of a prolix regulation, which begins already in Article 2.3 which stated: 'Municipalities, vegueries, and other local government bodies that may be determined by law also constitute the institutional system of the Generalitat, being the bodies according to which the latter is territorially organized, without prejudice to their autonomy.' Subsequently, it devotes a chapter to them in Title II of the institutions, in which it is reasserted that the municipalities form the basic territorial structure of the Community, its principles of organization are marked, affirming that its government will correspond to the municipalities chosen by citizens and are guaranteed a series of 'their own competences' to play with autonomy: town planning, basic services, etc., generally drafted in broad terms. Finally, the Statute confers on the Community a series of exclusive powers (Article 160).

140. The Statute of Autonomy of Andalusia of 2007 and the others approved subsequently follow the model of the Catalan Statute to regulate with amplitude the local entities, although expressly stating that it is a regulation that is carried out 'respecting Article 149.1.18 of the Constitution and the principle of local autonomy' (Article 60 EAA). That is why, in the statutory texts themselves, it is clear – without the need for legal interpretations as in the case of the Catalan Statute – the bifurcate nature of the local regime. It is also clear in the new Andalusian Statute – and in those containing similar assertions – that the Provincial Councils would no longer be the peripheral administrations of the Communities, but rather the governing bodies of the provinces.

Chapter 3. The Municipalities

141. In Spain there are more than 8,000 municipalities, a number that comes from the liberal territorial organization that was made in the first third of the twentieth century, but to date no reorganization has been carried out to reduce the number, which would serve to guarantee a better provision of public services, especially in the nearly 5,000 municipalities with a population of less than 1,000 inhabitants. Leaving aside the municipalities with less than 100 inhabitants, which operate in the Open Council – that is, in an assembly of all adult residents – the Constitution establishes that the governing body of municipalities throughout Spain is the Town or City Council, The mayors and councillors, whose number varies according to the number of inhabitants: from 5 councillors for municipalities of less than 250 inhabitants, to 51 for Madrid, the most populous in Spain. The councillors choose among them the mayor, bearing in mind that the candidates must be the heads of list of each party. A peculiar note of these elections, which does not occur in general or autonomous elections, is that since 1999 all citizens of the European Union can participate in them both as voters and candidates (Article 20 TEU).

142. Like the election and removal of the mayor, the distribution of competences of the institutional organization of the Spanish town councils responds to the model of parliamentary system of government: while the plenary (formed by all the councillors) has normative, planning and budgetary powers, the mayor and his/her government – known as the Local Government Council), have the executive functions. As in the State and in the Communities, the Plenary may dismiss the Mayor and he/she may present a question of confidence. However, the mayor cannot dissolve the Plenum and convene new local elections, as can the autonomous presidents and the central government.

143. The LBRL distinguishes between the competences of municipalities and other local authorities and those attributed by delegation. The former are exercised by local authorities with autonomy and can only be established by law, while the latter are exercised in the terms of the delegation, which can establish 'techniques of direction and control of opportunity that, in all cases, will have to respect the power of self-organization of the services of the local Entity' (Article 7). After making this distinction, the LBRL sets out a long list of subjects on which municipalities must have competences when the corresponding sectoral legislation so stipulates – State and Autonomous – regulates them: security in public places, traffic management, civil protection, town planning, parks and gardens, paving, culture, sport, etc. This formula has the advantage of fixing a minimum content of local autonomy, allowing the State and the Autonomous Communities – according to the division of competences of each subject – to determine exactly the extent of municipal competences. In addition to these mandates, the LBRL itself establishes the services that municipalities must provide to its citizens, which logically are increasing according to the number of inhabitants: all have to offer minimum services (lighting, cemetery, collection of vehicles), to which are being added new services according to size: those of more than 5,000 inhabitants must have a library, market etc., while those of more than 20,000 must have fire services, and sports facilities, etc., and those of more than 50,000 public transport and environmental protection.

Chapter 4. The Provinces

144. The province is a creation of the liberal state, which was created by the first Spanish Constitution, that of 1812. In 1833 Spain was divided into forty-nine provinces, which has not changed since then, apart from dividing the Canary Islands in 1927 into two provinces. Thus there are now fifty provinces, which the 1978 Constitution simultaneously configures as local entities with their own legal personality, determined by the grouping of municipalities, and as territorial divisions for the fulfilment of State activities (Article 141 SC). Among these activities, the Constitution itself emphasizes that the province is an electoral constituency for elections to both the Congress and the Senate, which the Communities with more than one province have also made their own. The areas of the Provinces can only be modified by Organic Act, which very rarely happens. An example is given by Organic Act 15/1995, 27 December, altering the provincial boundaries to change the municipality of Gátova from the province of Castellón to Valencia (both belonging to the Autonomous Community of Valencia).

145. Since the Constitution of 1812, the Provinces as local entities are governed and administered by the Provincial Councils (known in Spanish as *Diputaciones/* deputations). In the Autonomous State they do not exist in the seven uniprovincial Communities, whose self-governing bodies have assumed their competences and officials. Nor do they exist in the Canary Islands, replaced by the *Cabildos*, the governing bodies of each island. In the other nine Communities, the Deputations have been losing competences in favour of the Autonomous Administrations. According to LOREG, the Provincial Council consists of a number of deputies ranging from twenty-five in the provinces of less than 500,000 residents to fifty-one in those with more than 3,500,000 inhabitants (only Barcelona). These provincial deputies are elected by the local councillors, taking into account the results obtained by each party in the various electoral districts into which each province is divided. Subsequently, the deputies will choose among them the President of the Provincial Council. As in the Town Halls, the plenary can present a motion of censure against the President of the Provincial Council and this is a question of confidence. In this way another parliamentary system of government is created, also in the distribution of powers: the Plenum of the Provincial Council is in charge of approving the provincial norms, the budgets, the plans of public works and other important questions, while the President and the Governing Commission exercise executive functions.

146. The three Basque Provincial Councils of Álava, Guipúzcoa and Vizcaya have a special regime, based on their historical tradition, which recognizes both the Constitution and State legislation and the Statute of Autonomy for the Basque Country itself, which reserves for its Parliament of that Autonomous Community the power to regulate the direct elections to these three Provincial Councils. This direct legitimacy of the *foral* Provincial Councils is the basis of their normative capacity, especially in tax matters, which the Organic Act of the Constitutional Court has effectively equated to the autonomous laws in the sense that the tax rules can only be appealed to the Constitutional Court.

147. The main function of the Provincial Councils is to support the municipalities, especially those with less economic capacity. In general, the tendency of many Autonomous Communities is to reduce their functions as far as is constitutionally permissible, leaving them as little more than advisory institutions of the small municipalities, with few relevant competences in the environment, culture, tourism and sports. Thus, at present their most important competence is drawing up the provincial plans of cooperation for the works and services of municipal competence; however, this competence is not full since it is subject to the 'coordination' of the Autonomous Community.

Chapter 5. Other Local Governments

148. Article 141.4 of the Constitution stipulates that the islands shall have their own administration. The respective Statutes of Autonomy have regulated seven Island Councils in the Canary Islands (El Hierro, Fuerteventura, Gran Canaria, La Gomera, Lanzarote, La Palma and Tenerife) and four Island Councils in the Balearics (Mallorca, Menorca, Ibiza and Formentera). The Councillors of the Town Councils are elected directly by the citizens, its President being the first candidate of the most voted list in each Island. The Balearic Island Councillors are also directly elected by the citizens, and among them they elect the President of the Insular Council.

149. Article 141.3 of the Constitution authorizes the creation of groups of different municipalities of the province. For its part, Article 152.3 allows the Statutes of Autonomy to establish their own territorial constituencies. Under these provisions, most of the Statutes have established regions (called Comarcas in Spanish and *vegueries* in Catalan) as a territorial organization of the Autonomous Community, referring their specific regulation to regional laws. Autonomous legislators have behaved very differently when exercising this competence, since some have legislated intensely about the regions, extending them throughout the territory (Catalonia and Aragon, for example), others have not created a single one (Galicia and Andalusia) and some have created regions only for a specific territory (such as the *Comarca del Bierzo* in Castilla y León).

150. The LBRL allows the creation of local entities smaller than the municipality for the decentralized administration of separate population centres, of which over 3,500 have been created throughout Spain. Its specific legal regime is regulated by the Autonomous Communities; if they do not do it, the provisions of LOREG govern: the inhabitants will directly elect the Mayor of the small village, along with four or two councillors (depending on whether or not the village has 250 inhabitants or fewer) so making up the local or Parish council. These councillors are named by the Town Council to which the minor entity belongs, according to the electoral results of each party in that nucleus of population.

Part V. Representative Texts of Subnational Constitutions

§1. Statute of Autonomy of Catalonia

Organic Act 6/2006 of the 19th July, on the Reform of the Statute of Autonomy of Catalonia

Preamble

Catalonia has been shaped over the course of time through the contribution of the energy of many generations, traditions and cultures, which found in Catalonia a land of welcome.

The Catalan people have maintained a constant will to self-government over the course of the centuries, embodied in such institutions as the *Generalitat* – created in 1359 by the Cervera *Corts* – and in its own specific legal system, assembled, together with other legal compilations, in the *Constitucions i altres drets de Catalunya* (Constitutions and other laws of Catalonia). After 1714, various attempts were made to restore the institutions of self-government. Milestones in this historic route include the *Mancomunitat* of 1914, the recovery of the *Generalitat* with the 1932 Statute, the re-establishment of the *Generalitat* in 1977 and the 1979 Statute, coinciding with the return of democracy, the Constitution of 1978 and the State of Autonomies.

The collective liberty of Catalonia found in the institutions of the *Generalitat* a nexus with a history of affirmation of and respect for the fundamental rights and public liberties of the individual and of peoples; a history which the women and men of Catalonia wish to continue so as to enable the construction of a democratic and advanced society, one of wellbeing and progress, in solidarity with Spain as a whole and incorporated into Europe.

The Catalan people continues today to proclaim liberty, justice and equality as higher values of its collective life, and manifests its desire to advance in a way which will ensure a dignified quality of life for all those who live and work in Catalonia.

The public authorities are at the service of the general interest and the rights of the citizens, while respecting the principle of subsidiarity.

In the light of all the foregoing, and true to the spirit of the preamble to the 1979 Statute, this *Estatut* assumes that:

- Catalonia is a land rich in territories and peoples, a diversity that has defined and enriched it over the centuries and that strengthens it for the time to come.
- Catalonia is a community of free persons for free persons, in which each individual may live and express diverse identities, with a firm commitment to community based on respect for individual dignity.
- The contribution of its citizens has shaped an integrating society, which sees endeavor as a value and which is innovative and enterprising, values which continue to drive its progress.
- Catalonia's self-government is founded on the Constitution, and also on the historical rights of the Catalan people, which, in the framework of the Constitution, give rise to recognition in this *Estatut* of the unique position of the *Generalitat*. Catalonia wishes to develop its political personality within the framework of a State which recognizes and respects the diversity of identities of the peoples of Spain.
- The civil and associative tradition of Catalonia has always underlined the importance of Catalan language and culture, of rights and duties, of knowledge, of education, of social cohesion, of sustainable development and equality of rights, and today, especially, of equality between women and men.
- Catalonia, by means of the State, participates in the construction of the political project of the European Union, whose values and objectives it shares.
- Catalonia, with its humanistic tradition, affirms its commitment together with all peoples to constructing a peaceful and just world order.

In reflection of the feelings and the wishes of the citizens of Catalonia, the Parliament of Catalonia has defined Catalonia as a nation by an ample majority. The Spanish Constitution, in its second Article, recognizes the national reality of Catalonia as a nationality.

In exercise of the inalienable right of Catalonia to self-government, the members of the Catalan Parliament hereby propose, the Constitutional Committee of the Congress of Deputies agree and the people of Catalonia ratify this Statute.

Preliminary Title

Article 1. Catalonia

Catalonia, as a nationality, exercises its self-government constituted as an autonomous community in accordance with the Constitution and with this *Estatut*, which is its basic institutional law.

Article 2. The *Generalitat*

1. The *Generalitat* is the institutional system around which Catalonia's self-government is politically organized.
2. The *Generalitat* consists of Parliament, the Presidency of the *Generalitat*, Government and the other institutions established in Chapter V of Title II.

3. Municipalities, *vegueries*, *comarques* and other local government bodies that may be determined by law also constitute the institutional system of the *Generalitat*, being the bodies according to which the latter is territorially organized, without prejudice to their autonomy.
4. The powers of the *Generalitat* emanate from the people of Catalonia and are exercised according to this *Estatut* and the Constitution.

Article 3. Political Framework

1. The relationship of the *Generalitat* with the State is based on the principle of mutual institutional loyalty, is regulated by the general principle according to which the *Generalitat* is State, by the principle of autonomy, by that of bilateralism and by that of multilateralism.
2. Catalonia has its political and geographical space of reference in the Spanish State and the European Union, and it incorporates the values, principles and obligations implied by being a part thereof.

Article 4. Rights and Governing Principles

1. The public authorities of Catalonia shall promote the full exercise of the freedoms and rights recognized by this *Estatut*, the Constitution, the European Union, the Universal Declaration of Human Rights, the European Convention for the Protection of Human Rights and those other international treaties and conventions which Spain has signed that recognize and guarantee fundamental rights and freedoms.
2. The public authorities of Catalonia shall promote conditions in which individual and group freedom and equality are real and effective; they shall enable the participation of all people in political, economic, cultural and social life, and shall recognize the right of peoples to preserve and develop their identity.
3. The public authorities of Catalonia shall promote the values of freedom, democracy, equality, pluralism, peace, justice, solidarity, social cohesion, gender equity and sustainable development.

Article 5. Historical Rights

The self-government of Catalonia is also based on the historical rights of the Catalan people, on its secular institutions, and on the Catalan legal tradition, which this *Estatut* incorporates and modernizes under Article 2, Temporary Provision Two, and other precepts of the Constitution, from which derive recognition of the *Generalitat*'s unique position in relation to civil law, language, culture, the projection of these in the area of education, and the institutional system by means of which the *Generalitat* is organized.

Article 6. Catalonia's Own Language and official Languages

1. Catalonia's own language is Catalan. As such, Catalan is the language of normal and *preferential*[2] use in Public Administration bodies and in the public media of Catalonia, and is also the language of normal use for teaching and learning in the education system.
2. Catalan is the official language of Catalonia, together with Castilian, the official language of the Spanish State. All persons have the right to use the two official languages and citizens of Catalonia have the right and the duty to know them. The public authorities of Catalonia shall establish the necessary measures to enable the exercise of these rights and the fulfilment of this duty. In keeping with the provisions of Article 32, there shall be no discrimination on the basis of use of either of the two languages.
3. The *Generalitat* and the State shall undertake the necessary measures to obtain official status for Catalan within the European Union and its presence and use in international organizations and in international treaties of cultural or linguistic content.
4. The *Generalitat* shall promote communication and cooperation with the other communities and territories that share a linguistic heritage with Catalonia. To this end, the *Generalitat* and the State may, as appropriate, sign agreements, treaties, and other collaboration instruments for the promotion and external dissemination of Catalan.
5. The Occitan language, known as Aranese in Aran, is Aran's own language and is official in Catalonia, as established by this *Estatut* and by the laws of linguistic normalization.

Article 7. The Political Status of Catalans

1. Spanish citizens legally resident in Catalonia benefit from the political status of Catalans or citizens of Catalonia. Their political rights are exercised in accordance with this *Estatut* and the law.
2. Spanish citizens resident abroad whose last legal place of residence was Catalonia also enjoy, as Catalans, the political rights defined by this *Estatut*; their descendants, who maintain this citizenship, shall also enjoy these rights, if they so request, in the manner determined by law.

Article 8. The Symbols of Catalonia

1. The flag, the holiday and the anthem are the national symbols of Catalonia, defined as a nationality by Article 1.
2. The flag of Catalonia, which is the traditional flag with four red stripes on a yellow background, shall be present on public buildings and during official acts held in Catalonia.
3. The holiday of Catalonia is the *Diada* of the Eleventh of September.

2. The Constitutional Court has declared this word is unconstitutional and void (STC 31/2010, 28 June).

4. The anthem of Catalonia is *Els segadors*.
5. Parliament shall regulate the diverse expressions of the symbolic framework of Catalonia and shall define their order of protocol.
6. Legal protection for the symbols of Catalonia shall be the same as that for other symbols of the State.

Article 9. Territory

The territory of Catalonia is that which corresponds to the geographical and administrative limits of the *Generalitat* as of when this *Estatut* comes into force.

Article 10. The Capital

The capital of Catalonia is the city of Barcelona, which is the permanent seat of Parliament, of the Presidency of the *Generalitat* and of the Government, without prejudice to possible meetings of Parliament and Government in other locations in Catalonia, in accordance with the Parliament's Rules of Procedure and the law.

Article 11. Aran

1. The people of Aran exercise self-government through this *Estatut*, the *Conselh Generau d'Aran* and any other institutions of its own.
2. The citizens of Catalonia and their political institutions recognize Aran as an Occitan entity, with cultural, historical, geographical and linguistic identity as defended by the Aranese people over the centuries. This *Estatut* recognizes, protects and respects this uniqueness and recognizes Aran as a unique territorial entity within Catalonia, subject to specific protection under a special legal system.

Article 12. Territories with Historical, Linguistic and Cultural Links with Catalonia

The *Generalitat* shall promote communication, cultural exchange and cooperation with any communities and territories, whether or not they belong to the Spanish State, which have historical, linguistic and cultural links with Catalonia. For this purpose, the *Generalitat* and the Spanish State, as appropriate, may sign agreements, treaties and other collaboration instruments in any field, which may include the creation of joint entities.

Article 13. Catalan Communities Outside Catalonia

The *Generalitat*, within the terms established by law, shall foster social, economic and cultural links with Catalan communities outside Catalonia and shall provide them with any necessary assistance. To this end, the *Generalitat*, where appropriate, may establish cooperation agreements with public and private institutions in the territories and countries where these Catalan communities exist and may request the State to sign international treaties in this respect.

Article 14. Territorial Application of Rules

1. The rules and resolutions of the *Generalitat* and the civil law of Catalonia are applicable within the territory of Catalonia, without prejudice to any exceptions that may be established in relation to each matter and to any situations that are to be governed by private status or by other extraterritorial rules.
2. Foreign citizens who obtain Spanish nationality are subject to Catalan civil law while legally resident in Catalonia, unless they express a wish to the contrary.

Title I. Rights, Obligations and Governing Principles

Chapter I. Civil and Social Rights and Obligations

Article 15. The Rights of the Individual

1. The citizens of Catalonia have the rights and obligations recognized in the rules referred to in Article 4.1.
2. Each individual has the right to live in dignity, safety and autonomy, free from exploitation, from ill-treatment and from all types of discrimination, and has the right to freely develop his or her personality and personal abilities.
3. The rights of the citizens of Catalonia, as established in this *Estatut,* may be extended to other individuals, under the terms established by law.

Article 16. Rights in the Field of the Family

Each individual has the right, in accordance with the requirements established by law, to receive social benefits and public assistance in fulfilling family responsibilities.

Article 17. The Rights of Minors

All minors have the right to receive all the attention necessary for the development of their personality and for their welfare in both family and social contexts.

Article 18. The Rights of the Elderly

Elderly people have the right to live with dignity, free from exploitation and ill-treatment, and may not be discriminated against for reasons of age.

Article 19. The Rights of Women

1. All women have the right to freely develop their personality and personal abilities, and to live with dignity, confidence and autonomy, free from exploitation, ill-treatment and all types of discrimination.
2. Women have the right to participate equally with men in all private and public spheres.

Article 20. The Right to Undergo the Process of Death with Dignity

1. Each individual has the right to receive appropriate treatment of pain and complete palliative attention and to undergo the process of death with dignity.
2. Each individual has the right to express his or her will in advance in order to record instructions regarding any medical treatment or intervention that he or she may undergo. These instructions must be respected especially by medical staff, in accordance with the terms established by the law, if the individual is not able to express his or her wishes personally.

Article 21. Rights and Obligations in the Field of Education

1. Each individual has the right to a high-quality education and to equality of access. The *Generalitat* shall establish a model of education in the public interest that guarantees these rights.
2. In accordance with the principles established in Article 37.4, parents are guaranteed the right of their children to receive moral and religious education in accord with their convictions in State schools, in which the education is non-religious.
3. Private schools may be supported with public funds in accordance with the provisions of the law, in order to guarantee the rights to equal access and to a high-quality education.
4. Education is free at all compulsory stages and at other levels as may be established by law.
5. Each individual has the right to occupational and continuous training, under the terms established by law.
6. Each individual has the right to receive, under the terms and conditions which may be established by law, public assistance to meet his or her educational needs, and equal access to higher levels of education, in accordance with his or her economic resources, aptitudes and preferences.
7. Individuals with special educational needs have the right to receive the necessary support to gain access to the educational system, in accordance with the provisions of the law.
8. The members of the educational community have the right to participate in school and university affairs under the terms established by law.

Article 22. Rights and Obligations in the Cultural Field

1. Each individual has the right of equal access to culture and to the development of their individual and collective creative abilities.
2. Each individual has the duty to respect and preserve cultural heritage.

Article 23. Rights in the Field of Health

1. Each individual has the right of equal access, free of charge, to healthcare services provided under public responsibility, under the terms established by law.

2. Public healthcare users have the right to have their preferences respected in terms of choice of doctor and healthcare centre, under the terms and conditions established by law.
3. Each individual, with respect to public and private healthcare services, has the right to be informed of the services which he or she can have access to and of the requirements for using them; to be informed of medical therapies and their risks, prior to treatment; to give his or her consent for all medical interventions; to have access to his or her own medical records; and to confidentiality regarding information relating to his or her health, under the terms established by law.

Article 24. Rights in the Field of Welfare Services

1. Each individual has the right to equal access to the welfare service network provided under public responsibility, to be informed about those services, and to give his or her consent to any action that affects him or her personally, under the terms established by law.
2. Those individuals with special needs regarding personal autonomy in the activities of daily life have the right to receive attention which is appropriate to their condition, in accordance with legally established conditions.
3. Those individuals or families who are in a situation of poverty have the right to a minimum guaranteed income that ensures them the minimum necessary to live in dignity, in accordance with legally established conditions.
4. Third social sector organizations have the right to fulfil their functions in the spheres of social participation and collaboration.

Article 25. Rights in the Field of Labour

1. All workers have the right to professional training and promotion and the right of free access to public employment services.
2. Those individuals excluded from the job market because they have not been able to enter or re-enter it and without a means of subsistence have the right to receive non-contributory provisions and resources to alleviate their situation, under the terms established by law.
3. All workers have the right to perform their work and professional tasks in conditions that guarantee their health, safety and dignity.
4. Workers, or their representatives, have a right to information, consultation and participation in their companies.
5. Trade union and employer union organizations have the right to fulfil their functions in the spheres of social agreement, participation and social collaboration.

Article 26. Rights in the Field of Housing

Those individuals who lack sufficient resources have the right to a decent home, and public authorities shall, therefore, establish by law a system of measures to guarantee this right, within the terms determined by law.Article 27. Rights and Obligations Concerning the Environment

1. Each individual has the right to live in an environment that is balanced, sustainable and respectful of health, in accordance with the standards and levels of protection established by law. Each individual also has equal rights to enjoy the landscape and natural resources, and has the obligation to use these responsibly and to avoid squander and damage of natural resources.
2. Each individual has the right to protection from different forms of pollution, in accordance with the standards and levels determined by law. He or she also has the obligation to collaborate in the conservation of the natural heritage and in actions designed to eliminate any form of pollution, with the objective of maintaining and preserving the natural environment for future generations.
3. Each individual has the right of access to environmental information held by the public authorities. The right to information may only be limited for justifiable reasons of public order, within the terms established by law.

Article 28. The Rights of Consumer and Users

1. Each individual, as a consumer and user of goods and services, has the right to the protection of their health and safety. He or she also has the right to accurate and comprehensible information on the characteristics and prices of goods and services, to a system of guarantees for purchased products and contracted supplies, and to the protection of their economic interests against abusive, negligent or fraudulent conduct.
2. Consumers and users have the right to information and to participation, either directly or through their representatives, regarding the Public Administration bodies of Catalonia, under the terms established by law.

Chapter II. Rights in the Political and Administrative Field

Article 29. Right of Participation

1. The citizens of Catalonia have an equal right to participate in the public affairs of Catalonia, whether directly or through their representatives, on the assumptions and under the terms established by this *Estatut* and by law.
2. The citizens of Catalonia have the right to elect their representatives to the representative political bodies and to stand for election as candidates, in accordance with the conditions and the requirements established by law.
3. The citizens of Catalonia have the right to promote and present legislative initiatives to Parliament, under the terms established by this *Estatut* and the law.
4. The citizens of Catalonia have the right to participate, directly or through associative bodies, in the parliamentary process of drafting laws, by means of the procedures established by Parliament's Rules of Procedure.
5. Each individual has the right to present petitions and complaints, in the form and with the effects established by law, to the institutions and the Administration of the *Generalitat* and also to the local government entities of Catalonia in matters coming under the respective powers. The conditions for exercise of this

right and its effects, and the obligations of the receiving institutions shall be established by law.

6. The citizens of Catalonia have the right to promote the calling of public consultations by the *Generalitat* and the city councils in matters coming under the respective powers, in the form and under the terms established by law.

Article 30. Rights of Access to Public Services and to a Good Administration

1. Each individual has the right of equal access to public and economic services of general interest. Public Administration bodies shall set the access conditions and quality standards for these services, regardless of the system for their provision.
2. Each individual has the right to be treated impartially and objectively by the public authorities of Catalonia in matters affecting them, and that the action of the public authorities be proportional to the ends justifying it.
3. The law shall regulate the conditions for exercise and ensuring the rights referred to in Sections 1 and 2 above, and shall determine the circumstances in which Catalan Public Administration bodies and any public services dependent on them shall adopt a charter of user rights and service providers obligations.

Article 31. Right to the Protection of Personal Data

Each individual has the right to the protection of personal data contained in the records held by the *Generalitat*, and they have the right to access, examine and have these data corrected. An independent authority, designated by Parliament, shall ensure that these rights are respected under the terms established by law.

Chapter III. Linguistic Rights and Obligations

Article 32. Rights and Obligations Concerning the Knowledge and Use of Languages

Each individual has the right not to be discriminated against for linguistic reasons. Legal acts executed in either of the two official languages have, in linguistic terms, full validity and effect.

Article 33. Linguistic Rights in Dealings with Public Administration Bodies and State Institutions

1. Citizens have the right to linguistic choice. In their relations with institutions, organizations and Public Administration bodies in Catalonia, each individual has the right to use the official language of his or her choice. This right binds public institutions, organizations and administration bodies, including the electoral administration in Catalonia, and, in general, any private bodies depending on them when exercising public functions.
2. When dealing with the Administration of Justice, the Office of the Public Prosecutor, notaries and public registry offices, each individual has the right to use the official language of his or her choice in any judicial, notarial or registration

procedures, and to receive all official documentation issued in Catalonia in the language requested, without having to endure defenselessness or undue delay due to the language chosen, and without having to provide any type of translation.

3. To guarantee the right to linguistic choice, judges and magistrates, public prosecutors, notaries, registrars of property and companies, those responsible for the Civil Registry and those in the service of the Administration of Justice, must demonstrate, in order to serve in Catalonia, in the form established by law, that they have an adequate and sufficient knowledge of the official languages which renders them fit to fulfil the functions of their post or workplace.
4. To guarantee the right to linguistic choice, the Administration of the State in Catalonia must demonstrate that the staff in its service has an adequate and sufficient knowledge of the two official languages that renders it fit to fulfil the functions of their post.
5. The citizens of Catalonia have the right to communicate in writing in Catalan with the constitutional entities and with the State-wide jurisdictional bodies, in accordance with the procedures established by the corresponding legislation. These institutions shall attend to and process written communications in Catalan, which shall have in all cases, full legal validity.

Article 34. Linguistic Rights of Consumers and Users

Each individual, in his or her capacity as user or consumer of goods, products and services, has the right to be attended orally or in writing in the official language of his or her choice. Bodies, companies and establishments that are open to the public in Catalonia are bound by the obligation of linguistic availability within the terms established by law.

Article 35. Linguistic Rights in the Field of Education

1. Each individual has the right to receive an education in Catalan, as established in this *Estatut*. Catalan shall be used as the teaching and learning language for university and non-university education.
2. Pupils have the right to receive an education in Catalan at the non-university level. They also have the right and obligation to have a sufficient oral and written knowledge of Catalan and Castilian upon completing compulsory education, whatever their habitual language of use when starting their education. The Catalan and Castilian languages shall be sufficiently represented in the curricula.
3. Pupils have the right not to be separated into centres or different class groups on the basis of their habitual language of use.
4. Those pupils who join the school system in Catalonia at a later age than normal school starting age have the right to receive special linguistic support if their lack of comprehension skills makes it difficult for them to pursue their education normally.
5. The teaching staff and pupils of universities have the right to express themselves, orally and in writing, in the official language of their choice.

Article 36. Rights Concerning Aranese

1. In Aran each individual has the right to know and use Aranese and to be attended orally and in writing in Aranese in his or her dealings with the Public Administration bodies and public and private entities accountable to them.
2. The citizens of Aran have the right to use Aranese in their dealings with the *Generalitat*.
3. Other linguistic rights and obligations relating to Aranese shall be determined by law.

Chapter IV. Guarantees of Statutory Rights

Article 37. General Provisions

1. The rights recognized in Chapters I, II and III of this Title bind all the public authorities of Catalonia and, depending on the nature of each right, individual citizens. Regulations passed by the public authorities in Catalonia shall respect these rights and shall be interpreted and applied in the most appropriate way so as to ensure their full effectiveness.
   The rights recognized by Articles 32 and 33 also bind the General Administration of the State in Catalonia.
2. Parliament shall approve the Charter of Rights and Obligations of the Citizens of Catalonia by law. The provisions of this Article concerning the rights recognized in Chapters I, II and III of this Title shall also apply to the rights recognized in the above-mentioned Charter.
3. The essential regulation and the direct development of the rights recognized in Chapters I, II and III of this Title shall be effected through an Act of Parliament.
4. The rights and principles of this Title shall not imply any alteration to the system for distribution of powers nor the creation of new Titles regarding powers nor the modification of those that already exist. None of the provisions of this Title shall be enacted, applied or interpreted in any way that reduces or restricts the fundamental rights recognized in the Constitution and in international treaties and conventions ratified by Spain.

Article 38. Protection

1. The Council for Statutory Guarantees protects the rights recognized in Chapters I, II and III of this Title and the Charter of Rights and Obligations of the Citizens of Catalonia, in accordance with Article 76.2 *b* and *c*.
2. Any act that undermines the rights recognized in Chapters I, II and III of this Title and in the Charter of Rights and Obligations of the Citizens of Catalonia may be appealed before the Superior Court of Justice of Catalonia, in keeping with the procedure established by law.

Chapter V. Governing Principles

Article 39. General Provisions

1. The public authorities of Catalonia shall direct public policy in accordance with the governing principles established by the Constitution and this *Estatut*. In the exercise of their powers, the public authorities of Catalonia shall promote and adopt any measures necessary to guarantee their full effectiveness.
2. The recognition, respect and protection of these governing principles shall shape positive legislation, judicial practice and the actions of the public authorities.
3. The governing principles are invocable before the jurisdiction, in accordance with the provisions of the law and other regulations that develop them.

Article 40. Protection of the Individual and the Family

1. The public authorities shall have as their objective the improvement of the quality of life for all individuals.
2. The public authorities shall guarantee the legal, economic, and social protection of the various forms of family regulated by law, as a basic structure, as an element that favours social cohesion, and as the primary structure for coexistence between individuals. They shall, moreover, promote the economic measures and supportive regulations for families aimed at guaranteeing a balance between professional and family life and having children, with special attention to large families.
3. The public authorities shall guarantee the protection of children, in particular, from all forms of exploitation, abandonment, ill-treatment and cruelty, and from poverty and its effects. In all actions implemented by the public authorities or by private institutions, the interests of the child shall be awarded priority.
4. The public authorities shall promote public policies to encourage the emancipation of young people, by facilitating access to work and housing so that they may develop their own lives and participate with equal rights and obligations in social and cultural life.
5. The public authorities shall guarantee the legal protection of people with disabilities and shall promote their social, economic and occupational integration. They shall also adopt the necessary measures to replace or complement the support from their immediate family environment.
6. The public authorities shall guarantee the protection of the elderly so that they may lead a decent and independent life and be able to participate in social and cultural life. They shall also strive for full integration of the elderly in society by means of public policies based on the principle of inter-generational solidarity.
7. The public authorities shall promote the equality of the different stable forms of union established between couples, bearing in mind their characteristics, regardless of the sexual orientation of the partners. The law shall regulate these unions and other forms of cohabitation and their consequences.

8. The public authorities shall promote the equality of all individuals, regardless of background, nationality, gender, race, religion, social condition or sexual orientation, and shall also promote the eradication of racism, anti-Semitism, xenophobia, homophobia, and of any other manifestation that may constitute a violation of the equality and dignity of the individual.

Article 41. The Gender Perspective

1. The public authorities shall guarantee adherence to the principle of equal opportunities for women and men in access to work, training, professional promotion, working conditions, including salary, and in all other circumstances, and shall also guarantee that women will not be discriminated against as a consequence of pregnancy or motherhood.
2. The public authorities shall guarantee integration of the gender perspective and of women into all public policies so as to ensure real and effective equality and parity between women and men.
3. Public policies shall guarantee that all forms of violence against women and actions of a sexist and discriminatory nature shall be dealt with as a whole; they shall encourage the recognition of the role of women in the cultural, historical, social and economic fields, and shall promote the participation of women's groups and associations in drafting and evaluating these policies.
4. The public authorities shall recognize and take into account the economic value of domestic care and attention in establishing economic and social policies.
5. The public authorities, in the sphere of their powers, and in the cases established by law, shall ensure that the free choice of women is the determining factor in all matters that may affect their dignity, integrity and physical and mental welfare, most particularly in matters affecting their own bodies and their reproductive and sexual health.

Article 42. Social Cohesion and Welfare

1. The public authorities shall promote public policies that foster social cohesion and that guarantee a system of social services, whether public or private with public subsidies, which is appropriate to the economic and social indices of Catalonia.
2. The public authorities shall ensure full social, economic and occupational integration of the individuals and groups most in need of protection, particularly those who are in situations of poverty and at risk of social exclusion.
3. The public authorities shall ensure the dignity, safety, and full protection of all individuals, especially those who are most vulnerable.
4. The public authorities shall guarantee the quality of service and the free nature of public healthcare under the terms established by law.
5. The public authorities shall promote preventive and community policies and shall guarantee the quality and the free nature of any social service designated by law as basic.

6. The public authorities shall take the necessary measures to establish a system for receiving immigrants, and shall promote policies to guarantee recognition and effectiveness of their rights and obligations, equality of opportunity and the services and assistance that will facilitate their social and economic accommodation and their participation in public affairs.
7. The public authorities shall ensure social, cultural and religious harmony among individuals in Catalonia, and respect for diversity of belief and ethical and philosophical convictions. They shall foster intercultural relations through the encouragement and creation of forums for mutual awareness, dialogue and mediation. They shall also guarantee recognition of the culture of the Romany people so as to safeguard their historical heritage.

Article 43. Promotion of Participation

1. The public authorities shall promote social participation in drafting, providing and evaluating public policies, and also the participation of individuals and associations in civic, social, cultural, economic and political matters, with full respect for the principles of pluralism, free enterprise and autonomy.
2. The public authorities shall facilitate citizen and political participation and representation, with special attention to the less populated areas of the territory.
3. The public authorities shall ensure that institutional campaigns organized on the occasion of electoral processes have as their aim the encouragement of citizen participation and that the information on electoral candidates provided by the media to the electorate is accurate, objective and neutral and that it respects political pluralism.

Article 44. Education, Research and Culture

1. The public authorities shall guarantee the quality of the education system and shall provide a human, scientific and technical education for students that is based on the social values of equality, solidarity, freedom, pluralism and civil responsibility, and all other values that form the basis of democratic coexistence.
2. The public authorities shall ensure sufficient knowledge of a third language by completion of compulsory education.
3. The public authorities shall promote and encourage the involvement and the participation of the family in the education of children, within the framework of the education community, and shall facilitate and promote access to extracurricular educational activities.
4. The public authorities shall foster high-quality scientific investigation and research, artistic creativity, and the conservation and dissemination of the cultural heritage of Catalonia.
5. The public authorities shall take the necessary action to enable all individuals to have access to culture, to cultural goods and services, and to the cultural, archaeological, historical, industrial and artistic heritage of Catalonia.

Article 45. The Socio-economic Field

1. The public authorities shall adopt the necessary measures to promote the economic and social progress of Catalonia and its citizens, based on the principles of solidarity, cohesion, sustainable development and equal opportunities.
2. The public authorities shall promote a fairer distribution of personal and territorial wealth within the framework of a Catalan welfare system.
3. The public authorities shall adopt the measures necessary to guarantee the labour and trade union rights of workers, and shall encourage and promote their participation in companies, and policies of full employment, increased job stability, employee training, occupational risk prevention, occupational health and safety, the creation of decent workplace conditions, non-discrimination for reasons of gender, and the guarantee of necessary rest periods and paid holidays.
4. The *Generalitat* shall promote the creation of a Catalan labour relations space, established in accordance with the specific productive and business reality of Catalonia and of the social agents of Catalonia, in which the trade unions, employer organizations and the Administration of the *Generalitat* shall be represented. Within this framework, the public authorities shall foster the practice of social dialogue, agreement, collective bargaining, out-of-court settlement of labour disputes, and participation in the development and improvement of the productive fabric.
5. The *Generalitat* shall favour the development of business activity and the entrepreneurial spirit, taking into account the social responsibility of the company, free enterprise and the conditions for competitiveness, and shall protect in particular the productive economy and the activity of self-employed entrepreneurs, and of small and medium-sized enterprises. The *Generalitat* shall foster the action of cooperatives and labour associations and shall stimulate social economy initiatives.
6. Trade unions and employer organizations shall participate in the definition of public policies which affect them. The *Generalitat* shall promote mediation and arbitration for the resolution of conflicts of interest between different social agents.
7. Professional organizations and public law bodies representing economic and professional interests and third sector associations are to be consulted in the definition of public policies which affect them.
8. The *Generalitat*, taking into consideration the social, cultural and economic promotion functions of savings banks, shall protect their institutional autonomy and shall promote the social contribution of these entities to the economic and social strategies of the different territories of Catalonia.

Article 46. The Environment, Sustainable Development and Territorial Balance

1. The public authorities shall ensure the protection of the environment through the adoption of public policies based on sustainable development and on collective and inter-generational solidarity.

2. Environmental policies shall be particularly addressed to the reduction of different types of pollution, to establishing standards and minimum protection levels, outlining measures for the correction of environmental damage, the sensible use of natural resources, prevention and control of erosion and of activities that alter the atmospheric and climatic pattern, and respect for the principles of environmental protection, conservation of natural resources, responsibility, ecological control, and recycling and reuse of goods and products.
3. The public authorities shall create conditions for the preservation of nature and biodiversity, promote the integration of environmental objectives into sectoral policies, and establish conditions in which all individuals can enjoy the natural heritage and landscape.
4. The public authorities shall ensure economic and territorial cohesion by applying policies that ensure a special treatment for mountain zones, protection of the landscape and the coastline, the promotion of agriculture, livestock farming and forestry, and a balanced distribution of productive sectors, services of general interest and communication networks throughout the territory.
5. The public authorities shall provide citizens with environmental information and encourage education in values concerning the preservation and improvement of the environment as a common heritage.

Article 47. Housing

The public authorities shall facilitate access to housing by means of the provision of land and the promotion of public and subsidized housing, with special attention to young people and groups with the greatest needs.

Article 48. Mobility and Road Safety

1. The public authorities shall promote transport and communication policies based on sustainability criteria that encourage the use of public transportation and the improvement of mobility, and which guarantee access for people with reduced mobility.
2. The public authorities shall encourage, as a matter of priority, measures aimed at improving road safety and reducing the number of traffic accidents, placing particular emphasis on prevention, road safety education, and the care of accident victims.

Article 49. Protection of Consumers and Users

1. The public authorities shall guarantee the protection of health, safety, and the defence of the rights and legitimate interests of consumers and users.
2. The public authorities shall guarantee the existence of consumer mediation and arbitration instruments, promote awareness and use of these instruments, and provide support to consumers and user associations.

Article 50. Promotion and Dissemination of Catalan

1. The public authorities shall protect the Catalan language in all fields and sectors and shall foment its knowledge, use and dissemination. These principles shall also be applied to Aranese.
2. Government, universities and higher education institutions, in their respective powers, shall adopt the relevant measures to guarantee the use of the Catalan language in all teaching, administrative and research activities.
3. Policies for the promotion of the Catalan language shall be spread to the whole of the State, the European Union and the rest of the world.
4. The public authorities shall take steps to ensure that the information contained on labels, packaging and instructions for use of products distributed in Catalonia are also printed in Catalan.
5. The *Generalitat*, the local administration and other public corporations in Catalonia, the institutions and companies answerable to them and the franchisees of their services, shall use Catalan for their internal proceedings and for relations among themselves. They shall also use it in communications and notifications addressed to natural or legal persons resident in Catalonia, without prejudice to citizens' rights to receive them in Castilian should they ask for this.
6. The public authorities shall guarantee the use of Catalan sign language and conditions of equality for deaf people who chooses to use this language, which shall be the subject of education, protection and respect.
7. The State, in accordance with the provisions of the Constitution, shall support the application of the principles stated in this Article. Instruments for coordination and, where necessary, combined action for improved efficacy, shall be established.

Article 51. Cooperation for Promotion of Peace and Cooperation for Development

1. The *Generalitat* shall promote a culture of peace and actions that foster peace in the world.
2. The *Generalitat* shall promote cooperation actions and policies for the development of peoples and shall establish emergency humanitarian aid programmes.

Article 52. The Media

1. The public authorities shall promote the conditions which guarantee the right to information and the right to receive accurate information from the media and contents that respect personal dignity and political, social, cultural and religious pluralism. In the case of publicly-owned media, the information provided shall also be neutral.
2. The public authorities shall promote the conditions that guarantee equal access to audiovisual services in Catalonia.

Article 53. Access to Information and Communication Technologies

1. The public authorities shall facilitate knowledge of the information society and shall encourage equal access to communication and to information technologies in all areas of life, including the workplace; they shall encourage that these technologies are at the service of people and do not negatively affect their rights, and shall guarantee the provision of services by means of the above-mentioned technologies, in accordance with the principles of universality, continuity and modernization.
2. The *Generalitat* shall promote technological training, research and innovation so that the opportunities for progress offered by the knowledge and information society may contribute to improved social welfare and cohesion.

Article 54. Historical Memory

1. The *Generalitat* and the other public authorities shall work for the knowledge and the maintenance of the historical memory of Catalonia as a collective heritage that bears witness to its resistance and struggle for rights and democratic freedoms. To this end, they shall adopt the necessary institutional initiatives for the recognition and rehabilitation of all those citizens who have suffered persecution as a consequence of their defence of democracy and Catalan self-government.
2. The *Generalitat* shall strive to make its historical memory a permanent symbol of tolerance, of the dignity of democratic values, of the rejection of totalitarianism, and of recognition for all individuals who have suffered persecution as a consequence of personal, ideological or conscientious choices.

Title II. Institutions

Chapter I. Parliament

Article 55. General Provisions

1. Parliament represents the people of Catalonia.
2. Parliament exercises legislative power, approves the budget of the *Generalitat* and controls and promotes political and government action. It is the seat for the expression of pluralism and political debate.
3. Parliament is inviolable.

Article 56. Composition and Electoral System

1. Parliament consists of a minimum of one hundred and a maximum of one hundred and fifty members, elected for a period of four years by universal, free, equal, direct and secret suffrage, in accordance with this *Estatut* and with electoral legislation.

2. The electoral system is one of proportional representation and has to ensure adequate representation of all areas of the territory of Catalonia. Electoral Administration is independent and guarantees transparency and objectivity in the electoral process. The electoral system is regulated by an Act of Parliament approved by a final vote on the full text by a majority of two thirds of the Members of Parliament.
3. In accordance with electoral legislation, citizens of Catalonia, by virtue of their civil and political rights, are electors and eligible for election. The electoral law of Catalonia shall establish criteria for parity between women and men when preparing the electoral lists.
4. Fifteen days before the end of the legislative term, the President of the *Generalitat* shall call an election, which shall be held within from forty to sixty days after the call.

Article 57. Legal Status of Members of Parliament

1. Members of Parliament are inviolable with regard to the votes and opinions they may express in exercise of their position. During their term in office, they enjoy legal immunity and may not therefore be arrested unless in flagrant offence.
2. In lawsuits against Members of Parliament, the competent authority is the Superior Court of Justice of Catalonia. Outside the territory of Catalonia, penal responsibility shall be invocable on the same terms before the Criminal Chamber of the Spanish Supreme Court.
3. Members of Parliament are not subject to imperative mandate.

Article 58. Parliamentary Autonomy

1. Parliament has organizational, financial, administrative, and disciplinary autonomy.
2. Parliament drafts and approves its Rules of Procedure, its budget, and establishes the legal status of its staff.
3. Approval or reform of Parliament's Rules of Procedure is a matter for the Plenary Assembly and it requires the vote in favour of an absolute majority of Members of Parliament in a final vote on the full text.

Article 59. Organisation and Work

1. Parliament has a President and a Presiding Board elected by the Plenary Assembly. Their election and functions are regulated by Parliament's Rules of Procedure.
2. Parliament's Rules of Procedure establish the rights and obligations of the Members of Parliament, the requirements for the formation of parliamentary groups, the role of these groups in the exercise of parliamentary functions, and the powers of the Board of Spokespeople.

3. Parliament works in the Plenary Assembly and in committees. Parliamentary groups participate in all committees in numbers proportional to their representation.
4. Parliament has a standing committee, presided over by the President of Parliament and consisting of the number of members determined by Parliament's Rules of Procedure, in proportion to parliamentary group representation. The Standing Committee oversees exercise of parliamentary powers when Parliament is not in session, in the periods between sessions when the parliamentary mandate has ended, and when Parliament has been dissolved. At the end of a legislative term or upon dissolution of Parliament, the mandate of the Members of Parliament who form the Standing Committee is extended until a new Parliament is constituted.
5. Public office holders and staff in the employ of Public Administration bodies which operate in Catalonia are obliged to appear before Parliament when required.
6. Parliament may create investigative committees on any matter of public relevance or interest to the *Generalitat*. Those summoned to appear before them, are obliged to do so, in accordance with the procedure and guarantees established by Parliament's Rules of Procedure. Sanctions for non-fulfilment of this obligation shall be regulated by law.
7. Individual and group petitions addressed to Parliament shall be regulated by Parliament's Rules of Procedure. It shall also establish mechanisms for participation by citizens in the exercise of parliamentary functions.

Article 60. System of Meetings and Sessions

1. Parliament meets annually in two ordinary periods of sessions established by the Rules of Procedure. Parliament may meet in extraordinary sessions outside the ordinary session periods. Extraordinary parliamentary sessions are called by the President of Parliament with the approval of the Standing Committee, on the proposal of three parliamentary groups or of a quarter of the Members of Parliament, or at the request of parliamentary groups or Members of Parliament that represent an absolute majority. Parliament also meets in extraordinary sessions at the request of the President of the *Generalitat*. Extraordinary sessions are called to deal with a specific agenda and are adjourned when this has been dealt with.
2. Plenary sessions are public, except in the situations established by Parliament's Rules of Procedure.
3. For Parliament to adopt valid decisions, an absolute majority of Members of Parliament must be present. Decisions are valid if they have been approved by a simple majority of Members present, without prejudice to the special majorities established by this *Estatut*, by law or by Parliament's Rules of Procedure.

Article 61. Functions

In addition to the functions established in Article 55, it is also a matter for the Parliament:

a) To designate the senators that represent the *Generalitat* in the Senate. This designation shall be made through a specific sitting convened for this purpose and shall be proportional to the number of Members in each parliamentary group.
b) To draft Members' bills for presentation before the Presiding Board of Congress and to nominate the Members of Parliament charged with defending these bills.
c) To request the adoption of Government bills by the State Government.
d) To request the State to transfer or delegate powers and attribute authority, within the framework of Article 150 of the Constitution.
e) To lodge appeals on the basis of unconstitutionality and to appear before the Constitutional Court in other constitutional proceedings, in accordance with the Organic Act of the Constitutional Court.
f) Any other functions attributed to it by this *Estatut* and by law.

Article 62. Legislative Initiative and Exercise of the Legislative Function

1. Legislative initiative is a matter for Members of Parliament, parliamentary groups and the Government. It is also a matter for the citizens, under the terms established by the laws of Catalonia, by means of popular legislative initiative, and for the representative bodies of the supra-municipal entities of the territorial organization of Catalonia that this *Estatut* establishes.
2. The laws that directly regulate the matters mentioned in Articles 2.3, 6, 37.2, 56.2, 67.5, 68.3, 77.3, 79.3, 81.2 and 94.1 are laws concerning basic development of the *Estatut*. Approval, modification and repeal of these laws requires a vote in favour by an absolute majority of the Plenary Assembly in a final vote on the full text, except where the *Estatut* establishes another voting system.
3. The Plenary Assembly may delegate the processing and approval of legislative initiatives to legislative standing committees. This delegation may be revoked at any time. Matters that may not be delegated to the committees include the reform of the *Estatut*, the basic development laws, the budget of the *Generalitat,* and laws of legislative delegation to the Government.

Article 63. Delegation of Legislative Power to the Government

1. Parliament may delegate the power to enact rules of legal rank to the Government. Government regulations containing delegated legislation are termed *legislative decrees*. Matters that may not be subject to legislative delegation include the reform of the *Estatut*, the basic development laws, with the exception of the delegation of the establishment of a rewritten text, the basic regulation and direct development of the rights recognized in the *Estatut* and in the Charter of Rights and Obligations of the Citizens of Catalonia, and the budget of the *Generalitat*.
2. Legislative delegation may only be to the Government. Delegation shall be deliberate, by law, for a specific matter, and must specify the time period within which it applies. Delegation shall cease when the Government publishes the corresponding legislative decree or when the Government is an acting Government.

3. On authorizing the Government to write a new Articled text, the delegation laws shall lay down the bases for the Government to apply in the exercise of legislative delegation. On authorizing the Government to rewrite legal texts, the law shall determine both the scope and criteria of the rewriting.
4. Control of delegated legislation is regulated by Parliament's Rules of Procedure. The delegation laws may also establish a special control system for legislative decrees.

Article 64. Decree-laws

1. In the case of extraordinary and urgent need, the Government may enact provisional legal provisions in the form of a Decree-law. Matters that may not be subject to Decree-laws include the reform of the *Estatut*, subjects which are the object of basic development laws, basic regulation and the direct development of rights recognized in the *Estatut* and in the Charter of Rights and Obligations of the Citizens of Catalonia, and the budget of the *Generalitat.*
2. Decree-laws are repealed if, within thirty days of promulgation, a period which may not be extended, they are not specifically validated by Parliament following a debate and a full vote.
3. Parliament may process Decree-laws as Government bills by means of emergency procedures, within the period established in Section 2 above.

Article 65. Promulgation and Publication of Laws

The laws of Catalonia are promulgated, in the name of the King, by the President of the *Generalitat,* who orders their publication in the *Diari Oficial de la Generalitat de Catalunya* (Official Journal of the Generalitat of Catalonia) within fifteen days, and in the *Boletín Oficial del Estado* (Official Spanish State Bulletin). The date of publication in the *Diari Oficial de la Generalitat de Catalunya* is taken as the date of entry into force. The official version in Castilian is the translation produced by the *Generalitat.*

Article 66. Reasons for Termination of the Legislative Term

The legislative term ends due to expiry of the term of office once four years have passed from the date of the elections. The legislative term may also end early if the investiture of the President of the *Generalitat* fails to take place or if early dissolution has been agreed to by the President of the *Generalitat.*

Chapter II. The President of the Generalitat

Article 67. Election, Nomination, Personal Status, Cessation and Powers

1. The President is the highest representative of the *Generalitat* and directs the action of the Government. The President also embodies the ordinary representation of the State in Catalonia.

2. The President of the *Generalitat* is elected by Parliament from among its members. The limitation of terms of office may be regulated by law.
3. If after two months from the first investiture vote no candidate has been elected, Parliament shall be automatically dissolved and the acting President of the *Generalitat* shall call immediate elections which shall take place within from forty to sixty days.
4. The President of the *Generalitat* is appointed by the King.
5. The legal status of the President of the *Generalitat* is regulated by an Act of Parliament. For the purposes of precedence and protocol in Catalonia, the President of the *Generalitat* has the pre-eminent position as befits the representative of the *Generalitat* and the State in Catalonia.
6. As the ordinary representative of the State in Catalonia, the President has authority to:
   a) Promulgate, in the name of the King, laws, legal decrees and legislative decrees in Catalonia and give the order to publish them.
   b) Give the order to publish appointments to the institutional offices of the State in Catalonia.
   c) Request the collaboration of any State authorities that exercise public functions in Catalonia.
   d) Others as determined by law.
7. The President of the *Generalitat*'s term of office ends with renewal of Parliament following elections, the passing of a motion of censure or the defeat of a vote of confidence, death, resignation, permanent physical or mental disability acknowledged by Parliament rendering him or her unfit for office, or a confirmed criminal sentence rendering him or her unfit to hold any public office.
8. The First Minister, if there is one, or the Minister designated by law, replaces and substitutes for the President of the *Generalitat* in the event of absence, illness, or cessation due to disability or death. This replacement and substitution shall not include exercise of presidential functions with regard to proposal of votes of confidence, designation and cessation of Ministers, or early dissolution of Parliament.
9. The President of the *Generalitat* may, in cases where no First Minister has been appointed, temporarily delegate executive functions to another Minister.

Chapter III. The Government and the Administration of the Generalitat

Section One. The Government

Article 68. Functions, Composition, Organisation and Cessation

1. The Government is the superior collegiate body that directs political action and the Administration of the *Generalitat*. It exercises executive functions and regulatory power in accordance with this *Estatut* and the law.
2. The Government consists of the President of the *Generalitat*, the First Minister, if applicable, and the ministers.
3. A law shall regulate the organization, functions and powers of the Government.

4. Government ends when the office of the President of the *Generalitat* ends.
5. All acts, general regulations and rules emanating from the Government or from the Administration of the *Generalitat* shall be published in the *Diari Oficial de la Generalitat de Catalunya.* This is sufficient for all purposes for the efficacy of acts and for the entry into force of general regulations and rules.

Article 69. The First Minister

The President of the *Generalitat* may, by decree, appoint a First Minister. An account of this appointment shall be given to Parliament. The First Minister is a member of the Government. The office of First Minister, in accordance with the law, has functions of its own, in addition to those delegated by the President of the *Generalitat.*

Article 70. Personal Status of the Members of the Government

1. The President and the ministers of the *Generalitat* may not be arrested or detained during their term of office for presumed criminal offences committed in Catalan territory except in cases of flagrant offences.
2. The Superior Court of Justice of Catalonia has the authority to decide on the indictment, prosecution and trial of the President of the *Generalitat* and its ministers. Outside the territory of Catalonia, penal responsibility is invocable on the same terms before the Criminal Chamber of the Spanish Supreme Court.

Section Two. The Administration of the *Generalitat*

Article 71. General Provisions and Principles of Organisation and Functioning

1. The Administration of the *Generalitat* is the organization that exercises the executive functions that this *Estatut* attributes to the *Generalitat.* It is considered the ordinary administrative body in accordance with the provisions of this *Estatut* and the law, and without prejudice to the powers of the local administration.
2. The Administration of the *Generalitat* objectively serves the general interest and is fully subject to the law.
3. The Administration of the *Generalitat* acts in accordance with principles of coordination and comprehensive application, in order to guarantee the integration of public policies.
4. The Administration of the *Generalitat,* in accordance with the principle of transparency, shall make public the necessary information to enable citizens to evaluate its management.
5. The Administration of the *Generalitat* exercises its functions in the territory of Catalonia in accordance with the principles of deconcentration and decentralisation.
6. The law shall regulate the organization of the Administration of the *Generalitat* and shall determine in all cases:

a) The types of functional decentralisation and the various forms of public and private personification that the Administration of the *Generalitat* may adopt.
b) The forms of organization and management of public services.
c) The action of the Administration of the *Generalitat* in the field of private law, and also the participation of the private sector in the execution of public policies and the provision of public services.

7. The legal status of staff in the employ of the Administration of the *Generalitat* shall be regulated by law, and shall include in all cases the incompatibility requirements, the guaranteed provision of training and updating of knowledge, and the necessary praxis for the performance of public functions.

Article 72. Consultative Bodies of the Government

1. The Legal Advisory Commission is the highest consultative body of the Government. Its composition and functions are regulated by an Act of Parliament.
2. The Economic, Social and Work Council of Catalonia is the consultative and advisory body of the Government in socio-economic, labour, and employment matters. Its composition and functions are regulated by an Act of Parliament.

Chapter IV. Relations Between Parliament and Government

Article 73. Rights and Obligations of Members of the Government Towards Parliament

1. The President and the ministers of the *Generalitat* have the right to attend and speak at meetings of the Plenary Assembly and of the parliamentary committees.
2. Parliament may request that the Government and its members provide it with the information it considers necessary for the exercise of its functions. It may also request the presence of the Government at Plenary Assembly sessions and parliamentary committee meetings, under the terms established by Parliament's Rules of Procedure.

Article 74. Political Responsibility of the Government and Its Members

1. Politically, the President and the ministers of the *Generalitat* answer jointly to Parliament, without prejudice to the direct responsibility of each.
2. The delegation of functions of the President of the *Generalitat* does not exempt him or her from political responsibility before Parliament.

Article 75. Early Dissolution of Parliament

The President of the *Generalitat*, on prior deliberation with the Government and under his or her own exclusive responsibility, may dissolve Parliament. This power may not be exercised during the process of a vote of censure, nor may it be exercised if less than one year has passed since the last such dissolution of Parliament. The decree of dissolution shall establish the calling of new elections, which shall take place within forty to sixty days after the date of publication of the decree in the *Diari Oficial de la Generalitat de Catalunya.*

Chapter V. Other Institutions of the Generalitat

Section One. The Council for Statutory Guarantees

Article 76. Functions

1. The Council for Statutory Guarantees is the institution of the *Generalitat* that ensures that the regulations of the *Generalitat* comply with this *Estatut* and the Constitution, under the terms established in Section 2 below.
2. The Council for Statutory Guarantees may pass judgement, under the terms established by law, on the following cases:
   a) Compliance with the Constitution of draft bills and proposals to reform the Statute of Autonomy of Catalonia, prior to their approval by Parliament.
   b) Compliance with this *Estatut* and the Constitution of Government bills and Members' bills submitted for debate and approval by Parliament, and of legal decrees subject to validation by Parliament.
   c) Compliance with this *Estatut* and the Constitution of draft legislative decrees approved by the Government.
   d) Compliance of Government bills and Members' bills and draft legislative decrees approved by the Government with local autonomy under the terms guaranteed by this *Estatut.*
3. Prior to the lodging of appeals on the basis of unconstitutionality by Parliament or Government, the lodging of claims of conflict over jurisdiction by the Government, and the lodging of claims of conflict over the defence of local autonomy before the Constitutional Court, the Council for Statutory Guarantees shall pass judgement on the issue concerned.
4. *The judgements of the Council for Statutory Guarantees in relation to Government bills and Members' bills in Parliament that develop or affect the rights recognized in this Estatut, are binding in nature*[3].

Article 77. Composition and Functioning

1. The Council for Statutory Guarantees is composed of members appointed by the President of the *Generalitat* from among jurists of recognized competence, two thirds of whose members are nominated by Parliament, by a majority of three-fifths of the deputies, and the other third is nominated by Government.

3. The Constitutional Court has declared this section is unconstitutional and void (STC 31/2010, 28 June).

2. The Council for Statutory Guarantees shall elect a president from among its members.
3. An Act of Parliament regulates the composition and functioning of the Council for Statutory Guarantees, the status of its members, and the procedures relating to the exercise of its functions. The authority of the Council for Statutory Guarantees to pass judgement, as established by this *Estatut,* may be extended by law, without these judgements being binding in character.
4. The Council for Statutory Guarantees has organic, functional and budgetary autonomy in accordance with the law.

Section Two. The Ombudsman

Article 78. Functions and Relations with Other Similar Institutions

1. The Ombudsman has the function of protecting and defending the rights and freedoms recognized in the Constitution and in this *Estatut*. To this end, he or she oversees, *exclusively*[4], the activity of the Administration of the *Generalitat*, that of any public or private related bodies that are associated with or answerable to it, that of private companies that manage public services or that carry out activities of general or universal interest, or equivalent activities in a publicly-subsidized or indirect way, and that of other persons with a contractual relationship with the Administration of the *Generalitat* and with the public bodies which are answerable to it. He or she also oversees the activity of the local administration in Catalonia and that of the private or public bodies which are associated with or answerable to it.
2. The Ombudsman and the Spanish Ombudsman shall collaborate in the exercise of their functions.
3. The Ombudsman may request a report from the Council for Statutory Guarantees on Government bills and Members' bills presented for debate and approval by Parliament, and legal decrees presented for validation by Parliament, when these regulate rights recognized in this *Estatut*.
4. The Ombudsman may establish collaborative links with the local area ombudsmen and other similar figures created in the public and private spheres.
5. Public Administration bodies in Catalonia and other entities and individuals referred to in Section 1 above are obliged to cooperate with the Ombudsman. The sanctions and mechanisms intended to guarantee fulfilment of this obligation shall be regulated by law.

Article 79. Designation and Status of the Ombudsman

1. The Ombudsman is elected by Parliament by a majority of three-fifths of its members.
2. The Ombudsman exercises his or her functions with impartiality and independence, is inviolable in regard to any opinions expressed in carrying out his or

4. The Constitutional Court has declared this word is unconstitutional and void (STC 31/2010, 28 June).

her duties, is immovable, and may only be removed from office or suspended for the reasons established by law.

3. The personal status of the Ombudsman, incompatibilities, reasons for cessation, organization, and powers of the institution shall be regulated by law. The Ombudsman has regulatory, organizational, functional and budgetary autonomy in accordance with the law.

Section Three. The Audit Office

Article 80. Functions and Relations with the Accounts Court

1. The Audit Office is the external regulatory body for the finances, economic management and control of efficiency of the *Generalitat*, of the local bodies and of the remainder of the public sector in Catalonia.
2. In organizational terms, the Audit Office is answerable to Parliament, exercises its functions by parliamentary delegation, with full organizational, working and budgetary autonomy, in accordance with the law.
3. The Audit Office and the Accounts Court shall establish cooperative links by means of an agreement. This agreement shall establish the participation mechanisms in jurisdictional proceedings in regard to account liability.

Article 81. Composition, Work and Legal Status

1. The Audit Office is composed of auditors designated by Parliament by a majority of three-fifths of its members. The chief auditor is elected from among the auditors.
2. Legal status, incompatibilities, reasons for cessation, and the organization and work of the Audit Office shall be regulated by law.

Section Four. Regulation of the Catalan Broadcasting Authority

Article 82. The Catalan Broadcasting Authority

The Catalan Broadcasting Authority is the regulatory independent authority in the field of public and private audio-visual communication. The Catalan Broadcasting Authority acts with full independence from the Government of the *Generalitat* in carrying out its functions. The criteria for election of its members and its specific fields of action shall be established by an Act of Parliament.

Chapter VI. Local Government

Section One. Local Territorial Organisation

Article 83. Organization of Local Government in Catalonia

1. The territorial organization of Catalonia is based on municipalities and *vegueries*.

2. The supra-municipal area is constituted, in all cases, by *comarques*, which shall be regulated by an Act of Parliament.
3. Any other supra-municipal entity created by the *Generalitat* shall be based on the municipalities' desire for collaboration and association.

Article 84. Local Powers

1. This *Estatut* guarantees municipalities a core set of powers of their own which shall be exercised by them with full autonomy, subject only to controls of constitutionality and legality.
2. The local governments of Catalonia have in all cases their own powers in the following matters, in the terms determined by law:
   a) Territorial classification and management, town planning and planning restrictions, and the conservation and maintenance of local public property.
   b) Planning, programming and management of public housing and participation in the planning of subsidized housing on municipal land.
   c) Organization and provision of basic services to the community.
   d) Regulation and management of municipal facilities.
   e) Regulation of safety conditions for activities organized in public spaces and venues, and coordination of the various bodies and forces present in the municipality through the Security Board.
   f) Civil protection and fire prevention.
   g) Planning, organization and management of infant education, participation in the enrolment process in public and subsidized education centres within the municipal area, the upkeep and control of public centres outside school hours, and the school calendar.
   h) Traffic and mobility services and the management of municipal public transportation.
   i) Regulation of the establishment of authorizations and promotions for all types of economic activity, especially those related to retail, crafts and tourism, and those stimulating employment.
   j) Formulation and management of policies for the protection of the environment and sustainable development.
   k) Regulation and management of sports and leisure facilities, and the promotion of activities.
   l) Regulation of the establishment of telecommunications infrastructures and the provision of telecommunications services.
   m) Regulation and provision of care services, public primary care services and promotion of immigrant reception policies.
   n) Regulation, management and supervision of activities and uses that take place on beaches, rivers, lakes and mountains.
3. In matters referred to in Section 2 above, the distribution of administrative responsibilities between different local administrations shall take into account management capacities and is governed by the laws passed by Parliament, by the principle of subsidiarity, in accordance with the European Charter of Local

Self-Government, by the principle of differentiation, in accordance with the characteristics of the municipality, and by the principle of financial capacity.

4. The *Generalitat* shall determine and establish the mechanisms for the financing of new services deriving from the expansion of local government powers.

Article 85. The Council of Local Governments

The Council of Local Governments is the representative body for municipalities and *vegueries* in the institutions of the *Generalitat*. The Council shall be taken into account in parliamentary procedures for legislative initiatives that specifically affect local administrations, and in the processing of plans and regulatory rules of the same nature. An Act of Parliament regulates the composition, organization and functions of the Council of Local Governments.

Section Two. The Municipality

Article 86. The Municipality and Municipal Autonomy

1. The municipality is the basic local entity of territorial organization in Catalonia and the main channel for participation of the local community in public affairs.
2. Municipal government and administration are the responsibility of the city council, which is composed of a mayor or mayors and the city councillors. The requirements for the application of an open council system shall be established by law.
3. The municipality is guaranteed, in this *Estatut,* the necessary autonomy for the exercise of its powers and the defence of the interests of the community it represents.
4. The acts and the decisions adopted by the municipalities shall not be subject to control of appropriateness by any other administration.
5. The *Generalitat* has the authority to check that any act or decision adopted by municipalities complies with the legal system and, if appropriate, take the necessary action to bring the issue before the contentious-administrative courts, without prejudice to any actions which the State may take in defence of its powers.
6. City councillors are elected by the residents of the municipalities through a system of universal, equal, free, direct and secret suffrage.
7. Those concentrations of population within a municipality which form separate nuclei may become decentralized municipal entities. The law shall guarantee their decentralisation and that they have sufficient capacity to carry out the activities and provide the services corresponding to their jurisdiction.

Article 87. Principles of Organisation and Functioning and Regulatory Power

1. Municipalities have full authority for self-organization within the framework of the general provisions established by law in matters of municipal organization and functioning.

2. Municipalities have the right to associate with other municipalities and to cooperate with each other and with other public bodies in exercise of their powers, and also to carry out other tasks in the common interest. To this effect, they may enter into agreements and create and participate in *mancomunitats*, consortia and associations, and may also adopt other forms of joint action. The law may not restrict this right unless it is to guarantee the recognized autonomy of other entities.
3. As an expression of the democratic principle on which they are based, municipalities have regulatory power governing their sphere of powers and in other spheres where their autonomy is applicable.

Article 88. The Principle of Differentiation

The laws affecting the legal, organic, functional, jurisdictional and financial system of the municipalities shall take into account their different demographic, geographic, functional and organizational characteristics and also their size and capacity for management.

Article 89. Special System for the Municipality of Barcelona

The municipality of Barcelona has a special system established by an Act of Parliament. The City Council of Barcelona may propose the modification of this special system and, in accordance with laws passed by Parliament and Parliament's Rules of Procedure, shall participate in the preparation of Government bills affecting this special system and shall be consulted during the parliamentary proceedings of other legislative initiatives affecting the special system.

Section Three. The *Vegueria*

Article 90. The *Vegueria*

1. The *vegueria* is the specific territorial area for the exercise of inter-municipal government for local cooperation, and has legal personality. The *vegueria* is also the territorial division adopted by the *Generalitat* for the territorial organization of its services.
2. The *vegueria*, as local government, is territorial in nature and has autonomy in the management of its interests.

Article 91. The Council of the *Vegueria*

1. The government and the autonomous administration of the *vegueria* are the responsibility of the Council of the *Vegueria*, which is formed by the president and by the councillors of the *vegueria*.
2. The president of the *vegueria* is chosen by the councillors of the *vegueria* from among its members.
3. The councils of the *vegueria* replace the provincial councils.

4. The creation, modification, abolition, and also the implementation of the legal system of the *vegueries* is regulated by an Act of Parliament. Alteration of provincial boundaries, if required, shall be carried out within the terms established by Article 141.1 of the Constitution.

Section Four. The *Comarca* and the Other Supra-municipal Local Government Entities

Article 92. The *Comarca*

1. The *comarca* is a local government entity with legal personality. It is formed by municipalities for the purpose of managing local powers and services.
2. The creation, modification and abolition of the *comarques*, and also the establishment of their legal system, is regulated by an Act of Parliament.

Article 93. Others Supra-municipal Local Government Entities

The other supra-municipal local government entities are founded on the basis of the municipalities' wish to collaborate and enter into association and on recognition of the metropolitan areas. The creation, modification and abolition of these entities, and also the establishment of their legal system is regulated by an Act of Parliament.

Chapter VII. Aran's Own Institutional Organisation

Article 94. Legal System

1. Aran has a special legal system established by an Act of Parliament. The specific nature of the institutional and administrative organization of Aran is recognized by this system, which guarantees this territory autonomy in organizing and managing its public affairs.
2. The institution of government of Aran is the *Conselh Generau*, which consists of the *Síndic*, the *Plen des Conselhèrs e Conselhères Generaus* and the *Comission d'Auditors de Compdes*. The *Síndic* is the highest and ordinary representation of the *Generalitat* in Aran.
3. The institution of government of Aran is elected by universal, equal, free, direct and secret suffrage, in the form established by law.
4. The *Conselh Generau* has powers over the matters determined by the law regulating the special legal system of Aran and all the other laws approved by Parliament, and the authority attributed to it by law, especially that concerning the mountains. Aran, through its representative institution, shall participate in the elaboration of legislative initiatives affecting its special system.
5. An Act of Parliament establishes sufficient financial resources for the *Conselh Generau* to be able to provide the services corresponding to its powers.

Title III. Judicial Power in Catalonia

Chapter I. The Superior Court of Justice and the Public Prosecutor of Catalonia

Article 95. The High Court of Justice of Catalonia

1. The High Court of Justice of Catalonia is the supreme jurisdictional body of the legal system in Catalonia and it is competent, under the terms established by the corresponding organic act, to hear the appeals and cases of the different jurisdictional areas, and to protect the rights recognized in this *Estatut*. In all cases, the High Court of Justice of Catalonia is competent in the areas of civil, penal, contentious-administrative and social law and other areas of law which may be created in the future.
2. The High Court of Justice of Catalonia is the supreme jurisdictional court for all court proceedings initiated in Catalonia, and for all appeals processed within its territorial sphere, regardless of the right invoked as applicable, in the terms established by the Organic Act of Judicial Power and without prejudice to the powers reserved to the Supreme Court for the unification of doctrine. The Organic Act of Judicial Power shall determine the scope and content of the afore-mentioned appeals.
3. The High Court of Justice of Catalonia has exclusive authority to unify interpretation of the law in Catalonia.
4. The High Court of Justice of Catalonia has the authority to rule in the extraordinary review appeals authorized by law against the final, enforceable rulings of the judicial bodies of Catalonia.
5. The president of the High Court of Justice of Catalonia is the representative of judicial power in Catalonia. He or she is nominated by the King, on the proposal of the General Council of Judicial Power, *with the participation of the Council of Justice of Catalonia*[5], in the terms determined by the Organic Act of Judicial Power. The President of the *Generalitat* orders the publication of this appointment in the *Diari Oficial de la Generalitat de Catalunya.*
6. The presidents of the chambers of the High Court of Justice of Catalonia are appointed on the proposal of the General Council of Judicial Power *and with the participation of the Council of Justice of Catalonia*[6], in the terms established by the Organic Act of Judicial Power.

Article 96. The Public Prosecutor of Catalonia

1. The Public Prosecutor of Catalonia is the supreme prosecutor of the High Court of Justice of Catalonia, represents the Public Prosecution Service in Catalonia and is appointed under the terms established by his or her organic statute.

---

5. The Constitutional Court has declared this phrase is unconstitutional and void (STC 31/2010, 28 June).
6. The Constitutional Court has declared this phrase is unconstitutional and void (STC 31/2010, 28 June).

2. The President of the *Generalitat* orders the publication of the appointment of the Public Prosecutor of Catalonia in the *Diari Oficial de la Generalitat de Catalunya.*
3. The Public Prosecutor of Catalonia shall send a copy of the annual report of the Office of the Public Prosecutor of the High Court of Catalonia to the Government, to the Council of Justice of Catalonia and to Parliament, and shall present said report before the latter within six months of the date of publication.
4. The functions of the Public Prosecutor of Catalonia are those established by the Organic Statute of the Public Prosecution Service. The *Generalitat* may enter into agreements with the Public Prosecution Service.

Chapter II. The Council of Justice of Catalonia

Article 97. The Council of Justice of Catalonia

The Council of Justice of Catalonia is the body governing judicial power in Catalonia. It acts as a deconcentrated body of the General Council of Judicial Power, without prejudice to the powers of the latter, in keeping with the provisions of the Organic Act of Judicial Power[7].

Article 98. Powers

1. The powers of the Council of Justice of Catalonia are those established in this *Estatut*, in the Organic Act of Judicial Power, in the laws approved by Parliament, and those, where applicable, delegated by the General Council of Judicial Power.
2. The powers of the Council of Justice of Catalonia with respect to jurisdictional entities located in Catalan territory are, in accordance with the provisions of the Organic Act of Judicial Power as follows:
   a) Participation in the appointment of the president of the High Court of Justice of Catalonia, and in the appointment of the presidents of the chambers of the High Court and the presidents of the provincial courts.
   b) Proposal to the General Council of Judicial Power and announcement of the appointment and cessation of judges and magistrates temporarily incorporated into the judicial system for the purposes of assistance, support or substitution, and also determination of the nomination of these judges and magistrates to any judicial bodies that require reinforcement measures.
   c) *Instruction of proceedings and, in general, exercise of disciplinary functions against judges and magistrates, in the terms established by law.*
   d) Participation in the planning of inspection of courts and tribunals; ordering, where appropriate, their inspection and monitoring, and making proposals in this field; attending to the orders of inspection of courts and tribunals

7. The Constitutional Court has declared this article is unconstitutional and void (STC 31/2010, 28 June).

agreed by the Government, and reporting on the outcome and measures adopted[8].

e) Reporting on any appeals lodged against decisions of the governing bodies of the tribunals and courts of Catalonia.
f) Specification and application, where appropriate, of the regulations of the General Council of Judicial Power in Catalan territory.
g) Provision of information on proposals for revision, delimitation and modification of territorial demarcations of jurisdictional bodies, and on proposals for the creation of divisions and courts.
h) Presentation of an annual report to Parliament on the status and the functioning of the Administration of Justice in Catalonia.
i) All the functions attributed to it by the Organic Act of Judicial Power and the laws of Parliament, and those delegated to it by the General Council of Judicial Power.

3. Resolutions of the Council of Justice of Catalonia regarding appointments, authorizations, licences and leave shall be adopted in accordance with the criteria approved by the General Council of Judicial Power[9].
4. The Council of Justice of Catalonia, through its president, shall notify the General Council of Judicial Power of resolutions adopted and initiatives undertaken, and shall provide any information that may be requested.

Article 99. Composition, Organisation and Work

1. The Council of Justice of Catalonia is composed *of the president of the High Court of Justice of Catalonia, who chairs the Council*[10], and by the members appointed in accordance with the Organic Act of Judicial Power, from among judges, magistrates, prosecutors or jurists of recognized prestige. The Parliament of Catalonia appoints the members of the Council established by the Organic Act of Judicial Power.
2. The Council of Justice of Catalonia approves its own internal regulations governing organization and functioning, in accordance with applicable regulations.

Article 100. Control of the Acts of the Council of Justice of Catalonia

1. *The acts of the Council of Justice of Catalonia may be challenged by appeal to the General Council of Judicial Power, except those that have been issued in exercise of the powers of the autonomous community*[11].

---

8. The Constitutional Court has declared these points are unconstitutional and void STC 31/2010, 28 June).
9. The Constitutional Court has declared this section is unconstitutional and void (STC 31/2010, 28 June).
10. The Constitutional Court has declared this phrase is unconstitutional and void (STC 31/2010, 28 June).
11. The Constitutional Court has declared this section is unconstitutional and void (STC 31/2010, 28 June).

2. The acts of the Council of Justice of Catalonia that may not be challenged by appeal to the General Council of Judicial Power may be challenged jurisdictionally in the terms established by law.

Chapter III. Powers of the Generalitat over the Administration of Justice

Article 101. Public Entrance Examinations and Competitions

1. The *Generalitat* proposes to the State Government, the General Council of Judicial Power, *or the Council of Justice of Catalonia, as appropriate*[12], that public entrance examinations and competitions be held to fill vacancies for magistrates, judges and public prosecutors in Catalonia.
2. The Council of Justice of Catalonia announces public competitions to fill vacancies for judges and magistrates in Catalonia in the terms established by the Organic Act of Judicial Power[13].
3. Candidates may choose to take examinations in public competitions and entrance examinations regulated by this Article which take place in Catalonia, in either of the two official languages.

Article 102. Judicial and Other Staff in the Employ of the Administration of Justice in Catalonia

1. Magistrates, judges and public prosecutors who occupy a post in Catalonia shall prove an adequate and sufficient knowledge of Catalan to ensure the linguistic rights of the citizens, in the form and within the scope determined by law.
2. Magistrates, judges and public prosecutors who occupy a post in Catalonia shall prove a sufficient knowledge of Catalan law in the form and within the scope determined by law.
3. In all cases, sufficient knowledge of the Catalan language and law shall be specifically and uniquely evaluated for the award of a post in the corresponding transfer competitions.
4. Staff in the service of the Administration of Justice and the Office of the Public Prosecutor in Catalonia must demonstrate an adequate and sufficient knowledge of both official languages that qualifies them to perform the functions of their position or post.

Article 103. Human Resources

1. The *Generalitat* has regulatory power over the non-judicial staff in the employ of the Administration of Justice, while respecting the juridical status of these

---

12. The Constitutional Court has declared this phrase is unconstitutional and void (STC 31/2010, 28 June).
13. The Constitutional Court has declared this section is unconstitutional and void (STC 31/2010, 28 June).

personnel as established by the Organic Act of Judicial Power. In the said terms, this power includes regulation of:

a) Organization of these personnel into corps and grades.
b) The selection process.
c) Internal promotion, initial training, and continuous training.
d) The provision of posts and promotions.
e) Administrative situations.
f) Salaries.
g) The working day and the working schedule.
h) The planning of professional activity and functions.
i) Paid and unpaid leave, holidays, and incompatibilities.
j) Staff records.
k) Discipline.

2. In the same terms as established in Section 1, the *Generalitat* has executive and management power concerning non-judicial staff in the employ of the Administration of Justice. This power includes:
   a) Approving public announcement of employment vacancies.
   b) Calling and ruling on all selection processes and making appointments.
   c) Appointment of civil servants who are selected.
   d) Provision of preliminary and continuous training.
   e) Preparation of lists of posts of employment.
   f) Calling for and resolving all the processes for the provision of posts of employment.
   g) Calling and deciding on all internal promotion processes.
   h) Management of the Staff Registers, in coordination with those of the State.
   i) Management of this staff in application of its statutory and salary systems.
   j) Exercise of disciplinary power and imposing any necessary sanctions, including dismissal.
   k) Exercising all the other necessary functions to guarantee effective and efficient human resource management in the Administration of Justice.
3. Within the framework of the provisions of the Organic Act of Judicial Power, an Act of Parliament may create corps of civil servants in the employ of the Administration of Justice which will be answerable to the public function of the *Generalitat*.
4. The *Generalitat* has exclusive power over all contracted staff in the employ of the Administration of Justice.

Article 104. Material Resources

The material resources of the Administration of Justice in Catalonia correspond to the *Generalitat*. This power includes in all cases:

a) Construction and refurbishment of judicial buildings and the buildings of the Office of the Public Prosecutor.
b) Provision of goods and equipment for the judicial and public prosecution premises.

c) Configuration, implementation and maintenance of computer and communication systems, without prejudice to the powers of coordination and standardization which correspond to the State to ensure the compatibility of the system.
d) Management and custody of archives, exhibits and seized property, in all those matters that are not of a jurisdictional nature.
e) Participation in management of deposit accounts and judicial consignments and their returns, taking into account the volume of judicial activity taking place in the autonomous community and the effective costs of the services.
f) Management, settlement and collection of judicial charges established by the *Generalitat* within the sphere of its powers over the administration of justice.

Article 105. Judicial Office, and Institutions and Support Services

In accordance with the Organic Act of Judicial Power, the *Generalitat* has the authority to determine the creation, design, organization, resources, and management of judicial offices and support services for jurisdictional bodies, including the regulation of institutions, institutes and forensic medicine and toxicology services.

Article 106. Free Legal Service. Mediation and Conciliation Processes

1. The *Generalitat* has power to organize free legal services and free legal advice services.
2. The *Generalitat* may establish the instruments and procedures for mediation and for conciliation in the resolution of conflicts in matters within its powers.

Article 107. Judicial Demarcation, Organisation and Capitals

1. Subject to the report of the Council of Justice of Catalonia, the Government of the *Generalitat* shall propose to the State Government the determination and review of judicial demarcation and organization in Catalonia, at least every five years. This proposal, which is mandatory, shall accompany the Government bill sent by the Government to the *Cortes Generales*.
2. Modifications of judicial organization that do not involve legislative reform may correspond to the Government of the *Generalitat*. Similarly, the *Generalitat* may create sections and courts, under delegation by the Government of the State, in the terms established by the Organic Act of Judicial Power.
3. The capitals of the judicial demarcations are established by an Act of Parliament.

Article 108. Justice of the Peace and Justice of Proximity

1. The *Generalitat* has power over justice of the peace under the terms established by the Organic Act of Judicial Power. In the same terms, appointment of judges corresponds to the Council of Justice of Catalonia. The *Generalitat* is also responsible for their allowances and for the provision of the necessary resources

for them to carry out their duties. The creation of secretarial offices and their provision also corresponds to the *Generalitat*.
2. In the specified towns and in accordance with the provisions of the Organic Act of Judicial Power, the *Generalitat* may demand the establishment of a system of justice of proximity, with the aim of resolving minor conflicts speedily and efficiently.

Article 109. Subrogation Clause

In addition to the powers expressly attributed to it in this *Estatut*, the *Generalitat* exercises all the functions and powers that the Organic Act of Judicial Power recognizes for the State Government in relation to the Administration of Justice in Catalonia.

Title IV. Powers

Chapter I. Types of Power

Article 110. Exclusive Powers

1. In matters in which the *Generalitat* has exclusive power, legislative power, regulatory power and the executive function correspond fully to the *Generalitat*. The exercise of these powers and functions, by means of which it may establish its own policies, is the exclusive right of the *Generalitat*.
2. In matters regarding the exclusive power of the *Generalitat*, Catalan law is applicable in its territory and shall prevail over any other.

Article 111. Shared Powers

In matters in which the *Estatut* attributes powers to the *Generalitat* which are shared with the State, legislative power, regulatory power and the executive function are the responsibility of the *Generalitat*, within the framework of the basic conditions established by the State *as principles or lowest common legislative denominators in rules of legal rank, with the exception of those circumstances determined by the Constitution and this Estatut*[14]. The *Generalitat* may establish its own policies in the exercise of these powers. Parliament shall implement and specify said basic provisions by means of a law.

Article 112. Executive Powers

In matters in which the *Generalitat* has executive powers, the *Generalitat* has regulatory power, which includes the power to approve provisions for execution of State

14. The Constitutional Court has declared this phrase is unconstitutional and void (STC 31/2010, 28 June).

rules, and also the executive function, which in all cases includes the power to organize its own administration and, in general, all the functions and activities that the system attributes to the Public Administration.

Article 113. Powers of the *Generalitat* and European Union Rules

The *Generalitat* has the authority to enact, apply and implement European Union rules when these affect its powers, under the terms established in Title V.

Article 114. Promotional Activity

1. The *Generalitat* has the authority to carry out promotional activities in matters within its power. To this end, the *Generalitat* may grant subsidies from its own funds.
2. In matters where the *Generalitat* has exclusive power, the *Generalitat* has the authority to specify the purpose for which territorializable subsidies from the State and from European communities are used, and also to regulate the conditions for their assignment and management, including administration and award.
3. In matters where power is shared, the *Generalitat* has the authority to specify, in the form of a regulation, the purpose for which territorializable subsidies from the State and from European communities are used, and also to complete the regulation of the conditions for their assignment, including administration and award.
4. In matters where the *Generalitat* has executive power, the *Generalitat* has authority to manage territorializable subsidies from the State and from European communities, including their administration and award.
5. The *Generalitat* shall participate in determining the non-territorialisability of subsidies from the State and European communities. Similarly, it shall participate, under the terms established by the State, in the management and administration of these subsidies.

Article 115. Territorial Scope and Effects of Powers

1. The area of application of the powers of the *Generalitat* is the territory of Catalonia, except in the cases referred to by this *Estatut* and other legal regulations establishing the extraterritorial applicability of the provisions and actions of the *Generalitat*.
2. In matters where the object of its powers extends beyond the territory of Catalonia, the *Generalitat* exercises its powers over the part of this object within its territory, without prejudice to the collaboration instruments established with other territorial bodies, or, in a subsidiary way, to the coordination by the State of the affected autonomous communities.

Chapter II. Matters of Power

Article 116. Agriculture, Livestock Farming and Forestry

1. While respecting the provisions established by the State in exercise of the powers attributed to it by Article 149.1.13 and 16 of the Constitution, the *Generalitat* has exclusive power over agriculture and livestock farming. This power includes in any case:
   a) Regulation and development of agriculture, livestock farming and the food industry.
   b) Regulation and implementation of quality, traceability and requirements for agricultural and livestock farming products, and also the fight against fraud in the sphere of food production and sale.
   c) Regulation of participation of agricultural and stockbreeding organizations and agrarian chambers in public bodies.
   d) Plant and animal health, in those cases where there are no effects on human health, and the protection of animals.
   e) Seeds and seedbeds, in particular in all matters relating to genetically modified organisms.
   f) Regulation of production processes, cultivation, agricultural structures, and their corresponding legal systems.
   g) Integrated development and protection of the rural community.
   h) Research, development, technology transfer, innovation in cultivation, agriculture and food companies, and training in these areas.
   i) Trade fairs and agricultural, forestry and livestock shows.
2. The *Generalitat* has shared power for:
   a) The planning of agriculture and livestock farming and the food sector.
   b) The regulation and system of administrative intervention and uses of forests, forest exploitations and forestry services and drove roads of Catalonia.

Article 117. Water and Hydraulic Works

1. The *Generalitat* has exclusive authority in matters concerning water pertaining to intra-community basins, which includes in any case:
   a) Administrative organization, planning and management of surface and underground water, the uses and exploitations of water and also hydraulic works that are not qualified as being of general interest.
   b) Planning and adoption of measures and specific instruments for the management and protection of water resources and aquatic and water-associated terrestrial ecosystems.
   c) Extraordinary measures, when required, to guarantee water supply.
   d) Organization of water administration in Catalonia, including user participation.
   e) Regulation and implementation of activities related to land consolidation and irrigation works.

2. In the terms established by State legislation, the *Generalitat* shall have executive powers concerning public water resources and works of general interest. In the same terms, the *Generalitat* shall participate in planning and programming works of general interest.
3. The *Generalitat* participates in hydrological planning and in the State bodies managing water resources and harnessing resources in intra-community basins. The *Generalitat*, within its territorial area, has executive power over:
   a) Adoption of additional protection and sanitation measures for water resources and aquatic ecosystems.
   b) Execution and exploitation of State-owned works, where established by agreement.
   c) The policing powers concerning public water resources assigned by State legislation.
4. The *Generalitat* shall issue a mandatory report on all proposals for transfer from basins which imply a modification of water resources in its territory.
5. The *Generalitat* participates in hydrological planning for water resources and water exploitation installations located in Catalan territory or those of territories outside the Spanish State that terminate in Catalonia, in accordance with the mechanisms established in Title V and participates in the execution of said planning in the terms established by State legislation.

Article 118. Associations and Foundations

1. While respecting the basic conditions established by the State to guarantee equality in the exercise of law and the reservation to Organic Act, the *Generalitat* has exclusive power over the legal system of the associations that carry out their functions mainly in Catalonia. This power includes in any case:
   a) Regulation of the forms of association, denomination of associations, aims, constitution requirements, amendment, dissolution and liquidation, of content of the Articles of association, governing bodies, rights and obligations of members, and of the obligations of associations and of associations of a special nature.
   b) Determination of tax benefits for associations and the system for their application, as established by tax rules, and also declaration of public utility, the contents and requirements for obtaining this.
   c) The register of associations.
2. The *Generalitat* has exclusive power over the legal system of foundations that carry out their functions mainly in Catalonia. This power includes in any case:
   a) Regulation of the modalities of foundation, of denomination of foundations, of the aims and beneficiaries of the foundation; of funding capacity; of requirements for constitution, amendment, dissolution and liquidation; of the Articles of association; of the endowment and foundation system in the process of formation; of the board of trustees and supervisory body, patrimony, and the economic and financial system.
   b) Determination of tax benefits for foundations and the system for their application as established by tax rules.
   c) The registry of foundations.

3. The *Generalitat* has the authority to set the criteria for, regulate the conditions of, and to implement and control public grants to associations and foundations.

Article 119. Hunting, Fishing, Maritime Activities and Organisation of the Fishing Sector

1. The *Generalitat* has exclusive power over hunting and river fishing, which includes in any case:
   a) Planning and regulation.
   b) The regulation of the system for administrative intervention in hunting and fishing, of supervision, and of hunting and fishing uses.
2. The *Generalitat* has exclusive power over sea and recreational fishing in continental waters, and also over regulation and management of fish stocks and delimitation of protected areas.
3. The *Generalitat* has exclusive power over maritime activities, including in any case:
   a) Regulation and management of shellfish and fish farming and the establishment of requirements for the practice of these activities, and also the regulation and management of resources.
   b) The regulation and management of installations intended for these activities.
   c) Professional diving.
   d) Training and certification in matters of leisure activities.
4. The *Generalitat* has shared power over planning of the fishing sector. This power includes, in any case, the organization and administrative implementation measures in regard to the professional requirements for fishing activities, the construction, safety and official registry of vessels, fishing associations and fish markets.

Article 120. Savings Banks

1. The *Generalitat* has exclusive power over regulation of the organization of savings banks whose headquarters are in Catalonia, while respecting State provisions established in exercise of the powers attributed to it by Article 149.1.11 and 13 of the Constitution. This power includes in any case:
   a) Determination of governing bodies and the manner in which the different social interests are represented on them.
   b) The legal status of governing body members and other posts in savings banks.
   c) The legal system governing creation, mergers, liquidation and registration.
   d) Exercise of administrative powers in relation to any foundations they might create.
   e) Regulation of groups of savings banks with registered headquarters in Catalonia.
2. In matters concerning savings banks whose headquarters are in Catalonia, the *Generalitat* has shared power over financial activity, in accordance with *the*

principles, rules and minimum standards established by[15] the State basic law, which includes, in any case, regulation of the distribution of surplus and of the social activities of savings banks.
Similarly, the *Generalitat* shall monitor the process of issuing and distributing owner share titles, with the exception of those aspects relating to the system for public offerings, purchase of securities and admission to negotiation, to financial stability and to solvency.

3. In matters concerning saving banks whose headquarters are in Catalonia, the *Generalitat* has shared power over their discipline, inspection and sanctioning. This power includes in any case the establishment of additional infractions and sanctions in the sphere of its powers.
4. The *Generalitat*, in keeping with the provisions of State legislation, collaborates in the inspection and sanctioning of savings banks whose headquarters are in Catalonia implemented by the Ministry of the Treasury and the Bank of Spain.

Article 121. Trade and Trade Fairs

1. The *Generalitat* has exclusive power in matters of trade and trade fairs, including the regulation of non-international trade fair activities and the administrative planning of trading activity, which includes in any case:
   a) Determination of the administrative conditions for exercising the activity and the locations and establishments which comply and the administrative regulation of electronic commerce or of commerce by any other medium.
   b) Administrative regulation of all forms of sales and supply in relation to commercial activity, and promotional sales and sale at loss.
   c) Regulation of trading hours, while respecting the constitutional principle of market unity.
   d) Classification and territorial planning of commercial facilities and regulation of the requirements and the system for installation, extension and change of activity of the said commercial facilities.
   e) Establishment and implementation of norms and quality standards related to commercial activity.
   f) Adoption of administrative policing measures in relation to market discipline.
2. The *Generalitat* has exclusive power in matters of international trade fairs held in Catalonia. This power includes in any case:
   a) Authorization and declaration of an international trade fair.
   b) Promotion, management and coordination.
   c) Inspection, evaluation and accountability.
   d) Establishment of internal regulations.
   e) Appointment of a delegate to the management body for each trade fair.
3. The *Generalitat* collaborates with the State in establishing a calendar of international trade fairs.

---

15. The Constitutional Court has declared this phrase is unconstitutional and void (STC 31/2010, 28 June).

Article 122. Popular Consultation

The *Generalitat* has exclusive power over the establishment of the legal system, the modalities, the procedure, the implementation and the calling, whether by the *Generalitat* or by local bodies, acting within their jurisdiction, of public opinion polls, public hearings, participation forums and any other instruments of popular consultation, with the exception of those provided for by Article 149.1.32 of the Constitution.

Article 123. Consumer Affairs

The *Generalitat* has exclusive power in matters of consumer affairs. This power includes in any case:

a) Defence of consumers' and users' rights, as proclaimed in Article 28, and the establishment and application of administrative procedures for complaints and claims.
b) Regulation and promotion of consumer and user associations, and of their participation in any procedures and matters which affect them.
c) Regulation of mediation bodies and procedures in matters of consumer affairs.
d) Consumer training and education.
e) The regulation of information regarding consumers and users.

Article 124. Cooperatives and the Social Economy

1. The *Generalitat* has exclusive power over matters affecting cooperatives.
2. The power which Section 1 refers to includes the organization and functioning of cooperatives, which includes in any case:
   a) Their definition, denomination and classification.
   b) Criteria for the establishment of registered offices.
   c) Criteria governing operation.
   d) Requirements for constitution, modification of Articles of association, mergers, splits, transformation, dissolution and liquidation.
   e) Qualification, registration and certification in the corresponding registry.
   f) The rights and obligations of members.
   g) The economic system and company documentation.
   h) Conciliation and mediation.
   i) Cooperative groups and forms of economic cooperation for cooperatives.
3. The power referred to in Section 1 above includes in any case regulation and promotion of the cooperative movement especially to promote forms of participation in companies, access of workers to the means of production, and social and territorial cohesion. Regulation and promotion of the cooperative movement includes:
   a) The regulation of cooperative associations.
   b) Cooperative education and training.
   c) Establishment of criteria, the regulation of requirements, and the execution and control of public subsidies to cooperatives.

4. The *Generalitat* has exclusive power over the promotion and organization of the social economy sector.

Article 125. Public Law Corporations and Certified Professions

1. The *Generalitat* has exclusive power over matters affecting professional associations, academies, chambers of agriculture, chambers of commerce, industry and navigation, and other public law corporations representing economic and professional interests, with the exception provided for by Sections 2 and 3. While respecting the provisions of Articles 36 and 139 of the Constitution, this power includes in any case:
   a) Regulation of the internal organization, functioning, and economic, budgetary and accounting system, and also of the system of association and membership, the rights and obligations of members, and the disciplinary system.
   b) The creation and attribution of functions.
   c) Administrative supervision.
   d) The electoral system and electoral procedures applicable to the election of the corporation members.
   e) Determination of territorial limits and possible grouping within Catalonia.
2. The *Generalitat* has shared power over definition of the corporations referred to in Section 1 above, and over the requirements for their creation and for membership.
3. In the case of a previous agreement between the *Generalitat* and the State, the chambers of commerce, industry and navigation may carry out activities in relation to foreign trade for which they may allocate chamber resources.
4. While respecting the general rules on academic and professional qualifications and the provisions of Articles 36 and 139 of the Constitution, the *Generalitat* has exclusive power over the exercise of certified professions, which includes in any case:
   a) Determination of the requirements and conditions for practice of certified professions, and also the rights and obligations of certified professionals and of the system of incompatibilities.
   b) Regulation of administrative guarantees against practice without proper qualifications and irregular activities, and also regulation of mandatory professional service provision.
   c) The disciplinary system for the practice of certified professions.

Article 126. Credit, Banks, Insurance and Mutual Benefit Societies Not Included in the Social Security System

1. The *Generalitat* has exclusive power over the structure, organization and functioning of mutual pension societies not included in the social security system.
2. The *Generalitat* has shared power over the structure, organization and function of credit entities which are not savings banks, of credit cooperatives and pension plan and fund management entities and of physical and legal entities operating in the insurance market other than those referred to in Section 1, *in*

accordance with the principles, rules and minimum standards established by[16] the State basic law.

3. The *Generalitat* has shared power over the activity of the entities referred to in Sections 1 and 2. This power includes the regulated implementation acts attributed to it by State legislation.
4. The *Generalitat* has shared powers over discipline, inspection and sanction of the entities referred to in Section 2 above.

Article 127. Culture

1. The *Generalitat* has exclusive power over cultural matters. This exclusive power includes in any case:
   a) Artistic and cultural activities carried out in Catalonia, including:
      First. Measures related to the production and distribution of books and periodical publications in all forms, and management of copyright and the granting of identification codes.
      Second. Regulation and inspection of cinemas, protection measures for the film industry, and control over and award of dubbing licences to distribution companies whose headquarters are in Catalonia.
      Third. Rating of films and audiovisual material according to age and cultural values.
      Fourth. Promotion, planning, construction and management of cultural facilities located in Catalonia.
      Fifth. Establishment of tax incentive measures for those cultural activities over which the *Generalitat* has regulatory authority regarding taxes.
   b) Cultural heritage, including in any case:
      First. Regulation and execution of measures aimed at guaranteeing the enrichment and dissemination of the cultural heritage of Catalonia, and at facilitating access to it.
      Second. Inspection, inventory-keeping and restoration of architectural, archaeological, scientific, technical, historical, artistic, ethnological and general cultural heritage.
      Third. Establishment of the legal system for activities in relation to movable and unmovable assets that form part of the cultural heritage of Catalonia, determination of the legal system affecting unmovable assets, and declaration and management of these assets, with the exception of those in the ownership of the State.
      Fourth. Protection of the cultural heritage of Catalonia, which includes conservation, repair, supervision and control of assets, without prejudice to the State authority for the defence of assets comprising this cultural heritage against exportation and plundering.
   c) Archives, libraries, museums and other cultural heritage centres not owned by the State, including in any case:

16. The Constitutional Court has declared this phrase is unconstitutional and void (STC 31/2010, 28 June).

First. Creation, management, protection and establishment of the legal system concerning the centres that integrate the archive and library system, the museums, and other cultural heritage centres.
Second. Establishment of the legal system of documentary, bibliographical and cultural assets stored in these centres.
Third. The conservation and recovery of assets that form part of the Catalan bibliographic and documentary heritage.

d) The promotion of culture, including:
First. Promotion and dissemination of theatrical, musical, audiovisual, literary, dance, circus and combined-art creations and productions carried out in Catalonia.
Second. Promotion and dissemination of the cultural, artistic and monumental heritage and cultural heritage centres in Catalonia.
Third. The international projection of Catalan culture.

2. The *Generalitat* has executive power over archives, libraries, museums and cultural heritage centres owned by the State and located in Catalonia and whose management the State does not reserve for itself. This power includes in any case the regulation of their functioning, organization and staffing system.
3. In actions carried out by the State in Catalonia in matters of investment in cultural assets and equipment, previous agreement is required with the *Generalitat*. In the case of activities carried out by the State in relation to the international projection of culture, the Government of the State and the Government of the *Generalitat* shall articulate formulas for mutual collaboration and cooperation, in accordance with the provisions of Title V of this *Estatut*.

Article 128. Geographical and Quality Denominations and Indications

1. The *Generalitat*, while respecting the provisions of Article 149.1.13 of the Constitution, has exclusive power over denominations of origin and other quality indications, including the legal system covering their creation and functioning, which also includes:
   a) Determination of possible levels of protection for products, their associated system and requirements, and the rights and obligations arising from them.
   b) Ownership of the denominations, while respecting industrial property legislation.
   c) Regulation of forms and requirements for production and sale of corresponding products, and the applicable sanction system.
   d) The system of administrative organization of denominations of origin, or indications of quality, regarding both management and control of production and sale.
2. The power referred to in Section 1 above includes recognition of denominations or indications, approval of the regulations, and all the administrative powers of management and control over activities in relation to denominations or indications, especially those deriving from possible administrative supervision of the denomination bodies and from the exercise of sanctioning powers in relation to infractions of the denomination system.

3. Should the territory of a denomination of origin extend beyond Catalan borders, the *Generalitat* exercises its functions of management and control over the activities of the denomination bodies for land and facilities located in Catalonia, under the terms established by law. The *Generalitat* exercises the obligations of protection resulting from the recognition by the *Generalitat* itself of a denomination of origin or of a protected geographical indication. The corresponding authorities collaborate in the protection of Catalan geographical and quality denominations outside Catalan territory and before the corresponding European and international protection institutions.

Article 129. Civil Law

The *Generalitat* has exclusive power in matters of civil law, with the exception of those matters which Article 149.1.8 of the Constitution attributes to the State in any case. This power includes determination of the system of sources of the civil law of Catalonia.

Article 130. Prosecution Law

The *Generalitat* has authority to dictate the specific prosecution rules resulting from the particular nature of substantive law in Catalonia.

Article 131. Education

1. The *Generalitat* has exclusive power, in non-university education, over post-compulsory teaching that does not lead to academic or professional certification valid in all the State, and over the educational centres in which this teaching is carried out.
2. The *Generalitat* has exclusive power in non-university education, in relation to compulsory and non-compulsory subjects that lead to an academic or professional qualification valid in all the State and in relation to infant education, including:
   a) Regulation of participative and consultative bodies of the sectors involved in educational planning in its territory.
   b) Determination of the educational content of the first cycle of infant education and the regulation of the centres is which this cycle is taught, and also definition of the staffing arrangements and the qualifications and specializations of the other staff.
   c) Creation, organizational development and the overall system of public centres.
   d) Inspection, internal evaluation of the education system, educational innovation, research and experimentation, and also ensuring the quality of the education system.
   e) The system for promoting study, scholarships and grants through their own funds.
   f) Continuous training and improvement of teaching staff and other education system staff and approval of human resources directives.

g) The educational services and the complementary extra-curricular activities related to public educational centres and to private educational centres supported with public funds.
h) Organizational aspects of distance teaching aimed at students above the compulsory school-leaving age.

3. In those matters not regulated by Section 2 and in relation to the education referred to in said Section, the *Generalitat* has shared power, while respecting the fundamental aspects of the right to education and to freedom in teaching in non-university education and in accordance with the provisions of Article 149.1.30 of the Constitution. This power includes in any case:
   a) Programming of teaching, its definition and general evaluation of the education system.
   b) Organization of the education sector and of teaching and educational activity.
   c) Establishment of suitable syllabuses, including curriculum planning.
   d) The system to promote study, and State grants and aids.
   e) Access to education, and establishment and regulation of the criteria for admission and teaching of students in educational centres.
   f) The system for maintenance with public funds of the teaching provided in the education system and the centres providing it.
   g) Requirements and conditions of educational and teaching centres.
   h) Organization of public centres and private centres supported with public funds.
   i) Participation of the education community in control and in management of public educational centres and of private centres supported with public funds.
   j) Acquisition and loss of educational civil servant status for teachers in the employ of the education authorities, development of their basic rights and obligations and also the policy concerning personnel in the employ of the educational administration.
4. The *Generalitat* has executive power, in non-university education, over the issue and approval of State academic and professional qualifications.

Article 132. Emergencies and Civil Protection

1. The *Generalitat* has exclusive power over civil protection, which includes, in any case, regulation, planning and implementation of measures related to emergencies and civil security and safety matters, and management and coordination of civil protection services, including fire prevention and fire-fighting services, without prejudice to the powers of local government authorities in this matter and respecting State provisions established in exercise of its powers in matters of public safety.
2. For emergencies and civil protection issues which extend beyond Catalonia, the *Generalitat* shall promote mechanisms for cooperation with other autonomous communities and with the State.
3. The *Generalitat* has executive power in matters of maritime rescue operations, in the terms determined by State legislation.

4. The *Generalitat* participates in the execution of matters concerning nuclear safety, in the terms agreed in the agreements signed to this effect and, where appropriate, by law.

Article 133. Energy and Mines

1. The *Generalitat* has shared power over energy. This power includes in any case:
   a) Regulation of activities concerning energy production, storage and transport, the issue of licences to facilities operating wholly within Catalan territory, and inspection and control of all facilities located in Catalonia.
   b) Regulation of energy distribution within Catalonia, the issue of licences to the corresponding facilities, and inspection and control of all facilities located in Catalonia.
   c) Implementation of additional quality standards for energy supply services.
   d) Fostering and management of renewable energy sources and promotion of energy efficiency.
2. The *Generalitat* participates, by means of the issue of a preliminary report, in the proceedings for granting licences to energy production and transport facilities which extend beyond Catalan territory or if the energy is used outside this territory.
3. The *Generalitat* participates in energy sector regulation and planning at State level that affects the territory of Catalonia.
4. The *Generalitat* has shared power over the mining system. This power includes, in any case, regulation, the system for administrative intervention and control over mines and the mining resources located in the territory of Catalonia and over any mining activities that take place in Catalonia.

Article 134. Sport and Leisure

1. The *Generalitat* has exclusive power over sport, which includes in any case:
   a) Fostering, dissemination, planning, coordination, execution, consultancy, implantation and projection of the practice of physical activity and of sport throughout Catalonia, at all social levels.
   b) Organization of mediation bodies in matters concerning sports.
   c) Regulation of sports training and fostering of technical training and elite sports performance.
   d) Establishment of the legal system for sporting federations and clubs and Catalan entities that promote and organize the practice of sport and physical activity within Catalonia, and declaration of the public utility of sporting entities.
   e) Regulation in matters of sporting, competitive and electoral discipline of entities that promote and organize the practice of sport.
   f) Fostering and promotion of sports associations.
   g) Registration of entities that promote and organize the practice of physical and sporting activity and that have their headquarters in Catalonia.

h) Planning of the network of sports facilities in Catalonia and the promotion of its use.
i) Medical and health control and monitoring of individuals who practice physical and sporting activity.
j) Regulation in matters of prevention and control of violence at public sporting events, while respecting the powers reserved to the State concerning public safety.
k) Ensuring the health of spectators and other individuals involved in the organization and the carrying out of physical and sporting activity, and safety and health control of sporting facilities.
l) Development of scientific research in sport matters.

2. The *Generalitat* participates in entities and bodies, at State, European and international level, whose purpose is the development of sport.
3. The *Generalitat* has exclusive power over leisure and this includes, in any case, fostering and regulation of activities that take place in the territory of Catalonia and the legal system concerning entities whose purpose is the carrying out of leisure activities.
4. The *Generalitat* participates in entities and bodies, at the State, European and international level, whose purpose is development of leisure.

Article 135. Statistics

1. The *Generalitat* has exclusive power over statistics of interest to the *Generalitat*. This power includes in any case:
   a) Statistical planning.
   b) Administrative organization.
   c) The creation of the *Generalitat*'s own official statistical system.
2. The *Generalitat* participates in and cooperates with the preparation of statistics at supra-autonomous community level.

Article 136. Public Employment and Staff in the Employ of the Catalan Public Administration Bodies

While respecting the principle of local autonomy, in matters of public employment the *Generalitat* has:

a) Exclusive power over the statutory system for staff in the employ of the Catalan Public Administration bodies, and over classification and organization of public employment with the exception of the provisions of *b* below.
b) Shared power for development of organizing principles of public employment, over the acquisition and loss of civil service status, administrative situation and rights, obligations and incompatibilities of staff in the employ of the Public Administration bodies.
c) Exclusive power, in the area of contracted staff, for adaptation of the list of employment positions to the needs of administrative organization and over training of this staff.

Article 137. Housing

1. The *Generalitat* has exclusive power over housing, which includes in any case:
   a) Planning, classification, management, inspection and control over housing, in accordance with social needs and the need for territorial balance.
   b) Establishment of priorities and objectives in the promotional activity of Catalan Public Administration bodies in matters concerning housing, and the adoption of the necessary measures to achieve them, in relation to both the public and the private sectors.
   c) Provision of public housing.
   d) Administrative regulation of house sales and the establishment of protective and disciplinary measures in this field.
   e) Technical rules, inspection and control of construction quality.
   f) Rules on the suitability of housing for habitation.
   g) Technological innovation and sustainability applicable to housing.
   h) Regulations on house conservation and maintenance, and their application.
2. The *Generalitat* has power over the requirements of buildings in relation to the installation of common infrastructures for telecommunications, broadcasting, basic telephone and other cable services, while respecting State legislation in the area of telecommunications.

Article 138. Immigration

1. In matters concerning immigration, the *Generalitat* has:
   a) Exclusive power regarding the initial reception of immigrants, which includes sociosanitary attention and guidance.
   b) Development of the integration policy for immigrants in the framework of its powers.
   c) Establishment and regulation of the required measures for social and economic integration of immigrants and for their social participation.
   d) Establishment by law of a referential framework for the reception and integration of immigrants.
   e) Promotion and integration of returning immigrants and their assistance, and facilitation of their return to Catalonia through the pertinent policies and measures.
2. The *Generalitat* has executive power in authorizing work to foreigners whose employment is in Catalonia. This power, which shall be coordinated with that of the State regarding the entry and residence of foreigners, includes:
   a) Processing and assignation of initial work authorizations for employed and self-employed workers.
   b) Processing and resolution of appeals presented with regard to cases arising from paragraph *a)* above and application of the inspection and sanction system.
3. The *Generalitat* participates in State decisions concerning immigration which are especially important for Catalonia and, in particular, shall have preceptive participation in determining the contingent of foreign workers by means of the mechanisms established by Title V.

Article 139. Industry, Craftsmanship, Metrological Control and Evaluation of Metals

1. The *Generalitat* has exclusive power over industry, with the exception of the provisions of Section 2 below. This power includes, in any case, the classification of industrial sectors and processes in Catalonia, the safety of activities, facilities, equipment, processes and industrial products and the regulation of industrial activities which may have an impact on people's safety or health.
2. The *Generalitat* has shared power over planning of industry, in the framework of general planning of the economy.
3. The *Generalitat* has exclusive power over matters of craftsmanship.
4. The *Generalitat* has executive power over metrological control.
5. The *Generalitat* has executive power over the evaluation of metals.

Article 140. Transport and Communications Infrastructures

1. The *Generalitat* has exclusive power over any ports, airports, heliports and other transport infrastructures in the territory of Catalonia that are not legally classified as being of general interest. This power includes in any case:
   a) The legal system, planning and management of all ports and airports, port and airport facilities, minor maritime facilities, loading terminals in port and airport premises, and other transport infrastructures.
   b) Management of the public domain required to provide the service, and especially the issue of licences and concessions within port or airport premises.
   c) Financial system for port and airport services, and especially the power to establish tariffs and taxes and the charging and collecting of all kinds of taxes and charges related to the use of the infrastructure and the service it provides.
   d) Delimitation of the service areas for ports or airports and determination of the uses, equipment and complementary activities within port or airport premises or other transport infrastructures, while respecting the powers of the owner of the public domain.
2. The *Generalitat* participates in supra-autonomous community bodies that exercise functions concerning transport infrastructures located in Catalonia that are owned by the State.
3. The classification of a port, airport or other transport infrastructure located in Catalonia as of general interest is subject to a preliminary report by the *Generalitat*, which may participate in its management, or take responsibility for its management, in accordance with the provisions of law.
4. The *Generalitat* participates in the planning and programming of ports and airports of general interest, in the terms determined by State regulations.
5. The *Generalitat* has exclusive power over its road network throughout the territory of Catalonia, and may also participate in the management of the State's road network in Catalonia, in accordance with State regulations. This power includes in any case:

a) Organization, planning and integrated management of the road network of Catalonia.
b) The legal and financial system of all elements of the road network of which the *Generalitat* is owner.
c) Connectivity, whether with each other or with other transport infrastructures or networks, of the elements that make up the road network of Catalonia.

6. The *Generalitat* has exclusive power, in matters concerning the rail network, over the infrastructures of which it is the owner, and participates in the planning and management of infrastructures owned by the State that are located in Catalonia, in accordance with the provision of State regulations.
7. In accordance with State regulations, the *Generalitat* has executive power over electronic communications. This power includes in any case:
   a) Promotion of the existence of a minimum set of universally accessible services.
   b) Inspection of the shared telecommunications infrastructures and exercise of the corresponding power to sanction.
   c) Resolution of conflicts between broadcasting operators that share multiplexes and whose coverage does not extend beyond the territory of Catalonia.
   d) Management of the registry of installers of shared telecommunications infrastructures and the registry of multiplex managers whose sphere of activity does not extend beyond the territory of Catalonia.

Article 141. Gaming and Shows

1. The *Generalitat* has exclusive power over gaming, betting and casinos when these activities take place in Catalonia only, including in any case:
   a) Creation and authorization of gaming and betting and their regulation, and regulation of companies responsible for management, operation and practice of these activities or whose aim is to sell and distribute materials related to gaming in general, including computerized and online gambling.
   b) Regulation and control of the premises, facilities and equipment used in the performance of these activities.
   c) Determination, within the framework of its powers, of the fiscal system concerning the gaming activity of companies performing these activities.
2. Authorization of new forms of gaming and betting at State level, or modification of the already existing forms, requires deliberation by the *Generalitat* - State Bilateral Commission established by Title V and the decisive preliminary report of the *Generalitat.*
3. The *Generalitat* has exclusive power over shows and recreational activities. This power includes, in any case, organization of the sector, the system of administrative intervention, and control over all kinds of shows in public spaces and premises.

Article 142. Youth

1. The *Generalitat* has exclusive power over youth affairs, which includes in any case:
   a) Design, application and evaluation of policies, plans and programmes aimed at young people.
   b) Promotion of youth associations, initiatives to encourage youth participation, international mobility, and youth tourism.
   c) Regulation, management, intervention and administrative policing of activities and facilities aimed at young people.
2. The *Generalitat* is responsible for signing agreements with international entities and for participating in international bodies in cooperation with the State, or autonomously if the regulations of the entity so permit, and, in any case, processing of documents issued by international entities that affect individuals, facilities or entities with residence in Catalonia, while respecting State legislation.

Article 143. Catalonia's Own Language

1. The *Generalitat* of Catalonia has exclusive power over the matter of Catalonia's own language. This power includes, in any case, determination of the scope, uses and legal effects of its official status, and also the linguistic normalization of Catalan.
2. The *Generalitat* and also the *Conselh Generau d'Aran* have power over the linguistic normalization of Occitan, known as Aranese in Aran.

Article 144. The Environment, Natural Areas and Meteorology

1. The *Generalitat* has shared power over the environment, and power to establish additional protection rules. This shared power includes in any case:
   a) Establishment and regulation of the instruments of environmental planning and the proceedings for processing and approving these instruments.
   b) Establishment and regulation of environmental sustainability, tax and research measures.
   c) Regulation of natural resources, flora and fauna, biodiversity and marine and aquatic environment, except when for the purpose of preserving sea fish stocks.
   d) Regulation of prevention in the production of containers and packing throughout their lifecycle, from creation to conversion into waste material.
   e) Regulation of prevention and correction of the generation of waste material originating in or destined for Catalonia, and its management, movement and final disposal.
   f) Regulation of prevention, control, correction, recovery and compensation of soil and subsoil pollution.
   g) Regulation and management of dumping in the continental waters of Catalonia and into surface and underground waters that do not pass through

another autonomous community. In any case, the *Generalitat* has executive power over the administrative intervention of dumping in surface and underground waters in its territory.

h) Regulation of the atmospheric environment and the various kinds of pollution thereof, declaration of polluted atmospheric zones, and establishment of other instruments to control pollution, irrespective of the public authority with competence for authorizing the work, facility or activity causing the pollution.
i) Regulation of the system for authorizing and monitoring the emission of greenhouse gases.
j) Promotion of classification of products, activities, facilities, infrastructures, procedures, production processes and environmentally-friendly practices.
k) Prevention, restoration and repair of environmental damage and also the corresponding system of sanctions.
l) Measures to protect species and the system of sanctions.

2. While respecting the provisions of Article 149.1.23 of the Constitution, the *Generalitat* has exclusive power over natural areas. This power includes, in any case, the regulation and declaration of protection, delimitation, planning and management instruments for natural spaces and protected habitats located in Catalonia.
3. In the case of natural areas that extend beyond the territory of Catalonia, the *Generalitat* shall promote collaboration instruments with other autonomous communities in order to create, delimit, regulate and manage these areas.
4. Declaration and delimitation of natural areas with a State protection system requires the mandatory report of the *Generalitat* - State Bilateral Commission. If the area is located wholly within the territory of Catalonia, the *Generalitat* is responsible for its management.
5. The *Generalitat* shall establish its own meteorological service, shall supply meteorological and climatic information, including the forecasting, monitoring and follow-up of meteorological risk situations, and research in these fields and the production of climatic cartography.
6. The *Generalitat* exercises its powers by means of the Corps of Rural Agents responsible for surveillance, control, protection, overall prevention and cooperation in relation to environmental management. The members of this Corps have the status of agents of the authority and exercise special administrative and judicial policing functions, in the terms established by law.

Article 145. Stock Exchanges and Contracting Centres

The *Generalitat* has shared power over stock exchanges and contracting centres located in Catalonia. This power includes in any case:

a) Creation, denomination, authorization and supervision of stock exchanges and organized negotiation systems.
b) Regulation and administrative execution measures for the organization, operation, discipline and sanctioning system of the bodies governing stock exchanges.

c) Control over the issue, admission, suspension, exclusion, and establishment of additional requirements for the admission of securities to be negotiated exclusively in these markets, and inspection and control.
d) Accreditation of persons and entities for membership of these markets.
e) Establishment of deposits to be provided by members of the stock exchange as a guarantee in operations pending settlement.

Article 146. The Media and Audiovisual Content Services

1. In the area of radio and television services and also any other audiovisual communication service, the *Generalitat* has:
    a) Exclusive power over the organization of the provision of the public broadcasting services of the *Generalitat* and public broadcasting services at local level, while respecting the principle of local autonomy.
    b) Shared power over the regulation and control of broadcasting services that use any of the available formats and technologies aimed at the audience in Catalonia, and the supply of broadcasting services if distributed in the territory of Catalonia.
2. The *Generalitat* has shared power in matters of the media.
3. The *Generalitat* shall promote the linguistic and cultural pluralism of Catalonia in the media.

Article 147. Notarial Affairs and Public Registries

1. The *Generalitat* has executive power over notarial affairs and public property, mercantile and movable assets registries. This power includes in any case:
    a) Appointment of notaries and property, mercantile and movable assets registrars, by means of the calling, administration and resolution of open and restricted competitive examinations and competitions, which shall be called and implemented leading to formal appointment. Candidates for the post of notary or registrar shall be admitted on the basis of equality of rights, and shall provide proof of knowledge of the Catalan language and law in the form and to the extent established by the *Estatut* and by law.
    b) Participation in development of access programmes to the corps of notaries and property, mercantile and movable assets registrars of Spain, for the purpose of accreditation of their knowledge of Catalan law.
    c) Establishment of notarial and registration districts, including determination of mortgage districts and notarial territorial power districts.
    d) The appointment of district protocol notary archivists and the maintenance of mortgage account registers.
2. The *Generalitat* has exclusive power in matters concerning the system of appeals regarding the qualification of titles or specific clauses of Catalan law which must be inscribed in a property, mercantile or movable assets registrar of Catalonia.
3. In the framework of the general regulation, the *Generalitat* has executive power over the Civil Registry, including the appointment of officials in charge, temporary staff and substitutes, the exercise of disciplinary functions in relation to

them, and provision of the human and material resources required to carry out their functions. The officials in charge shall provide proof of knowledge of the Catalan language and Catalan law in the form and to the extent established by the *Estatut* and by law.

Article 148. Public Works

1. The *Generalitat* has exclusive power over public works that are carried out in the territory of Catalonia and that have not been classified as being of general interest or that do not affect another autonomous community. This power includes in any case the planning, construction and funding of such works.
2. Classification as being of general interest shall be subject to a preliminary report by the *Generalitat*. The *Generalitat* participates in planning and programming public works qualified as being of general interest, in accordance with State legislation and the provisions of Title V of this *Estatut*.
3. The *Generalitat* is responsible for the management of public services within its power to which all public works located in Catalonia and not categorized as of general interest are assigned or by which they are deemed affected. In the case of works classified as being of general interest or that affect another autonomous community, collaboration agreements may be signed to manage the corresponding services.

Article 149. Territorial, Landscape, Coastline and Urban Development Planning

1. The *Generalitat* has exclusive power over territorial and landscape planning. This power includes in any case:
   a) Establishment of guidelines for planning and management of the territory, and the landscape and of the actions that affect these areas.
   b) Establishment and regulation of the forms of territorial planning and of the procedures for their processing and approval.
   c) Establishment and regulation of the instruments to safeguard natural areas and biological corridors, in keeping with the provisions of Article 144.2.
   d) Planning for future location of infrastructures and equipment within the sphere of the power of the *Generalitat*.
   e) Determination of specific measures for the promotion of territorial, demographic, socio-economic and environmental balance.
2. Determination of locations for infrastructures and equipment under State ownership in Catalonia shall be subject to a report by the *Generalitat* - State Bilateral Commission.
3. The *Generalitat* has exclusive power over the management of the coastline, while respecting the general system for the public domain. This power includes in any case:
   a) Establishment and regulation of territorial plans for classification and use of the coastline and beaches and also the regulation of proceedings for processing and approving these instruments and plans.

b) Management of the licences to occupy and use the maritime-terrestrial public domain, and especially issue of authorizations and concessions and, in any case, concessions for fixed structures in the sea, while respecting the exceptions that may be established for environmental reasons in continental and transition coastal waters.
c) Regulation and management of the economic and financial system governing the maritime-terrestrial public domain, in the terms established by the general legislation.
d) Execution of works and actions on the Catalan coastline which are not of general interest.

4. The *Generalitat* is responsible for the execution and management of works of general interest on the Catalan coastline, in accordance with the provisions of Article 148.
5. The *Generalitat* has exclusive power over urban development. This power includes in any case:
   a) Regulation of the system for development of urban land, which includes, in any case, determination of the criteria for the different kinds of land and land use.
   b) Regulation of the legal land ownership system while respecting the basic conditions established by the State to guarantee equality in the exercise of the right to property.
   c) Establishment and regulation of urban planning and management instruments, and the procedures for their processing and approval.
   d) Land and housing policy, regulation of publicly-owned land and housing heritage, and the system for administrative intervention in building, urban development and land and subsoil use.
   e) Ensuring legality in urban development, which includes, in any case, urban inspection, orders for suspension of works and licences, measures to undo illegal physical alterations, and discipline in urban development.
6. The *Generalitat* has shared power over the right of escheat in urban expropriations within the framework of State legislation.

Article 150. Organisation of the Administration of the *Generalitat*

In relation to the organization of its Administration, the *Generalitat* has exclusive power over:

a) The structure and regulation of public bodies and managers, their functioning and territorial coordination.
b) The different organizational and instrumental modalities for administrative action.

Article 151. Territorial Organisation

While respecting the institutional guarantee established by Articles 140 and 141 of the Constitution, the *Generalitat* has exclusive power over territorial organization, which includes in any case:

a) Determination, creation, modification and abolition of the government entities that make up the territorial organization of Catalonia.
b) Creation, abolition and alteration of boundaries both of municipalities and local government entities of lesser territorial scope; denomination, determining the capital and symbols for municipalities and other local government entities; place-names, and determination of special systems.
c) Establishment by law of procedures for relations between local government entities and the population, respecting local autonomy.

Article 152. Planning, Organisation and Promotion of Economic Activity

1. The *Generalitat* has power to promote economic activity in Catalonia.
2. The *Generalitat* has shared power over the organization of economic activity in Catalonia.
3. The *Generalitat* may establish economic activity planning within the framework of the guidelines set by general State planning.
4. The *Generalitat* is responsible for the development and management of general economic activity planning. This power includes in any case:
   a) Implementation of State plans.
   b) Participation in State planning through the mechanisms established by Title V.
   c) Management of the plans, including funds and resources of State origin aimed at fostering economic activity, in the terms established by means of an agreement.

Article 153. Gender Policies

The *Generalitat* has exclusive power over gender policies. While respecting the provisions of the State in exercise of the power attributed to it by Article 149.1.1 of the Constitution, this power includes in any case:

a) Planning, design, execution, evaluation and control over rules, plans and general guidelines regarding policies for women, and establishment of positive action for elimination of gender-based discrimination to be implemented uniformly in the whole territory of Catalonia.
b) Promotion of associations of women that carry out activities related to equality and non-discrimination, and of participation initiatives.
c) Regulation of measures and instruments to raise awareness of gender-based violence and to detect and prevent it and regulation of services and its own resources aimed at overall protection of women who have experienced or who experience this kind of violence.

Article 154. Promotion and Defence of Competition

1. The *Generalitat* has exclusive power over the promotion of market competition in economic activities carried out mainly in Catalonia.
2. The *Generalitat* has executive power over defence of competition in the exercise of economic activities that alter or may alter free market competition within

an area not extending beyond the territory of Catalonia. This power includes in any case:

a) Execution in measures related to the economic processes which affect competition.
b) Inspection and implementation of the sanctioning procedure.
c) Defence of competition in the exercise of commercial activity.

3. The *Generalitat* has exclusive power over the establishment and regulation of the Catalan Court for the Defence of Competition, as an independent body with jurisdiction over the whole territory of Catalonia which is the sole responsible body for dealing with economic activities carried out mainly in Catalonia, which alter or may alter competition, in the terms established by Sections 1 and 2.

Article 155. Intellectual and Industrial Property

1. The *Generalitat de Catalunya* has executive power over intellectual property. This power includes in any case:
   a) Establishment and regulation, in coordination with that of the State, of a registry of intellectual property rights generated in Catalonia or owned by individuals usually resident in Catalonia; registration, modification or cancellation of these rights, and exercise of the administrative activity required to guarantee their protection in the whole territory of Catalonia. The *Generalitat* shall inform the State of the entries made in its register with a view to their inclusion in the State register, shall collaborate with the State registry and facilitate the exchange of information.
   b) Authorization and revocation of entities for the collective management of intellectual property rights acting mainly in Catalonia and also performance of complementary inspection and control tasks regarding the activity of these entities.
2. The *Generalitat* has executive power over industrial property. This power includes in any case:
   a) Establishment and regulation, in coordination with that of the State, of a register of industrial property rights for natural or legal persons.
   b) The legal and procedural defence of the place-names of Catalonia used in industry.

Article 156. Protection of Personal Data

While respecting the guarantees regarding fundamental rights in this area, the *Generalitat* has executive power over the protection of personal data. This power includes in any case:

a) Registration and control of files or processing of personal data created or managed by the public institutions of Catalonia, the Administration of the *Generalitat*, local public authorities of Catalonia, autonomous entities, and public or private law entities answerable to autonomous or local public authorities or providing services or carrying out activities on their own account by means of any form of direct or indirect management, and also the universities that make up the Catalan university system.

b) Registration, and control of files or the processing of personal data created or managed by natural or legal persons for the exercise of public functions in connection with matters that fall under the authority of the *Generalitat* or of the local government entities of Catalonia, provided the processing takes place in Catalonia.

c) Registration and control of files and the processing of data created or managed by the public law bodies which exercise their functions exclusively within the territory of Catalonia.

d) Establishment of an independent authority, appointed by Parliament, to supervise the safeguarding of the right to protection of personal data within the powers of the *Generalitat*.

Article 157. Advertising

Without prejudice to the mercantile legislation of the State, the *Generalitat* has exclusive power over the regulation of advertising.

Article 158. Research, Development and Technological Innovation

1. In matters concerning scientific and technical research, the *Generalitat* has exclusive power in matters concerning its own research centres and structures, and the projects it finances. This power includes in any case:
   a) Establishment of research areas of its own, and monitoring, control and evaluation of projects.
   b) Organization, functioning system, control, monitoring and accreditation of centres and structures in Catalonia.
   c) Regulation and management of grants and financial assistance organized and funded by the *Generalitat*.
   d) Regulation and professional training of research and research support personnel.
   e) Dissemination of science and the transfer of results.
2. The *Generalitat* has shared power over the coordination of the research centres and structures of Catalonia.
3. Collaboration criteria between the State and the *Generalitat* in research policy, development and innovation shall be established within the framework of the provisions of Title V. Likewise, systems shall be established for the participation of the *Generalitat* in determining policies affecting these matters at European Union level, and in other international bodies and institutions.

Article 159. Legal System, Legal Procedure, Public Contracts, Expropriation and Responsibility in the Catalan Public Administration Bodies

1. The *Generalitat* has exclusive power in matters concerning the legal system and legal procedure governing Catalan Public Administration bodies which are not affected by Article 149.1.18 of the Constitution. This power includes:

a) The means required to exercise administrative functions, including the system governing public and patrimonial property.
b) Control, inspection and sanctioning authority in all material areas that the *Generalitat* has power over.
c) The rules of administrative procedure arising from the particularities of the substantive law of Catalonia or from specialized areas of the organization of the *Generalitat*.

2. The *Generalitat* has shared power in all matters relating to the legal system and legal procedure of Catalan Public Administration bodies not included in Section 1 above.
3. In relation to the contracts of Public Administration bodies in Catalonia, the *Generalitat* has:
   a) Exclusive power over organization and jurisdiction in matters involving contracting by Catalan Public Administration bodies and over rules for execution, modification and termination of the Administration's contracts in those matters which are not affected by Article 149.1.18 of the Constitution.
   b) Shared power in all matters not attributed exclusively to the jurisdiction of the *Generalitat* according to *a)* above.
4. In matters concerning compulsory expropriation, the *Generalitat* has executive power, in any case, to:
   a) Determine cases, causes and conditions in which Catalan Administration bodies may exercise expropriatory authority.
   b) Establish the criteria for valuing the expropriated assets according to the nature and social function of these assets, in accordance with State legislation.
   c) Create and regulate an entity of its own for the purpose of determining a fair price, and to establish the procedure.
5. In matters of patrimonial responsibility, the *Generalitat* has shared power to establish the causes that may give rise to liability, in relation to claims brought against the *Generalitat*, in accordance with the general system of responsibility of all Public Administration bodies.
6. The powers of the *Generalitat* specified in Sections 1, 3, 4 and 5 above shall be exercised with respect for the principle of local autonomy.

Article 160. Local Government System

1. The *Generalitat* has exclusive power over the local government system, which, while respecting the principle of local autonomy, includes:
   a) Relations between the institutions of the *Generalitat* and local government entities, and also the methods for organization and liaison in regard to cooperation and collaboration between local government entities, and between these and the Administration of the *Generalitat*, and including the various forms: associations, *mancomunitats*, conventional associations and consortia.
   b) Determination of the powers and jurisdiction of municipalities and other local government entities, in the areas specified in Article 84.

c) The system of publicly-owned, communal and patrimonial property and the modalities of public service provision.
d) Determination of the governing bodies for local government entities created by the *Generalitat* and the functioning and decision-making system of these bodies.
e) The system governing complementary bodies in the organization of local government entities.

2. The *Generalitat* has shared power in all matters not established by Section 1 above.
3. The *Generalitat* has exclusive power in matters concerning the electoral system for the local entities it creates, with the exception of those which are constitutionally guaranteed.

Article 161. Relations with Religious Entities

1. The *Generalitat* has exclusive power over religious entities that carry out their activities in Catalonia. This power includes in any case regulation and establishment of collaboration and cooperation mechanisms for the carrying out of their activities within the jurisdiction of the *Generalitat.*
2. The *Generalitat* has executive authority over religious freedom. This power includes in any case:
   a) Participation in the management of the State Registry of Religious Entities in relation to churches, confessions and religious communities that carry out their activities in Catalonia, in the terms determined by law.
   b) Establishment of agreements and cooperation conventions with the churches, confessions and religious communities registered in the State Registry of Religious Entities within the jurisdiction of the *Generalitat.*
   c) Promotion, development and execution, within the jurisdiction of the *Generalitat,* of agreements and conventions signed between the State and the churches, confessions and religious communities registered in the State Registry of Religious Entities.
3. The *Generalitat* collaborates in bodies at State level to which functions have been attributed concerning religious entities.

Article 162. Healthcare, Public Health, Pharmaceutical Regulation and Pharmaceutical Products

1. The *Generalitat* has exclusive power in matters of healthcare and public health over the organization, internal functioning, evaluation, inspection and control of healthcare centres, services and establishments.
2. The *Generalitat* shall classify pharmaceuticals, in the framework of Article 149.1.16 of the Constitution.
3. The *Generalitat* has shared power in any case in the following areas:
   a) Classification, planning, determination, regulation and execution of public, social and mental health provisions and services, at all levels and for all citizens.

b) Classification, planning, determination, regulation and execution of measures and actions aimed at preserving, protecting and promoting public health in all areas, including health at work, animal health with effects on human health, food health, environmental health and epidemiological vigilance.
c) Planning of publicly provided healthcare resources and coordination of private healthcare activities with the public healthcare system.
d) Specialized healthcare training, which includes accreditation and evaluation of centres; planning to provide posts; participation in preparation of selection procedures and management of training programmes for specialties and other specific training, and the issue of diplomas for areas of specific training.
e) The statutory system and the training of the staff providing service in the public healthcare system services.

4. The *Generalitat* participates in planning and State coordination in matters of healthcare and public health, in accordance with the provisions of Title V.
5. The *Generalitat* has executive power over State legislation on pharmaceutical products.

Article 163. Private Security

The *Generalitat* executes the State legislation in the following matters:

a) Authorization of private security companies with head office in Catalonia whose area of activity does not extend beyond the territory of Catalonia.
b) Inspection and sanction of private security activities carried out in Catalonia.
c) Authorization of private security staff training centres.
d) Coordination of private security and investigation services with the Police of the *Generalitat* and the local police of Catalonia.

Article 164. Public Security

1. In matters of public security, the *Generalitat*, in accordance with State legislation, is responsible for:
   a) Planning and regulation of the public security system for Catalonia and organization of the local police.
   b) Creation and organization of the *Generalitat* Police Force - *Mossos d'Esquadra*.
   c) Traffic control and vigilance.
2. The *Generalitat* has supreme command over the *Generalitat* Police Force - *Mossos d'Esquadra* and coordinates the activities of the local police.
3. In the framework of State legislation on security, the *Generalitat* has the executive powers attributed to it by the State and in any case:
   a) Governing functions over the exercise of the rights of assembly and demonstration.
   b) Compliance with the provisions for the conservation of nature, the environment and water resources.

4. The *Generalitat* participates, through a Security Board with equal representation of the *Generalitat* and the State and chaired by the President of the *Generalitat*, in the coordination of security policies and of the activity of the State and Catalan police forces, and also in the exchange of information at international level, and in cooperating with and assisting the police authorities of other countries. In agreement with the State, the *Generalitat* shall be represented in the working groups working in collaboration with the police of other countries in which the State participates.
5. The scope of action of the *Generalitat* Police Force - *Mossos d'Esquadra* is the whole of the Catalan territory, and it exercises all the functions of a police force in the following fields:
   a) Public safety and public order.
   b) Administrative policing, including that deriving from State regulations.
   c) Judicial policing and criminal investigation, including the various forms of organized crime and terrorism, in the terms established by law.

Article 165. Social Security

1. While respecting the principles of the unity of economic patrimony and the financial solidarity of social security, the *Generalitat* has shared power over social security matters. This power includes:
   a) Implementation and execution of State legislation, with the exception of the rules which configure the economic system.
   b) Management of the social security economic system.
   c) Organization and administration of the assets and services that make up the healthcare and social services of the social security system in Catalonia.
   d) Organization and exercise of administrative jurisdiction over the institutions, companies and foundations that collaborate with the social security system in the matters referred to in *c*, and also coordination of workplace risk prevention activities carried out in Catalonia by the health funds for workplace accidents and occupational illness.
   e) Recognition and management of non-contributory pensions.
   f) The coordination of the health system actions linked to the social security service.
2. The *Generalitat* may organize and administer, to these effects and within its territory, all the services related to the matters specified above, and exercises the supervision of the institutions, entities and foundations in the area of health and social security, with the exception of high-level inspection, which is reserved to the State.

Article 166. Social Services, Volunteers, Minors and Promotion of Families

1. The *Generalitat* has exclusive power over the social services. This power includes in any case:

a) Regulation and organization of the social services activities, social service technical benefits and payments designed as welfare allowances or to supplement other public benefit support systems.
b) Regulation and organization of the entities, services and public and private establishments which provide social services in Catalonia.
c) Regulation and approval of specific plans and programmes addressed to individuals and groups in a situation of poverty or social need.
d) Supervision and control of private supplementary social protection systems.

2. The *Generalitat* has exclusive power over volunteers. This power includes, in any case, definition of the activity and regulation and promotion of actions to support solidarity and voluntary action carried out individually or through public or private institutions.
3. With regard to minors the *Generalitat* has:
   a) Exclusive power over the protection of minors, which includes, in any case, regulation of the protection system, and the public institutions for protection and guardianship of defenceless and at-risk minors and juvenile offenders, while respecting criminal legislation in this latter case.
   b) The *Generalitat* participates, in the preparation and reform of the penal and procedural legislation that affects powers concerning minors.
4. The *Generalitat* has exclusive power over promotion of families and children. This includes, in any case, social protection measures and their implementation.

Article 167. The Symbols of Catalonia

The *Generalitat* has exclusive power over the regulation, organization, configuration, and preservation of the symbols of Catalonia, in accordance with the provisions of this *Estatut*.

Article 168. The Prison System

1. The *Generalitat* has the executive power for State legislation regarding prison affairs. This includes in any case:
   a) The capacity to enact provisions adapting prison regulations to the social reality of Catalonia.
   b) All management of prison activity in Catalonia, especially directing, organization, overall system, operation, planning and inspection of prison institutions of any kind located in Catalonia.
   c) Planning, building and refurbishment of the prison buildings located in Catalonia.
   d) Administration and management of unmovable assets and facilities assigned to the Catalan prison administration, and of all material resources assigned to it.
   e) Planning and organization of paid work for the prison population, and implementation of alternative measures to prison and of reintegration measures.
2. The *Generalitat* may issue reports in the procedure for granting pardons.

Article 169. Transport

1. The *Generalitat* has exclusive power over land transport of passengers and goods by road, railway and cable entirely within Catalan territory, irrespective of ownership of the infrastructure. This power includes in any case:
   a) Regulation, planning, management, coordination and inspection of services and activities.
   b) Regulation of administrative supervision for the exercise of transport activities.
   c) Regulation of urban transport and of occasional transport services for passengers in tourist vehicles.
   d) Specific regulation of tourist transport, school transport or the transport of minors, health transport, funeral transport, transport of hazardous or perishable goods, and other transport requiring specific systems, while respecting State powers in the area of public safety.
   e) Regulation of a system of mediation in matters of transport.
   f) The power to set charges for land transport.
2. The integration of transport routes or services that lie entirely within the territory of Catalonia into higher level lines or services requires the preliminary report of the *Generalitat.*
3. The *Generalitat* participates in the establishment of rail services that ensure links with other autonomous communities or with international traffic, in accordance with the provisions of Title V.
4. The *Generalitat* has exclusive power over the transport, logistics and distribution centres located in Catalonia, including:
   a) Information and freight distribution centres.
   b) Road transport stations.
5. The *Generalitat* has exclusive power over operators in activities related to the organization of transport, logistics and distribution taking place in Catalonia.
6. While respecting the powers of the State in the areas of the merchant marine and ports, the *Generalitat* has exclusive power in maritime and river transport which lies entirely with the territory of Catalonia, including:
   a) Regulation, planning and management of maritime and river passenger transport.
   b) Administrative supervision for the provision of services and exercise of activities related to maritime and river transport.
   c) Requirements for exercise of the activity.

Article 170. Work and Labour Relations

1. The *Generalitat* has executive power in matters of work and labour relations. This power includes in any case:
   a) Labour relations and working conditions.
   b) Active employment policies, which include the training of jobseekers and active workers, and also management of the appropriate subsidies. The *Generalitat* participates in training plans or activities that extend beyond the territory of Catalonia.

c) Professional qualifications in Catalonia.
d) Employment brokerage, which includes regulation, authorization and control of employment agencies with head offices in Catalonia.
e) Collective negotiation and registration of collective bargaining agreements.
f) Procedures for regulating employment and for administrative action in collective transfers between work centres located in Catalonia.
g) Prevention of work risks, and health and safety in the workplace.
h) Power to apply sanctions for infringement of the social order, within its jurisdiction.
i) Determining minimum services for strikes that take place in Catalonia.
j) Ensuring the legality of and, if necessary, the subsequent registration of collective bargaining agreements for companies that exercise their activity exclusively in Catalonia.
k) Labour conciliation, mediation and arbitration instruments.
l) Preparation of the holiday calendar for the whole territory of Catalonia.

2. The *Generalitat* has executive power over public inspection in all matters regulated by this Article. To this end, the civil servants of the corps performing this function are structurally and functionally accountable to the *Generalitat*. Formulas guaranteeing effective exercise of the inspection function in the social sphere shall be established by means of the cooperation mechanisms determined by Title V.

Article 171. Tourism

The *Generalitat* has exclusive power in matters of tourism. This power includes in any case:

a) Organization and planning of the tourism sector.
b) Promotion of tourism, which includes the signing of agreements with foreign organizations and the creation of offices abroad.
c) Regulation and classification of tourism companies and establishments, and management of the network of *Generalitat*-owned tourism establishments. With a view to facilitating coordination between these establishments and those of the State network of *Paradores Nacionales* located in Catalonia, the *Generalitat* participates, in the terms established by State legislation, in the governing bodies of the *Paradores de Turismo de España*.
d) Regulation of the specific rights and obligations of users and providers of tourist services and of alternative means for conflict resolution.
e) Teaching and training in tourism that do not lead to the award of an official qualification.
f) Establishment of criteria, regulation of conditions and implementation and control over public funds for assistance and promotion of tourism.

Article 172. Universities

1. In matters of university education, the *Generalitat* has exclusive power, without prejudice to university autonomy, over:

a) Planning and coordination of the Catalan university system, in the framework of the general coordination.
b) The decision to create public universities and authorize private universities.
c) The approval of statutes of the public universities and of rules for organization and functioning of the private universities.
d) Coordination of the procedures for access to the universities.
e) The legal framework governing the university own qualifications, in accordance with the principle of university autonomy.
f) Its own funding for universities and, where appropriate, management of State funds for university education.
g) Regulation and management of its own grants and subsidies system for university education and, where appropriate, regulation and management of State funds in this area.
h) The system of remuneration of teaching and research staff employed by the universities and the establishment of additional remuneration for teaching staff in permanent public employment.

2. In matters of university education, the *Generalitat* has shared power, without prejudice to university autonomy, over all matters not referred to in Section 1 above, which include in any case:
   a) Regulation of the requirements for the creation and recognition of universities and university centres, and attachment of these centres to universities.
   b) The legal system for organization and functioning of the public universities, including the governing and representative bodies.
   c) Appointment and withdrawal of the capacity of public or private teaching centres to issue official university qualifications, and creation, modification and abolition of university centres in public universities, and also recognition of these centres in private universities and the introduction and abolition of teaching subjects.
   d) Regulation of the system of access to the universities.
   e) Regulation of the system governing contracted and permanent teaching and research personnel.
   f) Evaluating and ensuring the excellence and quality of university education, and also that of teaching and research personnel.
3. Executive power over issue of official university qualifications.

Article 173. Video and Sound Surveillance and Recordings

The *Generalitat* has responsibility for use of video and sound surveillance, recordings or other similar means, implemented by the police of Catalonia or by private companies or establishments in the public sphere. The *Generalitat* shall exercise this power while respecting the fundamental rights.

Title V. Institutional Relations of the *Generalitat*

Chapter I. Relations of the Generalitat with the State and with Other Autonomous Communities

Article 174. General Provisions

1. The *Generalitat* and the State provide mutual assistance to each other and collaborate when necessary so as to effectively exercise their respective powers and defend their respective interests.
2. The *Generalitat* may establish collaborative links with other autonomous communities for the establishment of common policies, for the effective exercise of its powers and for the handling of matters of common interest, especially when these are supra-territorial in scope. The *Generalitat* shall provide the necessary assistance to other autonomous communities for the effective exercise of their powers.
3. The *Generalitat* participates in any decision-making institutions, bodies and procedures of the State that affect its powers, in accordance with the provisions of this *Estatut* and the law.

Section One. Collaboration with the State and with Other Autonomous Communities

Article 175. Instruments for Collaboration Between the *Generalitat* and the State

1. Within their respective areas of powers, the *Generalitat* and the State may sign collaboration conventions and make use of other collaboration instruments as considered appropriate for the accomplishment of objectives of common interest.
2. The *Generalitat* also collaborates with the State through the multilateral bodies and procedures in areas and matters of common interest.

Article 176. Effects of Collaboration Between the *Generalitat* and the State

1. The participation of the *Generalitat* in bilateral and multilateral bodies and mechanisms of collaboration with the State and with other autonomous communities does not in any way alter the ownership of its powers.
2. The *Generalitat* is not bound by decisions taken within the framework of multilateral voluntary collaboration mechanisms with the State and with other autonomous communities with regard to which it has not manifested its agreement.
3. The *Generalitat* may state its reservations to agreements made within the framework of the multilateral voluntary collaboration mechanisms when these agreements have been made without its approval.

Article 177. System for Conventions Between the *Generalitat* and the State

1. The legal system governing conventions signed by the *Generalitat*, with regard to the *Generalitat*, shall be established by an Act of Parliament.
2. Conventions signed between the Government of the *Generalitat* and the State Government shall be published in the *Diari Oficial de la Generalitat de Catalunya* within one month of signing. The date of publication of the convention in the *Boletín Oficial del Estado* determines its applicability in relation to third parties.

Article 178. Conventions and Agreements with Other Autonomous Communities

1. The *Generalitat* may sign collaboration conventions and cooperation agreements with other autonomous communities.
2. The conventions and agreements with other autonomous communities may agree, among other matters, the creation of joint bodies and the establishment of joint projects, plans and programmes.
3. Entry into conventions and agreements requires prior approval of Parliament only in cases that affect its legislative powers. In other cases, the Government shall inform Parliament of the signing of conventions and agreements within one month of the date of signature.
4. Collaboration conventions signed by the *Generalitat* with other autonomous communities shall be notified to the *Cortes Generales* and shall come into effect sixty days after notification, unless the *Cortes Generales* decide that these are to be classified as cooperation agreements requiring the prior authorization referred to in Article 145.2 of the Constitution.
5. Conventions and agreements signed by the *Generalitat* with other autonomous communities shall be published, within forty-five days and one month, respectively, counting from the day on which they were signed, in the *Diari Oficial de la Generalitat de Catalunya.*

Section Two. Participation in State Decision-Making Institutions and Procedures

Article 179. Appearance of Senators Before Parliament

Senators elected in Catalonia and those who represent the *Generalitat* in the Senate may appear before Parliament at their own request to report on their activity in the Senate, within the terms set out in Parliament's Rules of Procedure.

Article 180. Designation of Members of the Constitutional Court and of the General Council of Judicial Power

The *Generalitat* participates in the processes for the designation of magistrates of the Constitutional Court and members of the General Council of Judicial Power in the terms established by law, or where appropriate, by parliamentary regulations.

Article 181. Participation in the General Regulation of Economic Activity

The *Generalitat* participates in any decision-making processes of the State that affect the general organization of economic activity, within the framework of the provisions of Article 131.2 of the Constitution.

Article 182. Designation of Representatives in Economic and Social Bodies

1. The *Generalitat* designates or participates in processes for designation of members of the management bodies of the Bank of Spain, the National Stock Market Commission and the Telecommunications Market Commission, any entities that may replace these and other State entities that have regulatory functions in matters of economic and social relevance affecting the powers of the *Generalitat*, under the terms established by applicable legislation.
2. The *Generalitat* designates or participates in processes for designation of members of economic and energy entities, financial institutions and publicly-owned State companies with jurisdiction in the territory of Catalonia and which are not the object of transfer, under the terms established by applicable legislation.
3. The *Generalitat* designates or participates in processes for designation of members of the Accounts Court, the Economic and Social Council, the Taxation Agency, the National Energy Commission, the Spanish Data Protection Agency, the Radio and Television Council, any entities that may replace these, and entities created in these fields, under the terms established by applicable legislation.
4. If the nature of the entity so requires, and if its main office is not in Catalonia, the *Generalitat* may ask the State to create territorial delegations of the bodies referred to in Section 1.

Section Three. The *Generalitat* - State Bilateral Commission

Article 183. Functions and Composition of the *Generalitat* - State Bilateral Commission

1. In accordance with the principles established by Articles 3.1 and 174, the *Generalitat* - State Bilateral Commission is the general and permanent framework for relations between the Government of the *Generalitat* and the Government of the State for the following purposes:
   a) Participation and collaboration of the *Generalitat* in the exercise of State powers affecting the autonomy of Catalonia.
   b) Exchange of information and establishment, when appropriate, of mechanisms for collaboration in their respective public policies and in matters of common interest.
2. The functions of the *Generalitat* - State Bilateral Commission are to deliberate, make proposals and, if appropriate, reach agreements in the cases established in this *Estatut* and, in general, in relation to the following areas:
   a) Government bills that uniquely affect the distribution of powers between the State and the *Generalitat*.

b) Planning of the general economic policy of the Government of the State in all matters that uniquely affect the interests and powers of the *Generalitat*, and application and development of this policy.
c) Promotion of appropriate measures to improve collaboration between the State and the *Generalitat* and to ensure more effective exercise of their respective powers in areas of common interest.
d) Conflicts over powers that arise between the two parties, and proposal, when appropriate, of measures to resolve them.
e) Evaluation of the functioning of the collaboration mechanisms established between the State and the *Generalitat* and proposal of measures to improve collaboration.
f) Proposal of a list of economic bodies, financial institutions and publicly-owned State companies in which the *Generalitat* may designate representatives, and the modalities and means of this representation.
g) Monitoring of European policy in order to ensure the effectiveness of the participation of the *Generalitat* in European Union affairs.
h) Monitoring of external State activities that affect the *Generalitat*'s own powers.
i) Questions of common interest established by law or raised by the parties.

3. The *Generalitat* - State Bilateral Commission is made up of an equal number of representatives of the State and of the *Generalitat*. It is chaired alternately by each of the two parties for periods of one year. The Commission has a permanent secretariat and may create sub-committees and committees as deemed necessary. The Bilateral Commission prepares an annual report, which is submitted to the State Government, the Government of the *Generalitat* and to Parliament.
4. The *Generalitat* - State Bilateral Commission meets in plenary session at least twice a year and whenever either of the parties requests a meeting.
5. Internal regulation and functioning of the *Generalitat* - State Bilateral Commission is by agreement between both parties.

Chapter II. Relations of the Generalitat with the European Union

Article 184. General Provision

The *Generalitat* participates, under the terms established by this *Estatut* and the legislation of the State, in affairs related to the European Union that affect the powers or interests of Catalonia.

Article 185. Participation in the Treaties of the European Union

1. The *Generalitat* shall be informed by the State Government of initiatives for review of European Union and of subsequent signing and ratification processes. The Government of the *Generalitat* and Parliament shall address, to the State Government and to the *Cortes Generales,* the observations that it deems pertinent to this effect.
2. The State Government may include representatives of the *Generalitat* in Spanish delegations taking part in processes for review and negotiation of original

treaties and those for adoption of new treaties, in matters affecting the exclusive powers of the *Generalitat*.

Article 186. Participation in the Formation of the State Position

1. The *Generalitat* participates in the formation of State positions before the European Union, especially before the Council of Ministers, in matters concerning the powers or interests of Catalonia, under the terms established by this *Estatut* and the legislation on these matters.
2. The *Generalitat* shall participate bilaterally in forming the State positions in those European affairs which affect it exclusively. In other cases, participation shall be in the framework of multilateral procedures to be established.
3. The position expressed by the *Generalitat* is decisive for the formation of the State position if it affects its exclusive powers and if the European proposal or initiative could lead to especially important financial or administrative consequences for Catalonia. In other cases, this position shall be heard by the State.
4. The State shall provide the *Generalitat* with complete and up-to-date information about the initiatives and proposals presented to the European Union. The Government of the *Generalitat* and the Parliament of Catalonia shall address to the State Government and the *Cortes Generales*, as the case may be, the observations and proposals deemed pertinent to these initiatives and proposals.

Article 187. Participation in European Institutions and Bodies

1. The *Generalitat* participates in Spanish delegations to the European Union that deal with affairs within the legislative power of the *Generalitat*, and especially to the Council of Ministers and the consultative and drafting bodies of the Council and the Commission.
2. In areas falling within the exclusive powers of the *Generalitat*, the participation established in Section 1, permits the *Generalitat*, by means of preliminary agreement, to represent and chair these bodies, in accordance with the applicable regulations.
3. The *Generalitat*, in accordance with the State, participates in designation of representatives in the framework of the permanent State representation in the European Union.
4. Parliament may establish relations with the European Parliament in areas of common interest.

Article 188. Participation in Overseeing the Principles of Subsidiarity and of Proportionality

Parliament participates in the processes to oversee the principles of subsidiarity and proportionality established by European Union Law in relation to European legislative proposals if these proposals affect powers of the *Generalitat*.

Article 189. Development and Application of European Union Law

1. The *Generalitat* applies and implements the law of the European Union within its jurisdiction. The existence of a European regulation does not modify the internal distribution of powers established by the Constitution and this *Estatut.*
2. If implementation of European Union law requires the adoption of internal measures that extend beyond Catalan territory which the competent autonomous communities are unable to adopt by means of collaboration or coordination mechanisms, the State shall consult the *Generalitat* on these circumstances prior to adopting the measures. The *Generalitat* shall participate in the bodies that adopt these measures or, should this participation be not possible, shall issue a preliminary report.
3. In the event that the European Union establishes legislation replacing the basic State regulations, the *Generalitat* may adopt the development legislation based on the European rules.

Article 190. Management of European Funds

The *Generalitat* is responsible for the management of European funds in matters within its jurisdiction, in the terms established by Articles 114 and 210.

Article 191. Actions Before the Court of Justice

1. The *Generalitat* has access to the Court of Justice of the European Union within the terms established by European regulations.
2. The Government of the *Generalitat* may demand that the State Government bring actions before the Court of Justice of the European Union in defence of the legitimate interests and powers of the *Generalitat*. The *Generalitat* shall collaborate in the legal defence.
3. The refusal of the State Government to bring the requested actions must be justified, and must be immediately communicated to the *Generalitat.*

Article 192. Delegation of the *Generalitat* to the European Union

1. The *Generalitat* may establish a delegation to better defend its interests before the institutions of the European Union.

Chapter III. Foreign Action of the Generalitat

Article 193. General Provisions

1. The *Generalitat* shall foster the external projection of Catalonia and promote its interests in this area, while respecting the powers of the State in foreign affairs.
2. The *Generalitat* has the capacity to carry out actions with external projection that derive directly from its powers, either directly or through the bodies of the General Administration of the State.

Article 194. Offices Abroad

In order to promote the interests of Catalonia, the *Generalitat* may establish offices abroad.

Article 195. Collaboration Agreements

In order to promote the interests of Catalonia, the *Generalitat* may sign collaboration agreements in areas falling within its powers. For this purpose, the external representative bodies of the State shall provide the necessary support to the initiatives of the *Generalitat.*

Article 196. International Treaties and Conventions

1. The Government of the State shall inform the *Generalitat* in advance of the signing of treaties which have a direct and singular effect on the powers of Catalonia. The *Generalitat* and Parliament may address the observations that they consider relevant to these matters to the Government.
2. In the case of treaties which have a direct and singular effect on Catalonia, the *Generalitat* may request that the Government include representatives of the *Generalitat* in the negotiating delegation.
3. The *Generalitat* may request that the Government sign international treaties in areas within its jurisdiction.
4. The *Generalitat* shall adopt the necessary measures to carry out any obligations arising from international treaties and conventions ratified by Spain or binding on the State within the area of its powers.

Article 197. Cross-Border, Inter-autonomous Community and Development Cooperation

1. The *Generalitat* shall promote cooperation and establish appropriate relations with the European regions with which it shares economic, social, environmental and cultural interests.
2. The *Generalitat* shall promote cooperation with other territories, under the terms established in Section 1 above.
3. The *Generalitat* shall promote development cooperation programmes.

Article 198. Participation in International Bodies

The *Generalitat* shall participate in the competent international bodies in matters of important interest for Catalonia, especially UNESCO and other cultural bodies, in the form established by the corresponding regulations.

Article 199. Coordination of Foreign Actions

The *Generalitat*, in areas falling within its powers, shall foster and coordinate the foreign actions of local government entities and of other bodies and public entities in Catalonia, without prejudice to their autonomy.

Article 200. The International Projection of Catalan Organisations

The *Generalitat* shall promote the international projection of social, cultural and sporting organizations in Catalonia and, when appropriate, their affiliation to similar entities at international level, in keeping with their objectives.

Title VI. Funding of the Generalitat

Chapter I. The Finances of the Generalitat

Article 201. Principles

1. Taxation and financial relations between the State and the *Generalitat* are regulated by the Constitution, by this *Estatut* and by the Organic Act referred to in Section 3 of Article 157 of the Constitution.
2. The funding of the *Generalitat* is governed by the principles of financial autonomy, coordination, solidarity and transparency in fiscal and financial relations between the Public Administration bodies, and also by the principles of sufficiency of resources, fiscal responsibility, equity and institutional loyalty between the afore-mentioned Public Administration bodies.
3. The development of the contents of this Title is the responsibility of the State - *Generalitat* Joint Economic and Fiscal Affairs Commission.
4. In accordance with Article 138.2 of the Constitution, the financing of the *Generalitat* shall not entail discriminatory effects for Catalonia with respect to other autonomous communities. This principle shall fully respect the criteria of solidarity set out in Article 206 of this *Estatut*.

Article 202. The Resources of the *Generalitat*

1. The *Generalitat* has autonomous finances and sufficient financial resources for the proper exercise of self-government.
2. The *Generalitat* enjoys full autonomy of expenditure so that it can use and apply its resources freely, in accordance with the political and social guidelines set by its self-government institutions.
3. The financial resources of the *Generalitat* consist of:
   a) Taxation income, rates, special charges and other taxes raised in Catalonia.
   b) The income of all ceded State taxes, in accordance with the provisions of Article 201 of this *Estatut*.
   c) Surcharges on State taxes.
   d) Revenues arising from the Inter-Territorial Compensation Fund and from other allocations established by the Constitution, as appropriate.
   e) Other transfers and allocations charged to the general budget of the State.
   f) Revenues from payments for public services.
   g) Incomes earned on the assets of the *Generalitat*.
   h) Private law revenues.
   i) Income yielded by debt issues and credit operations.

j) Revenues arising from fines and sanctions applied in areas falling within its powers.
k) Resources originating from the European Union and from community programmes.
l) Any other resource that may be established by virtue of the provisions of this *Estatut* and the Constitution.

Article 203. Financial Powers

1. The *Generalitat* has the capacity to determine the volume and composition of revenues falling within its financial powers, and also to freely apply its resources to expenditure items as it deems fit.
2. The *Generalitat* participates in the income arising from State taxes ceded to Catalonia. To this end, these taxes are as follows:
   a) Totally ceded taxes, that is, taxes the entire income and regulatory power of which corresponds to the *Generalitat.*
   b) Partially ceded taxes, that is, taxes part of the income of which and, where appropriate, regulatory power of which corresponds to the *Generalitat.*
3. Within the framework of the powers of the State and of the European Union, exercise of the regulatory power referred to in Section 2 includes participation in establishment of the tax rate, exemptions, reductions and rebates on the tax base and deductions in the quota.
4. The *Generalitat* is responsible for the management, collection, settlement and inspection of totally ceded State taxes and the same functions in the measure attributed, in accordance with the provisions of Article 204, regarding partially ceded taxes.
5. The *Generalitat* has the power to establish, by means of an Act of Parliament, its own taxes, over which it has regulatory power.
6. The regulatory power of the *Generalitat* to act in the taxation sphere is based on the principles of equity and efficiency. In its taxation policies, the *Generalitat* promotes social cohesion and welfare, economic progress and environmental sustainability.

Article 204. The Taxation Agency of Catalonia

1. The Taxation Agency of Catalonia is responsible for management, collection, settlement and inspection of all *Generalitat* of Catalonia taxes and also, when delegated by the State, of State taxes which are totally ceded to the *Generalitat.*
2. The Taxation Administration of the State is responsible for management, collection, settlement and inspection of other State taxes collected in Catalonia, without prejudice to any delegation to the *Generalitat* in this respect or to any collaboration that may be established especially when required by the nature of the tax.

   For implementation of the content of the previous paragraph, a consortium, or an equivalent entity, shall be constituted, within two years, with parity of participation by the Taxation Administration Agency of the State and the Taxation

Agency of Catalonia. The Consortium may be transformed into the Taxation Administration in Catalonia.

3. The two taxation administrations shall establish the necessary mechanisms to permit presentation and reception in the respective offices of tax forms and other taxation-related documentation which may have a bearing on the other administration, with a view to facilitating compliance with tax obligations on the part of taxpayers.
   The *Generalitat* participates, in the form to be established, in the State taxation entities or bodies with responsibility for management, collection, settlement and inspection of partially ceded State taxes.
4. The Taxation Agency of Catalonia shall be created by means of an Act of Parliament and shall have full power and attributes for organization and exercise of the functions referred to in Section 1.
5. Management functions in relation to local taxes may be delegated to the Taxation Agency of Catalonia by the municipalities.

Article 205. Economic-Administrative Bodies

The *Generalitat* shall assume, by means of its own economic-administrative bodies, the administrative review of claims that may be made by taxpayers against the acts of taxation management of the Taxation Agency of Catalonia.

The above shall be without prejudice to the powers of the General Administration of the State in relation to unification of criteria.

To this end, the *Generalitat* and the General Administration of the State may also agree the necessary cooperation mechanisms as necessary for appropriate exercise of the functions of economic-administrative revision.

Article 206. Participation in Income from State Taxes and Levelling and Solidarity Mechanisms

1. The level of financial resources available to the *Generalitat* for funding of its services and powers shall be based on criteria of expenditure needs and shall take its taxation capacity, among other criteria, into account. To this end, the resources of the *Generalitat* are, among others, those deriving from its taxation revenues, increased or reduced in accordance with its participation in the levelling and solidarity mechanisms.
2. The *Generalitat* participates in the income deriving from ceded State taxes. The percentage of participation is established taking its services and powers into account.
3. The financial resources available to the *Generalitat* may be adjusted to enable the State financing system to have sufficient resources to ensure levelling and solidarity with other autonomous communities, so that the education, health, and other essential social services of the welfare state provided by the different

autonomous governments can achieve similar levels throughout the State, *provided that they also make a similar fiscal effort*[17]. Similarly, where appropriate, the *Generalitat* receives resources from the levelling and solidarity mechanisms. The afore-mentioned levels shall be established by the State.

4. The levelling and solidarity mechanisms shall be determined in accordance with the principle of transparency, and the results shall be evaluated every five years.
5. The State shall guarantee that application of the levelling mechanisms shall in no case alter the position of Catalonia in the pre-levelling ranking of per capita earnings.
6. In determining the expenditure needs referred to in Section 1, the population, adjusted for differential costs and demographic variables, and in particular by means of a correction factor based on the percentage of immigrants in the population, shall be taken into account, as a basic variable. Likewise, population density, the size of urban nuclei and the socially excluded population shall also be taken into account.

Article 207. Fiscal Treatment

The *Generalitat* enjoys the fiscal treatment established by law for the State regarding State taxes.

Article 208. Updating of Funding

1. The State and the *Generalitat* shall update the funding system every five years, taking into account the evolution of the available public resources as a whole and that of the expenditure needs of the different administration bodies.
   This updating shall be carried out without prejudice to monitoring and possible updating of the basic variables employed for determination of the resources provided by the funding system.
2. The updating referred to in Section 1 shall be approved by the State - *Generalitat* Joint Economic and Fiscal Affairs Commission.

Article 209. Institutional Loyalty

1. In accordance with the principle of institutional loyalty, the financial impact, whether positive or negative, of the general provisions approved by the State on the *Generalitat*, and of those approved by the *Generalitat* on the State, shall be assessed, over a period of time in terms of variations of expenditure needs or fiscal capacity, with a view to establishing the necessary adjustment mechanisms.
2. Both administrations shall mutually facilitate access to the necessary statistical and management information for best exercise of their respective powers, in a framework of cooperation and transparency.

17. The Constitutional Court has declared this phrase is unconstitutional and void (STC 31/2010, 28 June).

Article 210. The State - *Generalitat* Joint Economic and Fiscal Affairs Commission

1. The State - *Generalitat* Joint Economic and Fiscal Affairs Commission is the bilateral body for relations between the Administration of the State and the *Generalitat* in the field of autonomous community funding. It is responsible for specification, application, updating and monitoring of the funding system, and also for channelling the entirety of fiscal and financial relations between the *Generalitat* and the State. It consists of an equal number of representatives of the State and of the *Generalitat*. Presidency of this Joint Commission rotates between the two parties for terms of one year.
   Internal regulation and functioning of the Commission is by agreement between the two delegations. The State - *Generalitat* Joint Economic and Fiscal Affairs Commission performs its functions without prejudice to agreements signed by the Government of Catalonia in this matter within multilateral institutions and bodies.
2. The State - *Generalitat* Joint Economic and Fiscal Affairs Commission is responsible for:
   a) Agreeing the scope and conditions for cession of taxes owned by the State and, especially, the percentages of participation in the partially ceded State taxes referred to in Article 206, and also their revision every five years.
   b) Agreeing the contribution to solidarity and levelling mechanisms referred to in Article 206.
   c) Establishing the mechanisms for collaboration between the Taxation Administration of Catalonia and the Taxation Administration of the State referred to in Article 204, and also the criteria for fiscal coordination and harmonization in accordance with the characteristics or the nature of the taxes ceded.
   d) Negotiating Catalonia's percentage of participation in the territorial distribution of European structural funds.
   e) Applying the updating mechanisms established by Article 208.
   f) Agreeing the valuation of services transferred by the State to the *Generalitat*.
   g) Establishing the necessary collaboration mechanisms between the *Generalitat* and the Administration of the State for appropriate exercise of the functions of economic-administrative revision referred to in Article 205.
   h) Agreeing the collaboration mechanisms between the *Generalitat* and the General Administration of the State for exercise of the land registry functions referred to in Article 221.
3. In accordance with the provisions of Article 209, the State - *Generalitat* Joint Economic and Fiscal Affairs Commission shall propose the co-operation measures necessary to ensure balance in the funding system established according to this Title when this may be altered by State or European Union legislative decisions.
4. The Catalan component of the State - *Generalitat* Joint Economic and Fiscal Affairs Commission is accountable to Parliament concerning compliance with the requirements of this Chapter.

Chapter II. The Budget of the Generalitat

Article 211. Powers of the *Generalitat*

The *Generalitat* has exclusive power over planning and regulating its finances.

Article 212. The Budget of the *Generalitat*

The *Generalitat* budget is annual, unique and includes all expenses and revenues of the *Generalitat*, and also those of the bodies, institutions and companies that are accountable to it. The Government is responsible for drawing up and executing the budget and Parliament is responsible for examining, amending, approving and controlling the budget. The Budget Act cannot create taxes, but can modify them if a substantive tax law so establishes.

Article 213. Resort to Debt

1. The *Generalitat* may have recourse to loans and may issue public debt to finance expenditure, within the limits set by the *Generalitat* itself and respecting the general principles and State regulations.
2. The securities issued shall, for all purposes and effects, be considered as public funds and shall enjoy the same benefits and conditions as those issued by the State.

Article 214. Budget Stability

The *Generalitat* is responsible for setting limits and conditions for achievement of the aim of budget stability, within the principles and regulations of the State and the European Union.

Article 215. The Assets of the *Generalitat*

1. The assets of the *Generalitat* consist of the goods and rights that it owns and those that it acquires by any legal title.
2. An Act of Parliament shall regulate the administration, protection and preservation of the assets of the *Generalitat*.

Article 216. Publicly-Owned Companies

The *Generalitat* may form publicly-owned companies to fulfil the functions that are within its powers, as established in the Acts of Parliament.

Chapter III. Local Government Finances

Article 217. Governing Principles

Local finances are governed by the principles of sufficiency of resources, equity, autonomy and fiscal responsibility. The *Generalitat* oversees compliance with these principles.

Article 218. Autonomy and Financial Powers

1. Local governments have autonomy over their budget and the use and application of their resources, including their share of the budgets of other Public Administration bodies, which they may dispose of freely in the exercise of their powers.
2. The *Generalitat* has power in matters of local financing, within the framework established by the Constitution and the State regulations. This power *may include the legislative capacity to establish and regulate local government taxes*[18] and includes the power to establish the criteria for distribution of shares of the budget of the *Generalitat*.
3. The local governments can regulate their own finances within the framework of the law. This includes the authority to set the quota or rate of local taxes, and also rebates and exemptions, within the limits established by law.
4. The local governments have the power, within the framework established by regulations governing the local taxation system, to manage and collect their taxes and implement inspections, without prejudice to their being able to delegate this function to the *Generalitat* and participate in the Taxation Agency of Catalonia.
5. The *Generalitat* is responsible for financial supervision of local governments, while respecting their autonomy as recognized by the Constitution.

Article 219. Sufficiency of Resources

1. The *Generalitat* shall establish a local co-operation fund for local governments. The fund, which is unconditional, shall be funded from the general taxation revenues of the *Generalitat* and shall be regulated by an Act of Parliament. Additionally, the *Generalitat* may establish specific financial cooperation programmes for specific matters.
2. Local government revenues which consist of shares in taxes and in unconditional State subsidies are received through the *Generalitat*, which shall distribute them in accordance with the law governing local finances in Catalonia for the passing of which a majority of three-fifth parts is required, and respecting the criteria of State legislation in this area. In the case of unconditional subventions, these criteria must enable Parliament to influence the distribution of resources with the aim of taking due account of the uniqueness of the institutional system of Catalonia referred to in Article 5 of this *Estatut*.
3. Local governments are guaranteed sufficient resources to be able to provide the services ownership or management of which is transferred or delegated to them. Any new attribution of powers shall be accompanied by allocation of the additional resources necessary for proper funding of these powers, in such a way that total and effective cost of the transferred services are taken into account.

18. The Constitutional Court has declared this phrase is unconstitutional and void (STC 31/2010, 28 June).

Compliance with this principle is a necessary condition for the transfer or delegation of a responsibility to take effect. To this end, various forms of funding may be established, including participation in the financial resources of the *Generalitat* or, as appropriate, of the State.

4. Distribution of resources originating from unconditional subsidies or from general participation in taxes shall be carried in accordance with the fiscal capacity and expenditure needs of local governments, while guaranteeing sufficiency in all cases.
5. Under no circumstances shall distribution of resources among local governments involve a reduction in the resources obtained by each, in terms of the criteria used in the financial accounting period before the requirements of this *Estatut* take effect.

Article 220. Local Finance Law

1. Parliament shall pass its own Local Finance Act to enact the principles and the provisions established by this Chapter.
2. Jurisdiction over local finances attributed by this Chapter to the *Generalitat* shall be exercised with due respect for local autonomy and with due consideration for the views of the Council of Local Governments, as established by Article 85.

Article 221. The Land Registry

The General Administration of the State and the *Generalitat* shall establish the necessary means of collaboration to ensure the participation of the *Generalitat* in the decisions and in the exchange of information required for the exercise of their powers. Similarly, consortial forms of management of the land registry shall be established between the State, the *Generalitat* and the municipalities, in keeping with the provisions of the State regulations and in a way that guarantees full availability of the databases to all administrations and the unity of the information.

Title VII. Reform of the Estatut

Article 222. Reform of the Titles That Do Not Affect Relations with the State

1. The reform of Titles I and II of the *Estatut* shall conform to the following procedures:
   a) The initiative for reform lies with the Parliament of Catalonia, on the proposal of one-fifth of its Members, and with the Government of the *Generalitat*. The city councils of Catalonia may propose exercise of the initiative to reform the *Estatut* to Parliament at the request of a minimum of 20% of the plenary city councils, representing at least 20% of the population. Reform may also be proposed by 300,000 accredited signatures of citizens of Catalonia entitled to vote.

Parliament shall regulate these two procedures to propose initiation of reform.

b) The approval of reform requires the favourable vote of two-thirds of the members of Parliament, submission to and consultation with the *Cortes Generales*, ratification by the *Cortes Generales* by means of an Organic Act, and approval in a referendum by the Catalan electorate.

c) If within thirty days of receipt of the request for consultation established in paragraph *b* above, the *Cortes Generales* declares itself affected by the reform, the reform shall follow the procedure established in Article 223.

d) Once the reform has been ratified by the *Cortes Generales*, the *Generalitat* shall submit it to a referendum.

2. If the proposed reform is not approved by Parliament or by the electorate, it cannot be re-submitted for debate and voting by Parliament until one year has elapsed.

Article 223. Reform of the Other Titles

1. The reform of the Titles of the *Estatut* not included in Article 222 shall conform to the following procedure:

a) The initiative for reform lies with Parliament, the Government of the *Generalitat* and the *Cortes Generales*. The city councils and individuals entitled to vote in elections to the Parliament may propose that Parliament exercise the initiative for reform under the terms established by Article 222.1.*a*.

b) Approval of the reform requires the favourable vote of two-thirds of the members of Parliament, approval by the *Cortes Generales* by means of an Organic Act and, finally, approval in a referendum by the electorate.

c) Once the proposed reform of the *Estatut* has been approved, Parliament shall refer it to the Congress of Deputies.

d) The proposed reform may be submitted to a vote of ratification by the Congress and Senate in accordance with the procedure established in the respective parliamentary Rules of Procedure. Parliament shall appoint a delegation to present the proposed reform of the *Estatut* to the Congress and the Senate. If the *Cortes Generales* ratify the proposed reform of the *Estatut*, the corresponding Organic Act is considered to have been passed.

e) If the procedure set out in paragraph *d* is not applied, a paritary joint commission shall be constituted, consisting of members of the competent commission of the Congress of Deputies and a delegation from Parliament proportionally representative of parliamentary groups, to formulate a joint proposal by common agreement in a period of two months, and applying the procedure established by the Rules of Procedure of the Congress of Deputies.

f) Presentation of the proposed reform of the *Estatut* to the Senate shall follow a similar procedure to that established in paragraph *e* above, in accordance with the terms of the Rules of Procedure of the Senate. In this case, the delegation from Parliament, adapted as appropriate, shall constitute, together with members of the competent commission of the Senate, a paritary joint commission to formulate a joint proposal by common agreement.

g) If the paritary joint commission is unable to formulate a joint proposal, the proposed reform of the *Estatut* shall be processed in accordance with the ordinary procedure established by the respective parliamentary Rules of Procedure.
h) Parliament may, by an absolute majority of its members, withdraw a proposal for reform that it has already approved at any time during presentation to the *Cortes Generales* and before this is definitively approved. Withdrawal of the proposed reform shall in no case involve application of the provisions of Section 2 below.
i) Approval of the reform by the *Cortes Generales* by means of an Organic Act shall include the authorization of the State for the *Generalitat* to call the referendum referred to in paragraph *b* above, within a period no longer than six months.

2. If the proposed reform is not approved by the Parliament, by the *Cortes Generales* or by the electorate, it may not be submitted again for debate and voting by the Parliament until one year has elapsed.

First Additional Provision. Appointment of Senators

1. The Parliament appoints Senators to represent the *Generalitat* in the Senate, under the terms established by a law approved by the absolute majority of the Plenary Assembly of Parliament in a final vote on the whole text. The appointment shall take place in a specially convened session and in proportion to the number of deputies of each parliamentary group.
2. Parliament shall, by means of a law approved by an absolute majority in a final vote on the whole text, bring the rules relating to the election of Senators into line with the constitutional reform of the Senate, in those aspects in which this is required.

Second Additional Provision. Agreements with the Government of the State

If the *Estatut* establishes that the position of the Government of the *Generalitat* is decisive for establishment of an agreement with the State Government and the latter rejects this position, the State Government shall justify its reasons before the *Generalitat* – State Bilateral Commission.

Third Additional Provision. Investment in Infrastructures

1. With the exception of the Inter-Territorial Compensation Fund, State investment in infrastructure in Catalonia, shall be equal to the relative participation of Catalonia's gross domestic product in the gross domestic product of the State for a period of seven years. These investments may also be employed in eliminating tolls or for construction of alternative expressway roads.
2. To this end, a committee representing the State, autonomous and local administrations shall be established.

Fourth Additional Provision. Funding Capacity

1. The State - *Generalitat* Joint Economic and Fiscal Affairs Commission shall prepare the necessary reports for evaluation of compliance with the provisions of Article 201.4.
2. The mechanisms to be eventually established to comply with the provisions of Article 201.4 may be applied gradually until the objective is reached.

Fifth Additional Provision. Review of the Special System of Aran

Within a period of four years after entry into force of this *Estatut*, there shall be a review and modification of the special system governing Aran to bring it into line, as necessary, with the provisions of this *Estatut*.

Sixth Additional Provision. Ordinary Administration

The *Generalitat* will become the ordinary Administration of the State in Catalonia as the executive functions performed by the Administration of the State through its territorial bodies in Catalonia are transferred to it, by means of the appropriate instruments.

Seventh Additional Provision. List of Ceded Taxes

The yield of the following taxes is ceded to the Autonomous Community of Catalonia:

a) Tax on personal income, partially (50 per cent).
b) Tax on patrimony.
c) Tax on successions and donations.
d) Tax on patrimonial transmissions and documented juridical acts.
e) Taxes on gambling.
f) Value Added Tax, partially (50 per cent).
g) Excise duty on beer, partially (58 per cent).
h) Excise duty on wine and fermented beverages, partially (58 per cent).
i) Excise duty on intermediate products, partially (58 per cent).
j) Excise duty on alcohol and derived beverages, partially (58 per cent).
k) Excise duty on hydrocarbons, partially (58 per cent).
l) Excise duty on tobacco products, partially (58 per cent).
m) Excise duty on electricity.
n) Excise duty on certain means of transport.
ñ) Tax on the retail sale of certain hydrocarbons[19].

19. The text of the first paragraph corresponds to the amendment made thereto under article 1 of State Law 16/2010, of the 16th July, on the system for the cession of State taxes to the Autonomous Community of Catalonia and for establishing the scope and conditions of such cession.

The content of this provision may be modified by means of an agreement between the Government of the *Generalitat* and the Government of the State, the latter presenting it as a Government bill. To this effect, modification of this provision is not considered to be a modification of the *Estatut*.

The scope and conditions of cession shall be established by the Joint Commission referred to in Article 210 which, in all cases, shall link this cession to the income in Catalonia. The Government shall process the Commission's accord as a Government bill.

Eighth Additional Provision. Cession of the Tax on Personal Income

The first Government bill on cession of taxes to be passed after the entry into force of this *Estatut* shall, in application of the previous provision, provide for cession of 50% of revenues from tax on personal income.

The ceded revenue from personal income tax corresponding to taxable persons whose normal residence is in Catalonia is considered to be produced in the territory of the autonomous community of Catalonia.

Similarly, an increase in the legislative powers of the community over the aforementioned tax shall be proposed.

Ninth Additional Provision. Cession of the Tax on Hydrocarbons, the Tax on Tobacco Products, the Tax on Alcohol and Derived Beverages, the Tax on Beer, the Tax on Wine and Fermented Beverages and the Tax on Intermediate Products

The first Government Bill on cession of taxes to be passed after the entry into force of this *Estatut* shall, in application of the seventh additional provision, provide for cession of 58% of the revenue from the following taxes: Tax on hydrocarbons, Tax on tobacco products, Tax on alcohol and derived beverages, Tax on beer, Tax on wine and fermented beverages, Tax on intermediate products. The attribution to the autonomous community of Catalonia shall be determined by the corresponding indices in each case.

Tenth Additional Provision. Cession of Value Added Tax

The first Government Bill on cession of taxes to be passed after the entry into force of this *Estatut* shall, in application of the seventh additional provision, provide for cession of 50% of the revenue from Value Added Tax. The attribution to the autonomous community of Catalonia shall be determined by consumption in its territory.

Eleventh Additional Provision. Regulatory Power

In the framework of the powers and the regulations of the European Union, the General Administration of the State shall cede regulatory powers over Value Added Tax in retail transactions the recipients of which are not classified as entrepreneurs or professionals and in retail taxes on products subject to special manufacturing taxes.

Twelfth Additional Provision. Harmonic Interpretation

The provisions of the Organic Act referred to in Article 157.3 of the Constitution and the provisions of this Estatut shall be interpreted harmonically.

Thirteenth Additional Provision. Catalonia's Own Collections and Collections Shared with Other Territories

Catalonia's own collections in the Archives of the Kingdom of Aragon and in the Royal Archives of Barcelona shall be integrated into the Catalan archive system. For effective management of the other collections held in common with other territories of the Kingdom of Aragon, the *Generalitat* shall collaborate with the Board of Archives of the Kingdom of Aragon, with the other autonomous communities with which it shares collections, and with the State, by means of mechanisms to be established by mutual agreement.

Fourteenth Additional Provision. Gaming and Betting

The provisions of Article 141.2 are not applicable to modification of the modalities of gaming and betting attributed, for social ends, to State-level organizations of a social and non-profit nature, in accordance with the provisions of the regulations applicable to said organizations.

Fifteenth Additional Provision. Transparency

In compliance with the principle of transparency, the State shall publish the provincial settlement of the various public expenditure programmes in Catalonia.

First Transitory Provision. Adaptation of the Laws and Rules of Legal Rank

1. Acts of Parliament and Government rules of legal rank that are valid when this *Estatut* enters into force and which might be incompatible with the rights recognized by Title I remain in effect for a maximum period of two years, during which time they shall be adapted to the regulation established by this *Estatut*.
2. Parliamentary groups, members of Parliament, the Government and the Ombudsman may, in the period established by Section 1 above, request a ruling from the Statutory Rights Council, under the terms established by law, in regard to compatibility with the *Estatut* of Acts of Parliament or of rules of legal rank made by the Government before the *Estatut* entered into force. The ruling is not binding and recommendations may be made to Parliament or to the Government to amend or repeal rules that are considered incompatible.

Second Transitory Provision. Validity of Previous Transitory Provisions

Transitory Provisions Three, Four and Six of Organic Act 4/1979 of the 18th December, on the Statute of Autonomy of Catalonia, maintain, where appropriate, their validity as transitory regulations.

Repeal Provision

Organic Act 4/1979, of the 18th December, on the Statute of Autonomy of Catalonia is hereby repealed.

First Final Provision. Application of the Precepts of Title VI

1. The State - *Generalitat* Joint Economic and Fiscal Affairs Commission shall, within two years of entry into force of this *Estatut*, specify the application of the precepts of Title VI.
2. The precepts of Title VI may be applied gradually in the light of their financial viability. In any case, application shall be fully effective within five years of the entry into force of this *Estatut*.

Second Final Provision. The Taxation Agency of Catalonia

The Taxation Agency of Catalonia, referred to in Article 204, shall be established by an Act of Parliament, within one year of entry into force of this *Estatut*. Until such time as the Taxation Agency of Catalonia is constituted, the functions corresponding to it in application of this *Estatut* shall be exercised by the bodies exercising them until then.

Third Final Provision. Period for Establishing the State - *Generalitat* Joint Economic and Fiscal Affairs Commission

The State - *Generalitat* Joint Economic and Fiscal Affairs Commission, provided for in Article 210, shall be created within six months of the entry into force of this *Estatut*. Until such time as it is established, the State - *Generalitat* Joint Valuations Commission shall assume its powers. The establishment of the State - *Generalitat* Joint Economic and Fiscal Affairs Commission implies the immediate extinction of the State - *Generalitat* Joint Valuations Commission.

Fourth Final Provision. List of Economic and Financial Entities

The State - *Generalitat* Joint Economic and Fiscal Affairs Commission shall, within six months of the entry into force of this *Estatut*, determine the list of those entities referred to in Article 182.

§2. Statute of Autonomy of Extremadura

Organic Act, 1/2011, 29 January, on the reform of the Statute of Autonomy of the Autonomous Community of Extremadura

The political, social and institutional reality of the constitution of Extremadura resulted in the creation of the Autonomous Community, implemented by the adoption of the Statute by Organic Act 1/1983, 25 February, has been intense and unequivocally has been altered greatly by the work of administrative decentralization of the 1978 Constitution, and establishment of the exercise of the competences of the Autonomous Community Government.

The Organic Act is not only a legal norm that governs the instruments of our Autonomous Community Government, but also a political, and social norm, that enables us to note our challenges as a community, that must be characteristic of this new society, and of a new era, the twenty-first century, and although the successive reforms of 1991, 1994 and 1999 helped specifically to update that original Statute it is now necessary to undertake a more fundamental and complete reform that allows it to be an effective instrument of social and political cohesion.

This reform reorders the traditional materials of the Statute and incorporates improvements dictated by the new trends of legislative technique, but chooses not to establish a set of differential rights and duties of the people/citizens of Extremadura, reflecting the new political goals of the public authorities in line with social changes, expands the list of competences taking into account the jurisprudential details, reinforces the institutions of self-governing Region and makes other relevant statutory changes that deepen mechanisms of vertical and horizontal cooperation, reflects and orders the exterior activity of the region, recognizes and reinforces the political and financial autonomy of local authorities, is exigent in matters of the financial relationships with the State Treasury and introduces guarantees for the successive reforms of the statute itself.

Consequently, in accordance with the provisions of Articles 62 and 63 of this Statute, the people of Extremadura represented by the Assembly propose to Parliament for its approval by Organic Act the reform of the Statute of Autonomy of Extremadura.Amending the Statute of Autonomy of Extremadura, approved by Organic Act 1/1983, 25 February, as amended by Organic Act 5/1991, 13 March, by Organic Act 8/1994, 24 March, and Organic Act 12/1999, 6 May, as follows:

Preamble

In the two great valleys of the Tagus and the Guadiana, from the prehistoric caves to technology centres, the chronicle of a will to feel, think, be and act in the world has been silently written. One task that the people of Extremadura have been forging, with or without awareness of doing so. The people of Extremadura face an ungenerous history of those who wrote so many of its lines in the first person, but did not give us the weight of a mandatory identity or a limited self-awareness or burden of a history that is imposed on us as an unfulfilled duty. And that makes our will present in the source and origin of our desire for Regional Self-Government.

We are Extremadura because we want to be its citizens of today, regardless of what our ancestors thought or felt, and because the inclusive project of Spain recognizes this and encourages us and the other peoples to be brothers. We are not tied to the past, nor do we owe it submission, it is only the varied mosaic of our history. And however hard it may have been, it was ordered to bring us to this hopeful present. We are not tied to the past; our nostalgia is for the future which is what we truly feel.

Extremadura has been as such in all the endeavours of modern Spanish politics, from the dawn of constitutionalism in Cadiz. But the foundation on which we build the present and future Extremadura is the recovery of democracy, with the 1978

Constitution. A people, yes, but a people of free and equal citizens. That is the foundation on which the Statute of Autonomy of 1983 embodies contemporaneously

The desire for Regional Self-Government of the people of Extremadura, the inalienable dignity of citizens who decide for themselves the challenge proposed by the Constitution and who rebel against a long history of dependence and political insignificance.

This text is the reference framework of our coexistence and the legal expression of our identity as a people, fully compatible with the unquestionable unity of a Spain that we love and to which we belong. It is the instrument to continue advancing as a people with roots, its own characteristics, history and defined personality. We can raise our voices and look with satisfaction that the path we have walked has made us greater without belittling anyone. Stone by stone, step by step, Extremadura has managed to be close and recognizable, able to defend its present and to fight for a future that belongs to us, able to demand its rights with no other merit than that which reason imposes. It is a reality that is emerging in the common horizon of Spain's solidarity, aimed at overcoming the atavisms of borders and seeks, in respect for uniqueness, equality in higher values of coexistence, peace, justice and freedom. All the people of Extremadura, those living within its territory and those of the Diaspora, have learned to reach a goal that could be glimpsed far off. Regional Self-Government has placed in our hands the direction of the collective destiny of the region and, with the conviction that we have the expertise to conduct this project, we are the present generations who should direct it to new heights, leaving to the future a more prosperous and freer Extremadura. And a quarter of a century of fruitful coexistence supports the success of the enterprise and encourages us to travel further on that road, also renewing the legal framework of our public life.

From the religious and American Guadalupe to the civic and European Yuste an arc of renewed collective identity is traced that is intended to embrace all traditions and sensitivities, roots and competences, all perspectives and aspirations of the new Extremadura.

An Extremadura definitively settled but more open to the world. An Extremadura comfortable and active in the project of the Spanish nation. An Extremadura that is the border of Europe and America. An Extremadura that shows solidarity with every corner of the planet. An Extremadura that finally is one.

Preliminary Title

Chapter I. General provisions

Article 1. The Autonomous Community of Extremadura

1. Extremadura, as an expression of its historical regional identity and by the Democratic will of the people of Extremadura constitutes itself into an Autonomous Community, within the unity of the Spanish nation, according to the Constitution and this Statute, which is its basic institutional Act.
2. The Autonomous Community of Extremadura, through its institutions, assumes the exercise of regional self-Government, the defence of its own identity and values, such as improving and promoting the welfare of Extremadura.

3. The competences of the Autonomous Community of Extremadura emanate from the people, from the Constitution and this present Statute.
4. There are differentiated elements of Extremadura, and this must guide the actions of the public authorities, the vitality of its recent collective identity, the quality of its environment and cultural heritage, the dominance of the countryside, its projection in Portugal and Latin America, the historical conditions of its socio-economy and the low population density and dispersion, defined by the relative difficulty of access to services and general facilities. The public authorities shall take the necessary measures to prevent such differences from resulting in inequalities as against the Spanish State and to correct existing ones.

Article 2. Territory

1. The territory of Extremadura, to which its competences extend, is the municipalities included within the present boundaries of the provinces of Badajoz and Cáceres.
2. However, the norms, provisions and acts of the institutions of Extremadura may have extraterritorial effects when necessary for the full exercise of such of their competences whose nature so requires.

Article 3. The People of Extremadura

1. For the purposes of this Statute, Spanish citizens have the political status of the people of Extremadura, which according to the general laws of the State, have their administrative residence in any of the towns of Extremadura.
2. Likewise, Spanish residents living abroad who have had their final administrative residence in Extremadura and can prove this condition in the diplomatic representation are people of Extremadura. Their descendants registered as Spanish will enjoy that status if they so request in the manner determined by a State law.
3. Extremaduran communities settled outside Extremadura in accordance with the provisions of the Act, may apply for recognition of Extremaduran identity,understood as the right to collaborate and share social and cultural life of the people of Extremadura and without, in any case implying the granting of political rights. The Autonomous Community may request the Spanish State for the appropriate celebration of international treaties or agreements with the States in which there are such communities.

Article 4. Symbols

1. The Extremadura flag consists of 3 equal horizontal stripes, green at the top, white in the centre and black at the bottom.
2. The coat of arms and anthem of Extremadura shall be regulated by law in the Assembly approved by a majority of two thirds of the deputies.
3. Extremadura Day is on 8 September.

4. The protection of the symbols of Extremadura shall correspond to the other State symbols, according to law.

Article 5. Capital

The capital of Extremadura is the city of Merida, the seat of the Assembly, the Presidency and the Regional Government.

Chapter II. Rights, Duties and Guiding Principles

Article 6. Rights and Duties of the People of Extremadura

1. The fundamental rights of Extremadura are those established in the Constitution. In addition, they may exercise against those public authorities of Extremadura other rights contained in this Statute or legislation, especially the right to participate in public affairs, directly or through representatives and by petition.
2. The duties of the people of Extremadura are those stipulated in the Constitution and other legislation in order to contribute to the collective well-being.

Article 7. Guiding Principles of Public Authorities of Extremadura

The Autonomous authorities shall:

1. Exercise their competences with the primary purposes of promoting conditions of social, political, cultural or economic order, for the freedom and equality of the people of Extremadura, both among themselves and with the rest of the Spanish people, so that they are real and effective, removing obstacles that prevent or hinder their fulfilment, and facilitate the participation of all in the political, economic, cultural and social life of Extremadura, in a context of freedom, justice and solidarity.
2. Promote the values of Extremadura and strength its identity through research, development and dissemination of social, historical, linguistic and cultural traits of Extremadura in all its variety and extent, with special attention to the rich heritage of traditional ways of life of the towns and people, in an inalienable framework of full rural social and economic development.
3. Actively boost territorial equity and social cohesion in its internal policies and in its relations with other Autonomous communities, with the general institutions of the State and Europe. Equally, it shall encourage population growth in the community support the returning of migrants and fight against depopulation in rural areas.
4. Promote consultation and social dialogue with trade unions and employers as instruments required in designing and implementing its policies of cohesion and development.
5. Actively adopt all types of policies to achieve full employment, particularly through measures to promote productive investment and adjust the supply and demand for labour within a framework of corporate social responsibility.

6. Stimulate scientific and technical research, the incorporation of innovative process by economic actors, access to new technologies by businesses and citizens and legal and technical mechanisms that facilitate free access of all the knowledge and culture.
7. Pursue a model of sustainable development and care for the preservation and improvement of environmental quality and biodiversity of the region, with special attention to its characteristic ecosystems such as pastures. Likewise, its policies shall contribute proportionately to the objectives of international agreements in the fight against climate change.
8. Ensure rational water use and its fair distribution among citizens who need it, according to the constitutional framework of competences and the priorities established by law, without impairing the quality of life of the people of Extremadura, the economic development of Extremadura confirmed by studies to ensure the current and future demands for all uses and land use, and without prejudice to compensation in such event.
9. Encourage measures to save energy, its efficient use and support renewable energy generation. Strictly to ensure the return to the community of the benefits of energy exports outside its territory.
10. Consider as an essential aim the dissemination of mass culture in its broadest sense and equal access to information, property and cultural services to the people of Extremadura. For this, Extremadura considers particularly useful instruments for mastering other languages, the management of information technology and communication, extension of open source operating systems and the use of free licences for copying and distribution. It shall ensure the conservation of goods of cultural, historical and artistic heritage.
11. Assume as an essential aspiration the strictest guarantees of the rights to health, education and public protection in the event of dependence.
12. Consider as an essential aim to inform all Autonomous Community policies and institutional practices of the full and effective equality of women in all areas of public, family, social, occupational, economic and cultural life. Also, to remove the obstacles that prevent or hinder real and effective equality through affirmative action as may be necessary.
13. Promote policies to ensure respect for sexual orientation and gender identity of all persons.
14. Ensure the special protection of those sectors of the population with special needs of any kind. Effective equality of the people of Extremadura passes inalienably to adopting specific policies for children, the elderly and any other social sector with specific needs.
15. Promote autonomy, equal opportunities, social integration and employment of people with disabilities, with particular attention to their active contribution to the whole society, to the teaching and the use of Spanish sign language and the removal of physical barriers.
16. Ensure the existence of channels for the expression of the views of young people, of the effectiveness of their systems and associations and promote their entrepreneurial capabilities, assume their participation in public life as an essential for the present and future development of the region. Also, ensure their professional orientation, family emancipation and access to housing.

17. The integration of immigrants living in Extremadura is a common goal of Autonomous Community public policy and will be guided by the principles of mutual knowledge, respect for differences, equality of rights and duties, within the framework of constitutional principles and values.
18. Ensure that the Autonomous Community of Extremadura is part of the process of European integration, through the mechanisms of participation in the institutions of the Union established by treaties, national laws or national or European agreements, through its intervention in European associations of regions and through the internal activities of dissemination of European policies and values.
19. Foster all forms of relationships with Portugal, both institutional and societal under the principles of loyalty, respect for the respective identity, solidarity and mutual benefit. Also, encourage relations of any nature with the peoples and institutions of the Latin American community of nations.
20. Understood as a collective ethical demand, make an active contribution of the Autonomous Community society and its institutions to peace and socio-political development and culture of all nations and peoples of the world, through its own actions of cooperation to development and its participation in the actions of other Spanish or international bodies.

Title I. The Competences of the Autonomous Community of Extremadura

Article 8. General Provisions

1. The Autonomous Community of Extremadura has competence over matters identified in the following Articles. Those competences include the functions that come in each case, without prejudice to any that may belong to the State under its own competence as set out in the Constitution.
2. It also assumes the responsibilities as assigned, delegated or transferred by the State, in accordance with the provisions of the Constitution, and any whatsoever that may fall under this, with the other titles of this Statute and with the rest of the legal system.
3. In exercising its competences the Autonomous Community may establish own policies.

Article 9. Exclusive Competences

1. The Autonomous Community of Extremadura has exclusive jurisdiction over the following matters:
   1. Creation, organization and functioning of legal system and institutions, as well as organizing its own administration and instrumental bodies on which it depends.
   2. Administration of justice, in accordance with the provisions of Title III of this Statute.
   3. Its own territorial organization of the Autonomous Community and local Regional Government in the terms of Title IV of this Statute.

4. Conservation, protection and defence of the local by-laws and institutions of customary law.
5. Specialties of administrative procedure. Procedural rules derived from its own law. Regulation of administrative remedy in applying the law of Extremadura against rating from property, commercial and property records.
6. Border and international cooperation for development, in coordination with the State.
7. Promoting social and economic development of the Autonomous Community within the aims of national economic policy.
8. Management/organization of the Treasury of the Autonomous Community.
9. Statistics for the purposes of the Autonomous Community.
10. Savings banks and cooperative credit institutions, as part of the overall management of the economy and credit. Organization and operation of mutual provident societies.
11. Chambers of commerce and industry and other public corporations representing economic and professional interests. Professional Associations and exercise of qualified professions.
12. Agriculture, livestock and pastures. Agribusiness.
13. Creation and control of designations of origin and other quality references.
14. Hunting and game preserves. River and lake fishing. Aquaculture.
15. Industry, except as governed by general legislation regarding safety, health, defence, mining and hydrocarbons.
16. Internal trade within the single market and under commercial law. Regulatory and administrative control of commercial activities and facilities, especially supermarkets. Non-international fairs and markets. Authorization for the establishment of centres of procurement of goods and stock exchanges in the territory of Extremadura.
17. Organization, operation and governance of cooperatives and assimilated bodies. The promotion of all forms of social economy.
18. Consumption. Regulation of prevention, protection and defence measures of users and consumers, of their rights and of mediation organs and procedures. Fight against fraud.
19. Tourism. Management, planning, and internal and external information and promotion. Regulation of the rights and obligations of tourist users and providers. Regulation and classification of tourist and catering businesses and establishments.
20. Crafts.
21. Commercial and institutional advertising.
22. Research, development and scientific and technical innovation, in coordination with the State. Coordination of research activities financed with public funds from the Self-regulating community. Innovation and technological development.
23. Regime of the new technologies of the information society and communication.
24. Health and public health, in terms of organization, internal functioning, coordination and control of health centres, services and establishments in

the Community. Participation in the planning and coordination of health system. Promoting health and biomedical research.

25. Pharmaceutical Management.
26. Childhood and youth. Protection and guardianship of minors.
27. Social action. In particular, the promotion and protection of the elderly and the prevention, care and social integration of groups affected by any type of disability, dependency or any other circumstances determining social exclusion. Financial assistance in addition to social security.
28. Policies of integration and social, cultural, economic and occupational participation of immigrants, in collaboration with the State, and participation in State immigration policies.
29. Gender equality policies, in particular the adoption of norms and implementation of plans for the establishment of affirmative action to eradicate gender inequalities.
30. Protection of the family and family mediation instruments.
31. Planning and housing. Norms on quality and technological innovation in buildings and conservation of traditional urban heritage.
32. Territorial Planning.
33. Norms and policies additional and complementary to those of the State in environmental protection and the fight against climate change. Regulating of its own protected natural areas and taking measures for their protection and enhancement in value. Service, maintenance and improvement of pastures.
34. Sustainable Rural Development. Special treatment for mountain areas.
35. Meteorological Service of the Autonomous Community.
36. Systemization, planning and management of the waters which run entirely within the territory of Extremadura, and their use and exploitation, including their concession. Planning, construction and operation of hydraulic works and infrastructure and irrigation channels that are not catalogued as of general interest by the State or that affect other Autonomous communities. Mineral and thermal waters. Participation in the manner determined by State law in managing the waters within intercommunity basins that flow through the territory of Extremadura.
37. Facilities for the production, storage, distribution and transportation of energies of whatever kind within its territory, including harnessing electricity when doing so does not affect other Autonomous communities. Additional norms guaranteeing the quality of the supply and participation in state agencies regulating the energy sector, in the terms established by State legislation.
38. Public works and infrastructure of interest to the Autonomous Community that are not classified as of general interest to the State and that do not affect other Autonomous communities and the participation in planning and, where appropriate, in the implementation and management of infrastructure of general interest in Extremadura, in the terms established by the State legislation.
39. Railways, highways and roads whose routes lie exclusively within the territory of the Autonomous Community and in the same area land and river

transport, regardless of the ownership of the infrastructure. Transportation, logistics and distribution centres located in Extremadura. Airports, heliports, marinas and other transport infrastructures not of general interest. Participation in planning and, where appropriate, implementation and management of infrastructure of general interest in the Autonomous Community, in the terms established by State law.

40. Monitoring and protection of its buildings and facilities.
41. Coordination and other competences under the relevant Organic Act on the local police force.
42. Civil Defence and Emergencies.
43. Entertainment and recreation. General organization of the sector and regime of administrative intervention and control of public entertainment.
44. Casinos and gambling, including by electronic means where the activity takes place exclusively in Extremadura.
45. Associations and foundations of all types that primarily develop their functions in Extremadura. Promotion of volunteering.
46. Sport. Promotion, regulation and planning of activities and sporting facilities and other leisure activities.
47. Culture in all its manifestations. Cultural and Historical Heritage of interest to the Autonomous Community. Folklore, festivals and traditions. Protection of local linguistic modalities. Scientific and cultural academies of Extremadura.
48. Museums, archives, libraries and other cultural centres and deposit of interest to the Autonomous Community not belonging to the State. Conservatories of Music and Dance, performing arts centres and the fine arts.
49. Encouragement, protection and promotion of artistic and literary production and creations by whatever means they are manifest and the medium in which they are communicated or contained, especially the publication of books and periodicals and audiovisual productions, films and musical performances as well as the regulation and inspection of showrooms.
50. Regime and call for non-binding public consultations different from referendums.

2. In these areas, where the legislative function, regulatory authority and in exercise of the executive function belongs to the Autonomous Community, the adoption of all measures, decisions and acts shall proceed.

Article 10. Competences of Policy Development and Implementation

1. The Autonomous Community of Extremadura has competences of policy development and implementation in the following areas:
   1. Legal system of its Public Administrations sector, of public procurement, concessions and publicly-owned property, the liability of the Administration in accordance with the general system of responsibility of public administrations and the statutory regime of public employees.
   2. Environment. Regulation and protection of flora, fauna and biodiversity. Prevention and correction of waste generation and dumps, and noise, air, light, soil and subsoil pollution. Regulation of water supply, sanitation and

purification. Mountains, woodlands, forestry and rights of way for livestock.

3. Management of credit, banking, insurance, mutual benefit societies, managing bodies of pension funds and plans.
4. Education and instruction in its entirety, at all levels, degrees, modalities and specialties. In particular the system, organization and control of schools, teaching staff, subjects of Autonomous Community interest, complementary activities and scholarship funds.
5. Public and private universities. In particular, programming and creation of public universities and the authorization of private ones, final approval of their statutes and performance standards, access procedures, staff emoluments and regulation of degrees, as well as financing of public universities and the system of control, supervision and monitoring of their accounts.
6. Social Security, with the exception of the rules that shape its economic regime and without prejudice to what is stipulated in the following Article.
7. Regime of mining and energy and radioactive facilities of the second and third categories.
8. Newspapers, radio and television and other media. Creation, regulation and maintenance of public social media, whose activity will be governed by the principles of independence, pluralism, neutrality, objectivity and public service.
9. Health and public health. Agricultural and animal health. Food safety.

2. In these areas, it is the duty of the Autonomous Community to develop, implement and where necessary, supplement the regulations of the State, through its own development legislation, regulatory competences and executive function.

Article 11. Competences of Implementation

1. The Autonomous Community of Extremadura has executive competences in the following matters:
   1. The prison system.
   2. Appointment of notaries, and commercial and property registrars and other persons authorized to authenticate documents. Participation in demarcating the boundaries of notaries and commercial and property registries. Civil Registry.
   3. Intellectual and industrial property.
   4. Weights and measures. Assay of metals.
   5. International fairs held in Extremadura.
   6. Pharmaceutical products.
   7. Work and labour relations, including public inspection, which shall be coordinated with the State. Active employment policies, labour mediation, health and safety at work, training for employment and, where appropriate, the management of funds for the unemployed.
   8. Management of the economic regime of social security and of the services that make up the system, with full respect for the principles of equity and economic unity and financial solidarity.

9. Airports, heliports and other transport infrastructure of general interest whose management is not reserved to the general State administration.
10. Museums, archives, libraries and other collections of similar nature owned by the State whose management is not reserved to the State.
11. Management of national and, where appropriate, the international parks in the territory of Extremadura, in the framework of the agreements signed by the State.
12. Antitrust legislation in the Extremadura market.
13. Fixing, in collaboration with the State, the needs of the labour market to determine the granting of work permits to foreigners.

2. In these areas the Autonomous Community has organizational regulatory power and the adoption of plans, programmes, measures, decisions and actions.

Article 12. Development and Implementation of Supranational Laws

1. The development, and where appropriate, the implementation of European Union legislation in the material fields of Autonomous competence are functions of the Autonomous Community of Extremadura.
2. The Autonomous Community shall likewise execute the international treaties and conventions ratified by the Kingdom of Spain in matters affecting its competence.

Article 13. Other Competences Associated with Competences

1. In the scope of its competences and in addition to those expressly provided, the Autonomous Community has all those inherent functions in their full exercise and, in particular, the management of special demand affected and the declaration of public utility or social interest of expropriations and determining assumptions, causes and conditions of the exercise of such power, the determination of objective criteria of evaluation and the establishment of bodies to implement them and set a just valuation.
2. In all matters within its competence the Autonomous Community shall exercise the competence of police activities, public service and promotion, being able to regulate the granting awarding and monitoring of subsidies from its own funds and, where appropriate, to those from other public bodies.
3. The Autonomous Community will participate in the exercise of State competences that determine the Autonomous Community's competences or affect natural resources or Autonomous Community's wealth

Article 14. Homogeneity of Competences

The statutory institutions shall ensure that the catalogue of competences of Extremadura be updated in terms of homogeneity with all other Autonomous communities. To this end, it shall take initiatives that lead to the reform of this Statute or to petition the State to expand Autonomous Community's competences by adoption of the relevant laws.

Title II. The Institutions of Extremadura

Article 15. Institutions of Regional Self-government and Other Statutory Bodies

1. The Autonomous Community shall exercise its competences through the Assembly, the President and the Autonomous Community Government of Extremadura.
2. The Advisory Council, the Autonomous Community Government of Auditors, the Economic and Social Council and the Representative of the Common are statutory bodies, endowed with organic, functional and budgetary autonomy.
3. The institutions of the Community shall exercise their functions and competences in compliance with the law and in accordance with the principles of institutional loyalty, solidarity, collaboration, coordination, cooperation and mutual assistance among themselves and with all the public competences.

Chapter I. Assembly of Extremadura

Article 16. Character and Competences

1. The Assembly, which represents the people of Extremadura, is elected for four years, is inviolable and shall not be dissolved except in the cases provided for in this Statute. It enjoys regulatory, budgetary, administrative and disciplinary autonomy in the terms of this Statute.
2. The Assembly of Extremadura shall:
   a) Exercise the reform initiatives of the Constitution and of this Statute.
   b) Exercise the legislative power of the Autonomous Community.
   c) Approve the budget of the Autonomous Community and authorize the use of public credit, pursuant to Title VI of this Statute.
   d) Develop its regulations, the approval and modification of which shall require an absolute majority of the House in a final vote on the entire project.
   e) Approve the statute of the Staff of the Assembly under the general scheme of public employees of the Autonomous Community.
   f) Control the exercise of legislative delegations granted to the Autonomous Community Government and validate its decree-laws.
   g) Request the Autonomous Community Government of the State to adopt bills or send proposals of laws to the Congress of Deputies, according to Article 87.2 of the Constitution.
   h) Promote and control the action of the President and the Autonomous Community Government of Extremadura, and where appropriate, demand its political responsibility in the terms provided in this Statute.
   i) Control the financial management of the Autonomous Community Income Tax Authority and examine its own accounts and those of other institutions, organizations, companies and public bodies including universities, subject to review by the appropriate Council of Auditors or, where appropriate, the State Court of Auditors.

j) To exercise control over the social media dependent on the Autonomous Community.
k) Review the service management Conventions and authorize the signing of cooperation agreements with other Autonomous Communities, in terms of Articles 65 and 66 of this Statute.
l) To appoint from among the members of the Assembly the senators referred to in Article 69.5 of the Constitution after the elections of the Autonomous Community according to the proportional representation of parliamentary groups and at their proposal. The appointed deputies may choose to keep their seats in the Assembly of the Autonomous Community or resign from the same, regardless of their condition as Senators linked to the Assembly of Autonomous Community.
m) Propose appointments to the high state institutions or Autonomous Community within its competence.
n) Lodge appeals of unconstitutionality and other procedures within the Constitutional Court's jurisdiction to which it is entitled, or to appear as a party in them, in the best interests of the Autonomous Community.
o) Exercise any other power or function that is derived from the Constitution, this Statute and the legal system.

Article 17. Elections

1. The deputies of the Assembly of Extremadura, the maximum number of which is 65, will be elected by universal, free, equal, direct and secret suffrage, according to criteria of proportional representation.
2. Elections shall be convened by order of the President of the Autonomous Community and voters and citizens in full use of their rights will be eligible, given the political status of Extremadura.
3. The province is the constituency. The law will distribute the number of Assembly deputies assigned to the provinces allocating an initial minimum representation in each constituency distributing the rest in proportion to population.
4. The electoral law, which shall be approved by a majority of three-fifths of the deputies of the Assembly, shall regulate the call of elections, the procedure and electoral systems; the formula for allocating seats, subsidies, election expenses and control, and a specific set of rule of ineligibility and incompatibility of candidates and deputies. In any case, applications must be made with criteria of gender equality.
5. The inaugural meeting of the elected assembly shall be convened by the retiring President within fifteen days after the elections.

Article 18. Statute of the Members of the Assembly

1. Members of the Assembly, whose rights and duties are set out in the Regulations hereunder, represent the entire region and shall not be subject to imperative mandate.

2. The Members of the Assembly have inviolability for votes and opinions expressed in the exercise of office even after leaving office. During tenure, they may not be arrested or detained in the territory of the Community except for flagrant offences, the Court of Justice of Extremadura deciding, in any case, on the arraignment, detention, prison and trial. Outside the territory of the Autonomous Community, criminal responsibility is enforceable in the same terms as that of the Criminal Division of the Supreme Court.
3. Members must be legally resident in Extremadura.
4. Without prejudice to other causes, Members cease after four years of their election or the date of official publication of the decree calling the election, both in the case of early dissolution as the termination of the legislature. However, members of the Permanent Deputation continue in the exercise of their functions until the constitution of the new Assembly.

Article 19. Organs

1. The Assembly shall elect from among its members the President, the Table/Council and the Permanent Deputation, whose legal systems/Standing Orders and election procedures shall be determined in those Orders.
2. The Assembly of Extremadura is represented by its President, who heads the sessions thereof, maintains its competence, executes its budget section taking into account Its Council, performs the administrative and police competences in its headquarters and carries out those other functions entrusted to it by the Statute, the Standing Orders or the Law.
3. The Council of the Assembly, which is composed of the President, Vice-Presidents, Secretaries of the House, in the number established by the Standing Orders, is the interior body and exercises the same functions attributed to it by the Standing Orders.
4. The Permanent Council shall substitute/replace the Plenary Assembly between regular ordinary sessions and assume all the functions of the Assembly when it has been dissolved early or has exhausted the legislature until the constitution of the new House.

Article 20. Parliamentary Groups

The Standing Orders shall require a minimum number of members to constitute parliamentary groups, regulate their operation in the activities in the Assembly and determine the duties of the Council of Spokesmen. The groups in the Assembly shall form part of all Commissions in proportion to the number of their members.

Article 21. Operating System

1. The Standing Orders shall regulate the operating system, periods and plenary sessions and Commissions in which the Assembly of Extremadura is organized.

2. Agreements are valid only in plenary sessions and committees when adopted in meetings convened according to regulations, attended by the majority of its members and are approved by a simple majority of the votes cast, except in cases where the statute or law shall require a qualified majority.
3. A law shall regulate the attendance of officials and public employees of Extremadura to report, at the request of the Assembly, on matters of interest to the Autonomous Community, and its citizens, before Parliamentary Research Committees, as well as the sanctions for noncompliance.

Article 22. Legislative Power

1. The legislative power of the Autonomous Community lies in the plenary Assembly, which may be delegated to the Committees on the terms and conditions set by the Standing Orders of the House, except in cases where the statute requires a qualified majority or on finance laws.
2. With the same limitations, the Plenary Assembly may expressly delegate to the Autonomous Community Government of Extremadura to issue rules with the force of law, called legislative decrees on specific matters and with the goals, objectives, scope, prohibitions, deadlines and forms laid down in Articles 82 and 83 of the Constitution.
3. Subject to additional parliamentary controls that may be established in the law on delegation, articulated or consolidated texts will be submitted prior to their entry into force, to a full vote in single reading procedure in the Assembly.

Article 23. Legislative Initiative

1. Deputies and the parliamentary groups of the Assembly hold the legislative initiative under the terms established by the Standing Orders of the House.
2. The Autonomous Community Government of Extremadura also has this initiative, and may, moreover, oppose the processing of legislative initiatives that affect a legislative delegation in force or might result in a reduction of income or increased expenditure in the current budgetary year.
3. Subject to the conditions and population numbers determined in a law passed by absolute majority, local entities may also submit legislative initiatives to the Assembly in matters within the Autonomous Community's competence.
4. The popular legislative initiative may be exercised in matters in which the Autonomous Community exercises competences, with the constitutional limitations provided for, in the terms determined by an Act of the Assembly of Extremadura approved by an absolute majority. In any case, the legislative initiatives that arise in this way must be supported by at least 45,000 signatures from the census accredited for elections to the Assembly.

Chapter II. The President of Extremadura

Article 24. Character and Functions

1. The President is the highest representative of the Autonomous Community, and exercises ordinary representation of the State therein and presides over the Autonomous Community Government of Extremadura.
2. A law will regulate the status of the President, the exercise regime of his functions and his relationships, and those of the Autonomous Community Government of Extremadura with the Assembly.

Article 25 Investiture

1. The President is elected by the Assembly of Extremadura from among its members and appointed by the King.
2. Within fifteen days from its constitution, the President of the Assembly, after consultation with the parliamentary groups, shall nominate a candidate for President from among those presented to it, by at least a quarter of the members of the House.
3. The nominee will present his programme to the full session of the Assembly within fifteen days of his nomination. After the relevant debate the vote of investiture will proceed, in which the candidate must obtain an absolute majority to be proclaimed president.
4. If the candidate fails to obtain such a majority, there will be a new vote forty-eight hours after the first in which a simple majority shall be required. The procedure may be repeated, with the same or different candidates, as often as deemed appropriate by the President of the Assembly. If within two months from the first ballot none of the candidates has been elected, the Assembly will be dissolved and the acting President of the Autonomous Community in office shall call new elections.
5. The same procedure will be followed in the event that the Presidency becomes vacant for any other cause.

Article 26. Competences

Any competences shall be vested in the President that are conferred by the Constitution, this Statute and laws, and in particular the following:

1. As supreme representative of the Autonomous Community:
   a) To represent Extremadura in its relations with State institutions, with other Autonomous Communities and with other public administrations, and in the international sphere where appropriate.
   b) To sign agreements of collaboration with the state and cooperative agreements with other Autonomous Communities, notwithstanding its delegation to other authorities.

c) To convene elections to the Assembly of Extremadura; to fix its constituent sessions and, if necessary, to dissolve it under the terms provided in this Statute.

2. As the ordinary representative of the State:
   a) Enact in the name of the King the laws passed by the Assembly of Extremadura and other regulations with force of law, ordering their publication in the Official Journal of Extremadura and, where appropriate, in the Official Gazette of the State.
   b) Order the publication in the Official Journal of Extremadura of the appointments of the Autonomous Community Government Commissioner and other senior Autonomous Community officials in Extremadura, in accordance with the provisions of this Statute.
   c) Ensure within the Autonomous Community respect for constitutional and other legislation, adopting measures that may be necessary in the framework of its own competences.
3. As President of the Autonomous Community of Extremadura:
   a) Establish, in accordance with its political programme, general guidelines for Autonomous Community action and foster, direct and coordinate its actions.
   b) Issue Presidential decrees for the creation or extinction of Vice-presidencies and Ministries, for changing the name of those then existing or distributing the competences among them, including reporting these matters to the Assembly and resolving conflicts of competences arising among members of the Autonomous Community.
   c) To call meetings of the Autonomous Community of Extremadura, setting the agenda, presiding, suspending and adjourning its sessions, directing its debates, and supervising the enforcement of the decisions taken.
   d) To sign the decrees and resolutions adopted by the Autonomous Community of Extremadura and order official publication where appropriate.
   e) Exercise appropriate action by judicial means, and reporting thereon to the Autonomous Community of Extremadura.
   f) Remit to the Assembly the information which is required of the Autonomous Community or Autonomous Community Administration

Article 27. Early Dissolution of the Assembly

1. The President, after deliberation by the Autonomous Community of Extremadura and under his exclusive responsibility, may provide early dissolution of the Assembly of Extremadura.
2. The dissolution decree cannot be approved when a motion of censorship is pending or before the expiry of one year from the previous dissolution, except in the case regulated in Article 25.4 of this Statute.
3. In the decree of dissolution new elections will be called, establishing what determinations are required by applicable election laws.

Article 28. Question of Confidence

1. The President, after deliberation by the Autonomous Community of Extremadura, provided that no motion of censure is pending, may raise with the Assembly the question of confidence on a policy statement within the competences of the Community.
2. Confidence will be deemed granted when a simple majority of Assembly members vote in favour of it.
3. If the Assembly rejects the vote of confidence in the President, he shall resign before the House, whose President shall, within fifteen days, call a plenary session for the election of new President, according to the procedure of investiture under this Statute.

Article 29. Motion of Censure

1. The Assembly of Extremadura may demand political responsibility from the President of the Autonomous Community through the adoption by a majority vote of motion of censure proposed by at least 15 percent of the members of the House and include a candidate for President who shall present his alternative programme.
2. A censure motion shall not be voted on until five days after its introduction. Alternative motions may be submitted in the first two days of this period.
3. If the Assembly passes a motion of censure, the President shall automatically cease in his functions and the candidate proposed in the motion shall be deemed to have the confidence of the House, informing the King of the appointment.
4. In the same legislature, the signatories of a rejected censure motion may not seek another until one year from the filing of the previous one.

Article 30. Other Causes for Removal of the President

1. The President, in addition to the adoption of a motion of censure, shall cease to be in office on the holding of new elections and on his voluntary resignation submitted in writing to the President of the Assembly. In these two cases, the outgoing president will continue acting in office until the election of person that will replace him.
2. He shall also cease on death, on disqualification arising from criminal conviction executive or judicial decision limiting his civil rights in a manner inconsistent with his high office, for incompatibility with other public office and those other causes provided by law, and shall be temporarily replaced by the member of the Extremadura Autonomous Community as established by law.
3. The law will regulate the status of ex-presidents.

Chapter III. The Government of the Autonomous Community of Extremadura and Administration

Section 1ª. The Government of the Autonomous Community

Article 31. Character and Function

1. The Government of the Autonomous Community is the official body that performs the functions appropriate for the Autonomous Community
2. The Government of Extremadura is politically answerable to the Assembly in solidarity, without prejudice to the direct responsibility of each one of its members for his or her management.

Article 32. Competences

The Government of Extremadura has the responsibility and authority to:

1. Establish the general policy of the Autonomous Community in relation to the competences assumed, to direct the Autonomous Community administration and exercise regulatory power and executive function.
2. To lodge Constitutional appeals and other procedures within the Constitutional Court's jurisdiction for which it is entitled or to represent the Autonomous Community in defence of the interests of the Community.
3. To execute the sections of the budget of the Community under the terms established by law.
4. To resolve conflicts of jurisdiction between local authorities when these have not been reserved to the State.
5. Perform such other competences and responsibilities assigned by the Statute and the laws.

Article 33. Emergency Legislation

1. In case of extraordinary and urgent necessity, the Extremadura Autonomous Community can issue temporary legislative provisions in the form of Decree-law.
2. The Budget, reform of the Statute or the subjects of law for which a qualified majority is required cannot be subject to Decree-law.
3. Decree-laws shall be repealed if within the mandatory time limit of one month from its official publication they are not validated by the Assembly, following debate and full vote.
4. The Assembly shall approve the Decree-laws as bills by emergency procedure within the period specified in the preceding paragraph.

Article 34. Composition

1. The Government is composed of the President, the Vice-presidents, if any, and the members of the Cabinet.

2. The President may appoint and dismiss freely the members of the Cabinet, informing the Assembly of Extremadura thereof. He may also appoint the substitutions among them.
3. The Vice-Presidents and, where appropriate, the members of the Cabinet will supply the President in case of vacancy, absence or illness, according to the precedence provided by law.

Article 35. Status of Members

1. The status of the members of the Government of the Community of Extremadura shall be regulated by law of the Assembly, which shall determine the causes of incompatibility.
2. In every case:
   a) The members of the Government of the Community shall reside in Extremadura.
   b) Members of the Government may not exercise representative functions other than their parliamentary mandate or any other public function not derived from office. They may not perform any type of work, professional or business activity, except representing public interests.
   c) The criminal responsibility of the President and members of the Government shall be tried before the High Court of Extremadura for criminal acts committed within the territory of the Autonomous Community. Beyond this, they may be tried before the corresponding Criminal Chamber of the Supreme Court. Civil liability formatters concerning its function shall be tried before that Supreme Court.

Article 36. Cessation

The Government of the Autonomous Community shall ceases when its President does, continuing in office until the installation of the new Government. The law shall regulate other grounds for termination of the Government.

Section 2ª. The Administration of the Autonomous Community

Article 37. Guiding Principles

1. The Autonomous Community administration under the authority of the Autonomous Community of Extremadura shall serve the general interests objectively and shall seek to meet public needs effectively and efficiently, and in accordance with constitutional and statutory principles.
2. In its action it shall observe the principles of good faith, legitimate trust, transparency, quality of service to citizens as well as those established in Article 15.3 of this Statute.

Article 38. Competences

In exercising its competences, the Administration of the Autonomous Community shall have the same authority and competences as the State. Inter alia, these shall include:

a) The presumption of legitimacy and enforceability of their actions and the enforcement competences
b) The power to expropriate, in the exercise of which the Autonomous Community may create a body for determining fair values.
c) The sanctioning authority, within the limits established by law and the rules that develop it.
d) The competences of investigation, survey and recovery of the heritage and attachment of its property and rights.
e) The right to use administrative urgency and priority privileges, preference and other rights recognized by the public treasury in credit collection in its favour.
f) The exemption from the obligation to provide all kinds of security or guarantees to the courts of any jurisdiction and to public bodies.
g) To appear in court in the same terms as the State Administration.
h) The public trust in its actions, agreements and contracts in the terms determined by law.
i) The official review of its actions and provisions administratively.
j) In general, any competences of self-governance that the legal order recognizes.

Article 39. Measurements of Sound Administration

1. By law of the Assembly the manner of creation and functioning of the administrative organs shall be regulated under the criteria of quality in the provision of public services, as well as forms of citizen participation in the processes of development of general provisions that affect them.
2. The Autonomous Community shall regulate its own administrative procedures and adapt the general procedures to give speed and transparency to administrative processes, and to extend inter-administrative relationships and with citizens by electronic means and the simplification of procedures.
3. The authorities of Extremadura shall draft its norms, agreements and acts simply and clearly. The permanent systematic arrangement and codification of autonomous norms shall be procured.

Chapter IV. Exercise and Control of the Competences of the Autonomous Community

Article 40. Publication of the Laws

1. The Laws of the Assembly of Extremadura will be issued on behalf of the King by the President of the Autonomous Community within ten days of their official remission by the Chamber by arranging immediate publication in the "Official Journal of Extremadura".

2. In every case, important provisions, and orders issued by institutions that need to be published, shall be inserted in the same Official Journal. Such publication will be sufficient to determine the entry into force of Autonomous Community laws and for the effectiveness of those Acts.
3. Assembly laws and decrees of legal effect issued by the Autonomous Community of Extremadura will also be published in the "Official Gazette". Other acts and provisions shall be published in the Official Journal referred to in accordance with State Regulations.
4. Laws of the Assembly of Extremadura and the laws of the President and the Government of the Autonomous Community shall enter into force on the twentieth day following their publication in the "Official Journal of Extremadura" unless otherwise stated.

Article 41. Judicial Review of Provisions and Acts

1. The Acts and Decree-laws of the Extremadura Assembly are excluded from the contentious-administrative appeal and subject only to the control of constitutionality, notwithstanding the dispute resolution system of Article 44 of this Statute.
2. Legislative decrees shall be audited by the constitutional court and, where appropriate, by the contentious-administrative system in cases of misuse or excess in the exercise of legislative delegation. There shall be no contentious review when the articulated text or any recast of it has been debated and passed by the Assembly of Extremadura.
3. Regulatory norms and the acts and resolutions of the administrative and executive organs of the Autonomous Community shall be appealable to the contentious-administrative courts or, where appropriate, to the competent jurisdiction.

Article 42. Liability of Public Authorities and the Administration

1. The application of laws and non-expropriation legislation does not generate liability for compensation unless expressly stated in such laws.
2. The liability of the Government and its officials and employees for the operation of public services is governed by the general laws of the State, without prejudice to additional compensation cases the Assembly may establish by law.

Article 43. Jurisdictional Conflicts

1. In defence of their authority, the President, the Government of Extremadura and any of its members, the President of the Assembly and the officers of other institutions referred to in this Title may raise conflicts to the courts in the way established in the applicable state law.
2. In case of conflict, the Autonomous Community shall be represented in the bodies that should resolve it in the terms prescribed by the Organic Act of jurisdictional conflicts.

Article 44. Conflict Between Autonomous Institutions

1. The President and the Government of the Community may remit conflict of competences to the Assembly of Extremadura and this claim to those competences set out in this Statute or conferred by law respectively.
2. Within one month from that notice of the alleged ultra vires, the institution that considers that its competences have been invaded shall require the other to admit the incompetence, giving a reasoned statement of its legal title, transferring it to the Advisory Council. In the same period from receipt of the above claim, after accepting the competence of the Advisory Council, it shall issue a non-binding opinion indicating ownership of the disputed competence.
3. The same procedure will be followed in cases where the President considers that the laws of the Assembly do not conform to the Constitution and this Statute, unless there has been initiated against them a procedure of an appeal of unconstitutionality or of another type before the Constitutional Court.

Chapter V. Other Statutory Bodies

Article 45. Advisory Council

1. The Advisory Council, located in the city of Badajoz, is the highest advisory body for the institutions and administrations of the Autonomous Community. A law adopted by an absolute majority of the Assembly, shall regulate its composition, its legal regime, organization and operation, determining the cases in which its opinion is binding.
2. The Advisory Council shall express its opinion on the conformity with the Constitution, the present Statutes and other legislation, the draft reform of the statute, of bills, drafts of other norms with the force of law, the lodging or maintenance of appeals and actions to the Plenary Constitutional Court and representation in them, and other cases provided for in this Statute. It shall also provide opinions in cases that this constitutive law lays down on the legality of the general provisions and acts of Autonomous Community institutions, the Autonomous Community administration, public universities and local authorities of Extremadura, and the agencies and bodies under public law or linked to them.
3. The Assembly of Extremadura, through its President, may request the Council's opinion in the cases provided for in the Rules for non-governmental legislative initiatives.

Article 46. Council of Auditors

1. The Council of Auditors, located in the city of Cáceres and dependent on the Assembly, shall control externally the financial and budgetary activities of the institutions, the Autonomous Community, local authorities, the public enterprises dependent on them, as well as public universities of Extremadura,

overseeing accounts with criteria of legality, economy and efficiency in spending, subject to the jurisdiction of the state Court of Accounts, which may delegate to the Council those judicial functions that allowed by its constitutive law.

2. An Act of the Assembly of Extremadura approved by an absolute majority shall regulate the Council's composition, competences, legal status, organization and operation.

Article 47. Economic and Social Council

An Act of the Assembly shall regulate the composition, competences, legal status, the organization and functioning of the Economic and Social Council of Extremadura, with its headquarters in the city of Mérida, of the consultative body of the Autonomous Community on socioeconomic matters.

Article 48. The Ombudsman

An Act of the Assembly shall regulate the legal status of the Representative of the Joint Commissioner with functions in respect of Autonomous Community and local institutions, based in the city of Plasencia, similar to the Ombudsman as provided in the Constitution. The Representative of the Commons shall be elected by three-fifths of the members of the Assembly of Extremadura.

Title III. Judicial Power in Extremadura

Article 49. Competencies of the Autonomous Community

1. Regarding Administration of Justice, the Autonomous Community assumes the competencies that the Organic Act of Judicial Power attributes to the state Government.
2. Particularly, in the terms established by the Organic Act on Judicial Power, the authorities of Extremadura shall exercise the following functions:
   a) Define the territorial boundaries of their courts and establish their headquarters by an Act of the Assembly.
   b) Request, after hearings by the Council of Justice of Extremadura, to review the situation of the courts to suit the needs of the region. In this case, by delegation of the Government of the Nation, Extremadura can create sections and courts.
   c) To exercise the regulatory and executive competences in the creation, design and organization of judicial offices and administrative units, as well as non-judicial staff serving the administration of justice.
   d) To exercise those same competences in relation to the organizations and institutions collaborating in the Administration of Justice, including forensic services and toxicology.
   e) Provide adequate means of staff and economic administration media and materials for the administration of Justice within the framework of its competences.

f) Arrange free legal aid services and legal advice, as well as those of attention to crime victims in the terms established by law.
g) Order the system of the justices of the peace.
h) Develop tools and procedures for mediation and conciliation in conflict resolution in matters of Autonomous Community competences. In particular, to create family mediation services.
i) Propose to the competent authorities the notice of competitive examinations and contests to fill vacancies for judges, magistrates, clerks and prosecutors in the Autonomous Community. In their resolution specialization and knowledge of Extremadura's own law, especially in the vacancies of the Superior Court of Justice of Extremadura, will be considered a preferential merit.
j) Promote the participation of Extremadura in the Administration of Justice as provided by law.
k) Those derived from the other competences under State law.

Article 50. Superior Court of Justice of Extremadura

1. The Superior Court of Extremadura, located in the city of Caceres, is the main organ of the judicial organization of Extremadura and constitutes the court of last appeal of all proceedings in the territory, without prejudice to the competences of the Supreme Court.
2. The Superior Court of Extremadura shall deal with the cases and exercise the functions in state law established by the laws of the State and in the terms established by the Organic Act of Judicial Power, in the following issues:
   a) In appeals alleging an infringement of Extremadura's own law and the extraordinary appeals that includes judicial review of final decisions of the courts of Extremadura.
   b) In appeals and reviews related to the special laws of Baylío.
   c) In any criminal proceedings in which the Members of the Assembly are involved and the members of the Autonomous Community of Extremadura, liability claims against same for events arising from the exercise of their duties and civil cases on the capacity to act of the President. Outside the territory of Extremadura, criminal responsibility shall be enforceable in the same terms, before the Criminal Chamber of the Supreme Court.
   d) The claims of liability against the Autonomous Community for the implementation of provisions and non-expropriation legislative acts, as provided in Article 42.1.

Article 51. On the Highest Judicial Offices and the Public Prosecutor in Extremadura

1. The President of the Superior Court of Extremadura represents ordinarily the judiciary in the region. He shall be appointed by the King as proposed by the General Council of the Judiciary, after hearing the Council of Justice of

Extremadura, and his appointment will be published in the Official Journal of Extremadura.

2. At the same hearing the Presidents of the Superior Court of Extremadura shall be appointed in the terms determined by the Organic Act of Judicial Power.
3. In the manner prescribed in the Organic Act of Judicial Power, in each of the Courts of the Superior Court judges shall be appointed by the existing General Council of the Judicial Power, after hearing the Justice Council of Extremadura, and choosing from a list proposed by three-fifths of the deputies of the Assembly among jurists of recognized standing with over fifteen years of professional activity
4. In accordance with Organic Acts and as maximum representative of the Prosecutor in the region, there will be a Special Prosecutor in the Autonomous Community whose appointment shall be published in the Official Journal of Extremadura.

Article 52. Council of Justice of Extremadura

The Council of Justice of Extremadura is the organ of institutional participation of the Autonomous Community in the government and administration of justice in the Autonomous Community, in accordance with the provisions of the Organic Act on Judicial Power.

Title IV. Of Territorial Organization

Article 53. Local Authorities and Legal System

1. Extremadura is organized territorially into municipalities, provinces and, where appropriate, in other forms under this Statute.
2. Under the basic law of the State, the Autonomous Community shall regulate the legal framework for local authorities of Extremadura, taking into consideration their different characteristics and different capacity managing their competences.
3. The local government authorities have regulatory power, the prerogatives of public law and autonomy to set its own organizational structure, in the terms established by law.

Article 54. Municipalities.

1. The municipality is the basic territorial entity of Extremadura and an essential tool for the participation of citizens in public affairs. Municipalities have political autonomy and legal personality.
2. The Autonomous Community of Extremadura shall regulate by a law passed by an absolute majority, the procedures for creating, merging, segregating and suppressing municipalities and change the territory of municipalities.

3. The representation, government and municipal administration are the responsibility of its council, which exercises the management and defence of local interests with full autonomy. By law Assembly requirements will be established operating in an open council system.
4. Municipalities can associate freely with others and cooperate with other public authorities to exercise their competences and undertake aims of common interest.

Article 55. Local Autonomy

Subject to full political autonomy and adequate financial resources for the management of issues of local interest within the overall policy framework, a law of the Assembly adopted by an absolute majority shall determine the matters and functions of Autonomous competences that can be managed by municipalities and, where appropriate, the minimum division of faculties or competences the councils shall have and which sectoral laws and regulations of the Autonomous Community must be envisaged and respected.

Article 56. Provinces

1. The province has its own legal personality, autonomy and full capacity to manage its own interests. Their government and administration are entrusted to the respective *Deputation*.
2. Competencies of the Deputations shall be fixed by the basic law of the State and the Autonomous Community. In any case, the Deputations shall exercise competences in the field of cooperation, advice and assistance to municipalities and local entities. They shall also provide supra-municipal services, without prejudice to those which they may delegate or entrust to local bodies in their territory or autonomous institutions.

Article 57. Counties

By law passed by an absolute majority, the Autonomous Community may structure its organization in territorial districts. The law shall regulate the competences, organization and legal status of such entities.

Article 58. Other Local Entities

By law, the Autonomous Community shall regulate the forms of constitution, organization, competences and legal and financial regimes of the smaller local authorities, metropolitan areas, local authority associations, consortia and other voluntary or necessary groups for the municipalities that may be established, recognizing, in any case, their administrative autonomy and legal personality.

Article 59. Relations with Local Authorities

1. The Autonomous Community and the local authorities shall adjust their reciprocal relationships on the principles of institutional and financial loyalty, respect for their areas of competence, coordination, cooperation, mutual information, subsidiarity and inter-territorial solidarity.
2. The Autonomous Community may articulate the ordinary management of the services of their competences through its local authorities, in the terms of an Act of the Assembly to establish the direction and control mechanisms to ensure that material, financial and human resources are available.
3. Equally through the law of the Assembly, Extremadura may transfer or delegate to its local authorities competences on matters of competence of the Autonomous Community. These laws shall provide, in each case, the corresponding transfer of financial and human resources, materials that are necessary to ensure sufficiency in the provision of decentralized public services and forms of direction and control that are reserved to the competences of the Community.
4. The Autonomous Community shall coordinate the functions of the Deputations that are of general interest to Extremadura. To this end, and within the law of the State, by an Act of the Assembly passed by absolute majority the general formulas of coordination and relationship functions to be coordinated shall be laid down.
5. The Autonomous Community recognizes the right to participate in discussions of Extremadura Federation of Municipalities and Provinces in the matters of local interest, subject to the establishment of other general or specific forums for the same purpose.

Article 60. Local Finance

1. The finances of local authorities of Extremadura are governed by the principles of adequacy of resources, solidarity, autonomy and fiscal responsibility.
2. The Autonomous Community of Extremadura shall ensure regional balance and effective implementation of the principle of solidarity. To this end and by law of the Assembly it shall establish a fund of unconditional purpose, provided that it is financed from the tax revenue of the Community and it is to be distributed to municipalities taking into account, among other factors its population, its expenditure needs and its fiscal ability.
3. The Autonomous Community shall necessarily compensate local entities of Extremadura when setting tax measures that involve a real reduction in their income.
4. Notwithstanding agreements with other administrations, local authorities may delegate to the Extremadura Autonomous Community the application of its taxes and establish other forms of cooperation in the matter.

Title V. Institutional Relations of the Autonomous Community

Article 61. General Principles

1. The Autonomous Community of Extremadura may establish relationships with the State, other Autonomous Communities and foreign or supranational entities in the exercise of its competences and defence of its interests under the principles of institutional loyalty, solidarity, collaboration, cooperation and mutual help.
2. Participation of the Autonomous Community in the bodies and mechanisms of bilateral and multilateral cooperation with the State and other Autonomous Communities that do not alter the ownership of the respective competences.

Chapter 1. Relations with State Institutions

Article 62. Instruments of Relationship with the State

1. The Autonomous Community of Extremadura and the State, in the scope of their respective competences, shall sign cooperation agreements and use other means to achieve objectives of common interest.
2. The Autonomous Community of Extremadura shall participate in the affairs of general interest of the State through the procedures or multilateral organs that are constituted.
3. In issues of specific interest of the Autonomous Community of Extremadura, it may create organs and specific collaborative relationship with the State, without prejudice to the functions assigned to other existing bodies.

Article 63. Participation in State Institutions and Procedures

1. The Autonomous Community of Extremadura shall participate in institutions, agencies and decision-making procedures of the State affecting its competences skills and interests in accordance with the provisions of the relevant State legislation and this Statute.
2. The Autonomous Community of Extremadura shall participate in procedures in the appointment of members of constitutional bodies and institutions of the State in terms provided by law.
3. The Autonomous Community of Extremadura shall appoint representatives in management, control and administration bodies of public enterprises, institutions and State agencies having their headquarters or conducting their activities in Extremadura in the terms established in state law and this Statute.

Article 64. Commission on Bilateral Cooperation

1. For the purposes provided in this chapter, the Cooperation Committee will be created between the State and the Autonomous Community of Extremadura,

which shall constitute the general, permanent framework of the relationship between the Autonomous Community of Extremadura and the State.

2. The Committee on Cooperation shall:
   a) Establish mechanisms for information and collaboration for the exercise of its own respective competences.
   b) Assist in the drafting of State legislation that particularly affects the competences and interests of Extremadura.
   c) Be the legal means and scope of conflict resolution between the two administrations.
   d) Perform any other duties of a similar nature at the initiative of either of the parties.
3. The Laws of organization and operation of the Committee on Cooperation shall be established by agreement of both parties.

Chapter II. On Relations with Other Autonomous Communities

Article 65. Agreements with Other Autonomous Communities

1. The Autonomous Community of Extremadura may propose, negotiate and conclude with other Autonomous Governments agreements for the planning, management and delivery of administrative or executive services in all matters within its competence. To this end it is likewise understood that the related regulatory competences and especially of self-organization for the creation or modification of its own administrative bodies or mixed agreements related to the content of the agreement are hereby authorized.
2. Such agreements shall be communicated simultaneously to the Congress of the Deputies and the Senate, for the eventual issuance of non-binding recommendations.
   After the period of one month if no recommendations shall have been received, the Convention shall enter into force, subject to the provisions below.
3. At the same time, it shall be communicated to the Assembly of Extremadura for mere consideration of a possible collision with its statutory competences. If within a month the Assembly claims the need for approval by plenary vote by absolute majority, the conflict resolution procedure shall apply between institutions by the Advisory Council, as set out in Article 44 of this Statute.

Article 66. Cooperation Agreements with Other Autonomous Communities

1. At the proposal of the Autonomous Community, it may enter into cooperation agreements with other Autonomous Communities within the scope of their respective competences and for the joint exercise of their different normative, institutional and policy functions of a purely regulatory, executive or administrative nature as regulated in the previous Article.
2. Before its final formalization by signature of the President of the Community such agreements must be submitted to the Assembly of Extremadura for

approval without amendment within one month and simultaneously, to the Congress of Deputies and the Senate for final approval within the same period.

Article 67. Multilateral Forums of Horizontal Cooperation

The institutions of the Autonomous Community shall promote and participate in as many horizontal cooperation forums as may be useful for a better performance of its respective competences and better overall functioning of the autonomous system. Without prejudice to purely programmatic or political commitments, the cooperation and management agreements that are negotiated in these areas by the Autonomous Community shall be processed in accordance with the procedures provided for in the preceding Articles.

Chapter III. External Action of Extremadura

Article 68. Principles and Objectives

The external action of the institutions of the Autonomous Community will serve the Autonomous Community interests of Extremadura and the people of Extremadura abroad, under the Autonomous Community competences and with respect for the unity of action of the State. It shall also contribute to the promotion of democracy, respect for human rights, promotion of international peace and concord, and the comprehensive, harmonious, balanced and sustainable development of all peoples and nations of the world.

Article 69. Instruments and Procedures

1. For the development of the external action of Extremadura, the following instruments will be used, including:
   a) Participation in State multilateral forums and conferences competent in the matter.
   b) Establishment of branches or representative offices and in defence of its interests.
   c) Participation in international organizations, either by representation or by itself, or within the Spanish representation.
   d) Subscription to agreements with regions and territorial entities of other States.
   e) Promoting the conclusion of international treaties by the State in matters of interest of the Autonomous Community.
   f) Participation in Autonomous Community associations for the defence of common interests.
   g) Financing cooperation to development activities, either directly or through specialized NGOs.
   h) Contribution to the maintenance of the activity of communities of the people of Extremadura living abroad and in relationships of all kinds with Extremadura.

2. In any case, the Autonomous Community will be informed in advance by the State of acts preparatory to the conclusion of international agreements that affect its specific interests and may request the State to include its representatives in negotiating delegations.

Article 70. Representation and Participation in the European Union

In the framework of national and European regulation, the Autonomous Community of Extremadura shall be represented and participate in the decisions and policies of the European Union according to the following procedures, among others:

a) The State shall inform the Autonomous Community of the initiatives, proposals, draft regulations and other decisions pending in the European Union when they affect the interests or competences of the Autonomous Community.
b) The Autonomous Community of Extremadura shall participate in the formation of State decisions relating to the European Union in the framework of existing internal multilateral procedures.
c) According to the laws of the State, the Autonomous Community of Extremadura may form part of the Spanish delegation in the institutions of the European Union which negotiates issues of Autonomous Community interest.
d) The Autonomous Community of Extremadura, in defence of Autonomous Community interests may urge organs so entitled to the exercise of the relevant action before the Court of Justice of the European Union and may intervene in proceedings substantiated before it, in accordance with EU and Spanish legal systems.
e) The Autonomous Community will maintain channels of direct relevance to the institutions of the European Union and will have a permanent office in charge of relationships with institutions and bodies on matters affecting the interests of Extremadura.

Article 71. Cooperation with Portugal

In the framework of its competences and with respect to those involving the State, the Autonomous Community shall develop and encourage cooperation with Portuguese institutions and society in all areas of common interest according to the following procedures, including:

a) The creation of a specific organ of the Autonomous Community in charge of its relations with Portugal and with its territorial authorities.
b) Participation in Spanish or mixed organizations, forums of institutions that are develop policies relating to Autonomous Community competences.
c) The planning, negotiation and execution of actions and shared programmes with Portuguese institutions, whatever the source of funding.
d) The planning, negotiation and implementation of its own policy of cross-border cooperation.
e) The creation of agencies and mixed services of common interest of any nature.

f) Dissemination and promotion of Portuguese and Portuguese culture in Extremadura, under the principle of reciprocity.
g) Making agreements with Portuguese institutions and local authorities, under relevant laws and treaties.
h) Participation in Spanish-Portuguese governmental meetings on a regular basis which may affect the region in the framework of corresponding bilateral agreements.
i) The promotion of balanced and mutually beneficial economic, trade and business relations.

Article 72. Development to Cooperation

The Autonomous Community shall conceive and implement its development to cooperation policy according to the following procedures, among others:

a) The planning, coordination and control of the actions of the autonomous Administration and instrumental bodies on the subject.
b) The coordination of Extremadura's development to cooperation policy with the State and, where appropriate, with the other communities in the context of multilateral procedures.
c) Direct implementation of development to cooperation activities by transfer of technology, the allocation of human and material resources or expert advice.
d) Direct transfer of its own funds or transferred from other entities or administrations.
e) Funding, evaluation and control of proposed development actions or implemented by companies, organizations or entities.
f) The promotion and awareness of citizens in this area through campaigns, outreach programmes, educational activities and promotion of volunteerism.

Title VI. Economy and Finance

Chapter I. Economy of Extremadura

Article 73. General Principles

1. The entire wealth of the region, in its various forms and whatever its ownership, is subordinate to the general interest. Free enterprise is protected and public initiative in economic activity is recognized.
2. The authorities of the Autonomous Community shall promote and, where appropriate, will regulate the participation of social and economic actors in organizations and institutions development functions in Extremadura. Likewise, it will foster the establishment and development of social economy companies and promote and protect self-employment.

Article 74. Economic Planning

1. The Autonomous Community may, by law, plan Autonomous Community economic activity as part of the overall planning of the State and with special attention to the needs of sustainable development and the rural environment.
2. The Autonomous Community shall participate in the preparation of economic plans and programmes of the State affecting Extremadura. It may also develop and submit to the National Government proposals for competences, businesses and public utility companies of the State. The reports, studies or proposals will be submitted to the Assembly of Extremadura, and this agreement, duly notified, shall be adopted and lead to a resolution motivated the Government of the Nation or relevant agencies or entities.

Article 75. Public Sector

For Autonomous Community development and the best exercise of its competences, the Autonomous Community of Extremadura may establish public enterprises and autonomous bodies and other public entities of public or private law, in the forms and with the controls provided by an Act of the Assembly in all cases to ensure transparency and adequate oversight of these entities.

Article 76. Financial Institutions

The Autonomous Community shall exercise its competences on Savings and Credit Banks based in Extremadura and, where appropriate, on the activity of these and other financial institutions in the region, in order to strengthen the Autonomous Community's financial system, ensuring compliance of their economic and social functions, encourage their participation in the strategic economic objectives of the region and ensure the impact of savings of the people of Extremadura in developing Extremadura.

Chapter II. The Treasury of Extremadura

Article 77. General Principles and Legal Regime

1. The Treasury of the Autonomous Community is constituted by the set of financial rights and obligations which shall belong to the administrations, agencies, organizations and autonomous institutions of Extremadura.
2. The principles of the Treasury are those of financial sufficiency and autonomy, solidarity, coordination, efficiency and budget foresight. In the application of rights and in fulfilment of its obligations it shall follow the principles of legality, austerity, efficiency, coordination economy and economy in procedures.
3. Autonomous tax authorities shall have the same competences and guarantees as those of the State Treasury, including the tax regime applicable to State resources.

4. The provisions contained in this Chapter shall be interpreted and integrated in accordance with provisions of the Organic Act under paragraph 3 of Article 157 of the Constitution.

Section 1. The Budget and Public Expenditure

Article 78. The Budget

1. All income and expenditure of the Autonomous Community of Extremadura shall be set out in a single, annual budget, which shall contain the amount of tax benefits provided by Autonomous Community laws.
2. The Budget shall include, as separate sections, the budget of the Assembly and those of other statutory bodies, which will be prepared by the relevant organs according to the general guidelines on public spending fixed by the Autonomous Community of Extremadura for the corresponding year.
3. The Budget shall be balanced, aimed at meeting economic policy objectives, subject to the principle of budgetary stability and its drafting and management criteria shall be such as to enable its consolidation with State criteria.
4. The Autonomous Community of Extremadura shall make the final preparation and presentation of the Draft Budget for processing and the Assembly shall be responsible for its debate, amendment, approval and control.
5. The draft Budget will be presented to the Assembly of Extremadura before 15th October of the year before it comes into force. If the draft Budget is not published before the first day of the fiscal year, the previous year's budget is deemed automatically extended until the adoption of the new one.
6. The Budgetary laws shall in no case establish new taxes or modify the essential elements of those already established, except as authorized by law regulating these.
7. The Assembly of Extremadura shall not pass legislative initiatives or amendments for the current financial year that involve increased expenses or decreased income without having the prior approval of the Autonomous Community of Extremadura.
8. Notwithstanding the annual nature of the budget, economic and financial plans of a multiannual nature of resource allocation may be approved.

Article 79. Government Expenditure

1. The Autonomous Community of Extremadura has full autonomy in spending and in the framework of its competences, is free to determine the fate of economic and financial resources.
2. The public expenditure of the Autonomous Community of Extremadura shall make an equitable allocation of public resources and programming and execution shall satisfy the criteria of transparency, efficiency and economy. Measures will be taken for an appropriate economic and financial control.
3. The public spending throughout the territory shall contribute to the economic and social cohesion of the region by substantial equalization of public services

and investments in different Autonomous Community areas, seeking homogeneity in the municipalities of similar population and equivalent needs.

Section 2. Financial Resources

Article 80. Revenue

1. The Autonomous Community of Extremadura shall have sufficient resources to meet expenditure needs arising from the exercise of its competences.
2. The income of the Autonomous Community of Extremadura consists of:
   a) Its own taxes, special assessments, fees and charges.
   b) Taxes assigned in whole or in part by the State.
   c) Surcharges on State taxes.
   d) Investments in government revenue.
   e) Allocations from the State Budget.
   f) Transfers from Inter-territorial Compensation Fund, according to its own laws, or other funds.
   g) Assignments and transfers from the EU programmes and community programmes and from international legal organizations and bodies.
   h) Income from its assets and other private property.
   i) The proceeds from the issuance of debt and credit operations.
   j) The proceeds from fines and penalties in the field of its competences.
   k) Any others as may be established in accordance with the Constitution and this Statute.

Article 81. Autonomous Community's Own Taxes

1. The Autonomous Community of Extremadura is competent to establish, regulate and implement its own taxes, under the Constitution and this Statute.
2. The Autonomous Community may impose its own taxes on the performance of acts, facts or businesses that demonstrate the economic capacity of the taxpayer or that cause expense, environmental or social costs which have to be supported by the Autonomous Community of Extremadura or its inhabitants and any others that do not fall on taxable events effectively taxed by the state, whether or not for non-tax purposes.

Article 82. Assigned Taxes and Surcharges

1. The Autonomous Community of Extremadura has competence to regulate and enforce State taxes assigned to it, within the limits and conditions of the Constitution.
2. The Autonomous Community shall regulate and implement fully assigned taxes, without prejudice to the competences of the state to general tax harmonization and the establishment of territorial allocation criteria.

3. Similarly, the Autonomous Community may establish and apply surcharges on State taxes with the limitations established by the pertinent Organic Act.

Article 83. Economic-Administrative Review

In the Autonomous Community of Extremadura a body shall be established to hear economic and administrative claims deducted against any acts of the Administration taught in Autonomous Community tax application that it manages and acts against other economic content determined by law.

Section 3. Patrimony and Public Credit

Article 84. Patrimony

1. The Autonomous Community of Extremadura has its own assets and public goods, heritage and other special domains held under the legal regime of an Act of the Assembly.
2. Property and rights received from public administrations on the occasion of the transfer of functions and services and those acquired by any other valid legal title form part of the assets of the Community.

Article 85. Public Credit

1. To obtain credit for and to issue debt, the Autonomous Community of Extremadura shall be authorized by law of the Assembly which shall determine their volume and characteristics within the general ordering of credit policy. Such authorization shall not be necessary to carry out treasury operations or other forms of short-term debt, which must be redeemed in any event, within the financial year or the next in which it is granted. An account of all this will be given to the Assembly of Extremadura.
2. The public debt of the Autonomous Community of Extremadura will be destined exclusively to investment costs and their holders shall have the same benefits and conditions as State public debt.
3. The Budget of the Autonomous Community shall assign the necessary appropriations to meet the payment of interest and principal on the public debt, amounts that may not be reduced while complying with the terms of issue.

Chapter III. Relations with the State Treasury

Article 86. General principles of Autonomous Community Funding

1. Relations between the Treasury of the Autonomous Community of Extremadura and the State shall be informed by the principles of solidarity, coordination, collaboration, transparency and institutional loyalty, and governed by the

Constitution, this Statute and, where appropriate, by the Organic Act provided for in paragraph 3 of Article 157 of the Constitution.

2. The State guarantees the necessary resources to enable the Autonomous Community of Extremadura to provide services and exercise its competences in a position of substantial equality with the rest of the Autonomous Communities, without different statutory formulations that might pose harm to the region.
3. The State shall also ensures the update of the basic variables applicable and to the five-yearly review of the system, which will take into account the evolution of spending needs and available resources.
4. The Autonomous Community of Extremadura shall participate in state revenues not transferred through the Sufficiency Fund or other financial instruments that may be established.
5. To determining expenditure needs and the funding of the Autonomous Community the most relevant variables shall be considered such as the Autonomous Community area relative to the national, low population density, aging population, the low income level, the population in poverty or exclusion, the weight of rural areas and the distance and time of access of citizens to public services.

Article 87. Financial Levelling

Without prejudice to the above basic funding and in order to correct territorial imbalances, the following financial resources will be transferred to the Autonomous Community:

a) The allocations earmarked for equality and fund derivatives, both regulated in Article 158 of the Constitution.
b) The resulting programmes, funds, initiatives and any other financing instruments established by the European Union or its total contribution or in part, with the principle of additionality.
c) From the territorialized participation in State funds established by Parliament and related to the competences of the Autonomous Community. The management of such funds shall, in any event, be the responsibility of the Autonomous Community of Extremadura.

Article 88. Participation and Institutional Loyalty

1. The Autonomous Community of Extremadura shall participate and vote in all bodies in relation to the State having conferred competences of proposal or decision on the autonomous financing system or on the distribution of funds of whatever origin between Autonomous Communities, especially in the Fiscal and Financial Policy Council, subject to the Joint Commission of Article 90 of this Statute. When the allocation decision belongs exclusively to the State, the Autonomous Community of Extremadura must first be heard Periodically the financial impact that the laws and measures adopted by the State on the Treasury of Extremadura shall be assessed and, conversely, the measures that are

approved by the Autonomous Community of Extremadura have on the State Treasury, adopting the appropriate compensatory measures.

2. The Autonomous Community shall contribute to the revenue corresponding to the taxes that the State establishes on polluting or potential risk-generating activities against the environment or the social environment of Extremadura.

Article 89. Cooperation in Tax Matters

1. The Autonomous Community, the State and local authorities of Extremadura shall collaborate in the respective taxation and facilitate the exchange of information required for the exercise of their respective competences in this area and especially the management of local taxes and rates including the joint use of information and databases.
2. The Autonomous Community, in the manner determined by law, shall be integrated into State agencies to coordinate the administration of assigned taxes.

Article 90. Joint Commission on Economic and Fiscal Affairs

1. The State - Autonomous Community of Extremadura Joint Commission on Economic and Fiscal Affairs is a bilateral organ between the two administrations in the financial field.
2. The Commission shall be in charge of the completion, approval, development, maintenance and monitoring of the financial system and for channelling the fiscal and financial relations between the two administrations, and in particular:
   a) Approve the scope and terms of the assignment of ownership of state taxes, and in particular, the percentage of participation in the performance of state taxes partially assigned.
   b) Establish mechanisms for collaboration between tax administrations of Extremadura and the State, and the criteria of coordination and fiscal harmonization appropriate to the nature of the taxes assigned.
   c) Negotiate the percentage of participation of Extremadura in the territorial distribution European structural funds.
   d) Consider investments that the State shall hold in the Autonomous Community of Extremadura.
   e) Approve the valuation of transfers of government services to the Autonomous Community.
   f) Establish mechanisms for collaboration between the Autonomous Community and the General Administration of the State for the proper performance of the functions on cadastral and revision through economic administrative proceedings.
   g) Propose measures to maintain balance on the funding system when it can be altered by State or European Union legislative decisions.
   h) Any other appropriate function appropriate to the nature of the body and agreed to by both parties.
3. The Joint Committee shall consist of an equal number of representatives from the State and the Autonomous Community. The Chair shall be held in rotation

by both parties in annual turns. Its rules of procedure and operation will be adopted by agreement between both Administrations.

Title VII. The Reform of the Statute

Article 91. Procedure for Statutory Reform

1. The reform initiative of this Statute is for the Autonomous Community of Extremadura and the Assembly, on the initiative of at least one third of its members, and of the Congress of the Deputies or the Senate.
2. If the reform is proposed by institutions of the Autonomous Community, it shall be processed in accordance with the following rules:
   a) The special legislative procedure laid down by the Assembly will be followed, where approval of the reform proposal of two-thirds majority of Members of the House for a final vote will be required.
   b) In the same meeting at which the proposed amendment is adopted it will choose a delegation of deputies representing the Assembly in the Congress of the Deputies and Senate.
   c) In the Congress the text of the reform will follow the special legislative process established by their Standing Orders having to obtain an absolute majority in the Congress of Deputies for approval.
   d) The Autonomous Community of Extremadura, by a vote of the absolute majority of the Plenary Session, may withdraw from Parliament the reform proposal at any time of processing prior to final full vote.
   e) The approval of the reform by Parliament through an Organic Act shall include State authorization for the Autonomous Community to convene a ratification referendum within six months after the final vote in Parliament, if the Assembly has previously agreed to it with the favourable vote of two-thirds of its members.
   f) The statutory reform requires, in any case, the form of an Organic Act.
3. If the initiative is adopted by the Congress of Deputies or the Senate, then it will be adopted by an absolute majority in the relevant House and after choosing a delegation of supporters thereof, the proposal shall be remitted to the Assembly of Extremadura for processing according to the rules set out in paragraph above.
4. If a reform proposal is not approved, the institution promoting it may not reformulate it until one year from the earlier proposal.

First Additional Provision. Supplemental Appropriations

1. The second additional provision of the Statute of Autonomy of Organic Act 1/1983, 25 February, as originally drafted, determined that the General Budget of the State should assign, specifying the destination and source of exceptional funding, supplemental appropriations to address the socioeconomic circumstances of Extremadura.

2. The Joint Commission of Transferences between the State Administration and the Autonomous Community of Extremadura approved the Agreement between the State Administration and the said Autonomous Community the latter receiving an advance of the above appropriations assignments. In that Agreement the existence of a partial agreement was recognized as a possible methodology to be used in determining the criteria, scope and amount of outstanding appropriations referred to in the paragraph above.
3. In the event that, at the date of approval of this Statute, the amounts derived as stated in the paragraph above, have not been determined and paid in full, the Joint Committee envisaged in Article 90 shall, within eighteen months, establish the criteria, scope and amount leading to the final implementation thereof. In this case, the implementation of the resolutions will made within 3 years from the entry into force of this Statute.
4. The procedure provided for in the preceding paragraph, the General Administration of the State may grant advance payments.

Second Additional provision. Ordinary State Investment

1. To secure regular annual State investment in infrastructure in Extremadura the extent of its territory in relation to that of the State will be taken into account, as well as the distance and time of access of the population to infrastructure and services.
2. Moreover, in order to accelerate the convergence of the region with the nation, the State shall make, each year, for a period of seven complementary investments equivalent to at least one percent of Autonomous Community gross domestic product. At the conclusion of this period, the Joint Commission on Economic and Fiscal Affairs established by Article 90 will examine the degree of convergence, being able to determine if new instruments designed to achieve it are needed.
3. The Autonomous Community shall promote the adoption by the State of active policies of promotion and implementation of investments for the principle of equality to make it real and effective for all Spaniards in the accessibility of public services and infrastructure, as well as ensuring the principle of territorial cohesion.

Third Additional Provision. Allocation of Taxes

1. The Autonomous Community will be granted the taxes that have been fully assigned to Extremadura by applicable law, and the performance of those of partially transferred as provided therein or in the instruments approving a new Autonomous Community financing system.
2. By agreement between the Autonomous Community and the State, which shall be passed as an ordinary draft law, the list of the taxes transferred may be amended determining the percentage of assignment and the scope and conditions of the same, subject, in both cases, to the provisions of this Statute and

under the Organic Act envisaged in paragraph 3 of Article 157 of the Constitution.

3. In any case, the removal or modification by the State of any of the taxes assigned shall involve the termination or modification of the allocation, subject to the compensation mechanisms referred to in Article 88 of this Statute.

Fourth Additional Provision. Transfer of Material and Financial Resources

The transfer of State services inherent to the competences of the Autonomous Community shall be done according to the following rules:

a) The Joint Committee on Transfers will make an inventory of the assets and rights
State to be subject to transfer to the Autonomous Community of Extremadura, specifying the services and staff to be transferred and shall adjust, if necessary, those passing to the competence of the Autonomous Community.
b) The Joint Committee shall meet at the request of the Government or the Autonomous Community of Extremadura, to establish its own rules of operation and remit their agreements to the Government for enactment as a royal decree.
c) The Joint Committee shall establish schedules and deadlines for the transfer of each service, so that the Autonomous Community shall receive organic materials and blocks of competences enabling it to organize a rational and consistent management of public services from their reception.
d) To prepare and verify the transfer, the Joint Committee on Transfers will also be assisted by sectoral joint committees whose primary role will be to determine for each subject the transfer of competences and human, financial and material resources that the Autonomous Community should receive. The sectoral commissions shall send their agreed proposals to the Joint Commission, which shall ratify them, all without prejudice to the competences assigned to the bilateral commission provided for in Article 90 of this Statute.
e) The assets and rights shall be transferred without other conditions than those resulting from the Registry of Property. Public certification of the Joint Commission of agreements on transfer of real property will be sufficient title for the entry in the records, which shall meet the requirements of the Mortgage Law. The cadastral changes shall be made officially.
f) The change of ownership of the leases of premises for government departments to be transferred shall not entitle the landlord to terminate, modify or renew the contract or to demand compensation of any kind.

Fifth Additional Provision. Transfers of Staff

1. Civil servants assigned to the State Administration or other public administrations that are affected by the transfer to the Autonomous Community of Extremadura will depend on this, their consolidated rights of whatever nature assigned at the time of transfer being respected according to the specific legal regime in each case without prejudice to its adjustment in accordance with the legal order. In particular, they retain their administrative status, salary level and

right to participate in competitive transfer examinations that are called by the respective Administrations with equality to the remaining members of the body or scale to which they belong and may exercise their permanent right of option under the legislation in force.

2. The Autonomous Administration shall be subrogated to the holders of contracts subject to administrative law and employment law, binding on the staff of this nature and which are affected by the entry into force of this Statute and the transfer to the Autonomous Community of Extremadura.

Sixth Additional Provision. Constitution of the Joint Economic and Fiscal Affairs Committee

The Committee referred to in Article 90 shall be established for a maximum period of six months from the entry into force of this Statute. Until its constitution, the Joint Commission of Transfers shall exercise its competences.

Seventh Additional Provision. Public Safety

The Autonomous Community of Extremadura, in matters of public safety, shall create a body of its own local police or permanent assignment or enter into a temporary or permanent partnership with units of the National Police, in both cases on the terms provided in State law, and shall be responsible for the authorization, inspection and sanction of private security companies that have activity in the region and the training of personnel performing such functions. Coordination of measures of the security services and private investigation with local police and where appropriate, with police depending on the Autonomous Community.

Repeal Provisions

Upon entry into force of this organic reform law any provisions of equal rank or less that oppose it are repealed.

Final Provision

The Organic Act shall enter into force on the day of its publication in the Official State Gazette and also published in the Official Journal of Extremadura.

Selected Bibliography

§1. System-Wide Materials

The bibliography on such a legally complicated and controversial subject as the Autonomous State is enormous. This is only a sample of the works considered most representative.

Aja Fernández, Eliseo. *Estado autonómico y reforma federal.* Madrid: Alianza, 2014.

Albertí Rovira, Enoch. *Autonomía política y unidad económica.* Madrid: Civitas, 1995.

Álvarez Conde, Enrique. *Reforma constitucional y reformas estatutarias.* Madrid: Iustel, 2007.

Biglino Campos, Paloma. *Federalismo de integración y de devolución. El debate sobre la competencia.* Madrid: CEPC, 2007.

Blanco Valdez, Roberto. *Los rostros del federalismo.* Madrid: Ariel, 2012.

Carrasco Durán, Manuel. *El reparto de competencias entre el Estado y las Comunidades Autónomas.* Valencia: Tirant lo Blanch, 2005.

Castellà Andreu, Josep Maria & Olivetti, Marco (coords). *Nuevos Estatutos y reforma del Estado. Las experiencias de España e Italia a debate.* Barcelona: Atelier, 2009.

Fernández Segado, Francisco (ed.). *The Spanish Constitution in the European Constitutional context.* Madrid: Dykinson, 2003.

Ferreres Comella, Victor. *The Constitution of Spain. A Contextual Analysis.* Oxford: Hart Publishing, 2013.

Fossas Espadaler, Enric. *El principio dispositivo en el Estado autonómico.* Madrid: Marcial Pons, 2007.

García Morillo, Joaquín. *La configuración constitucional de la autonomía local.* Madrid: Marcial Pons, 1998.

Gerpe Landín, Manuel and Cabellos Espiérrez, Miguel Ángel (eds.). *Poder Judicial y modelo de Estado.* Barcelona: Atelier, 2013.

Lago Montero, José María and Gil Rodríguez, Isabel. *El sistema de financiación de las Comunidades Autónomas. Comentario a la Ley 22/2009 de 28 de diciembre, tras la sentencia del Estatuto catalán*: Madrid, Dykinson, 2011.

Muñoz Machado, Santiago. *Derecho Público de las Comunidades Autónomas.* 2 vols., 2nd, Madrid: Iustel, 2007.

Ruipérez Alamillo, Javier. *División de competencias y forma territorial del Estado.* Madrid: Reus Editorial, 2012.

Solozábal Echavarría, Juan José (ed.). *La reforma federal: España y sus siete espejos.* Madrid: Biblioteca Nueva, 2014.

Tomás Font i Llovet (coord.), *El régimen local en la reforma de los estatutos de autonomía.* Madrid: CEPC, 2006.

Viver Pi-Sunyer, Carles. *Materias competenciales y Tribunal Constitucional.* Barcelona: Ariel, 1989.

§2. Materials Concerning Individual Subnational Components

Several institutions follow the development of the activities of the Autonomous Communities. Thus, the central government itself through the *Secretaría de Estado de Administraciones Públicas*:

http://www.seat.mpr.gob.es/portal/areas/politica_autonomica.html

There are also specialized research centres whose web pages allow access to the study documents, reviews, etc. For example, the Instituto de Derecho Público de Barcelona, with a very complete annual report on the Autonomous Communities http://www.idpbarcelona.net.

Many Communities have their own organs dedicated to research on the autonomous legal order. Among the most important are those of the Catalan and Basque governments:

- Institut d'Estudis de l'Autogovern:

http://presidencia.gencat.cat/ca/ambits_d_actuacio/desenvolupament_autogovern/institut-destudis-autogovern/

-Instituto Vasco de Administración Pública:

http://www.ivap.euskadi.eus

The Centro de Estudios Políticos y Constitucionales, a Spanish government organization also has a research centre studying the evolution of the Autonomous State: http://www.cepc.es.

§3. Information on Obtaining Subnational Constitutional Texts and Primary Sources

A current version of individual Statutes is available on line in the different Communities web pages. They can be seen altogether with synopses and bibliography on the Congress web page http://www.congreso.es/consti/estatutos/. And also on the Government web page: http://www.seat.mpr.gob.es/portal/areas/politica_autonomica/Estatutos_Autonomia.html

Almost all Autonomous States have published all the details of the drafting and procedures that gave rise to their basic institutional norm. Likewise, they have financed the publication of exhaustive commentaries. For example, those of Andalucía are:

- Cruz Villalón, Pedro (dir.), *Comentarios al Estatuto de Autonomía para Andalucía*, Sevilla: Centro de Publicaciones no Oficiales del Parlamento de Andalucía, 2012.

- Ruiz Robledo, Agustín, *La elaboración del nuevo Estatuto de Autonomía para Andalucía en sus documentos*, 2 vols, Seville: Centro de Publicaciones no Oficiales del Parlamento de Andalucía, 2007.

Selected Bibliography

Index

The numbers here refer to paragraph numbers.

Index

Made in the USA
Monee, IL
18 October 2026

66037598R10136